Anthony Giddens and Modern Social Theory

KENNETH H. TUCKER, JR

SAGE Publications
London • Thousand Oaks • New Delhi

SAGE Publications Ltd
6 Bonhill Street
London EC2A 4PU

SAGE Publications Inc.
2455 Teller Road
Thousand Oaks, California 91320

SAGE Publications India Pvt Ltd
32, M-Block Market
Greater Kailash – I
New Delhi 110 048

British Library Cataloguing in Publication data

A catalogue record for this book is available
from the British Library

ISBN 0 8039 7550 3
ISBN 0 8039 7551 1 (pbk)

Library of Congress catalog card number 98–060536

Typeset by Mayhew Typesetting, Rhayader, Powys
Printed in Great Britain by The Cromwell Press Ltd,
Trowbridge, Wiltshire

To my parents, Ann and Ken Tucker

CONTENTS

ACKNOWLEDGMENTS

I am indebted to Chris Rojek for suggesting this project and supporting it to its conclusion. Robert Rojek and Jane Evans of Sage Publications helped enormously with shepherding the book through the review process, and editing the manuscript. Anthony Giddens graciously granted me an interview which allowed me to clarify many issues regarding his work. A faculty grant from Mount Holyoke College assisted with travel and research expenses.

For emotional and intellectual support, I wish to thank Barbara Tucker and Michael Barker. For my spouse, Sherry, no thanks can be enough. A perceptive critic and wonderful companion, the book could not have been completed without her care and insight.

INTRODUCTION

Anthony Giddens is one of the leading practitioners of contemporary social theory. He has created a challenging and complex version of sociological theory that explores a range of perspectives, from feminism to ethnomethodology. He incorporates insights from these different approaches into his sociology, which accents the reflexive role of people in fashioning and reproducing social institutions.

Giddens advocates a sociology aimed at "reclaiming . . . the grand questions."[1] His sociology has never been content with cautious, empirical studies of clearly delimited scope. Rather, Giddens constructs a sociology that tries to grasp the "overall 'systemness'" of the modern social world. Giddens's sociological perspective attempts to overcome the dualities of structure and agency that so often inform social theory. He draws on theorists such as Wittgenstein and Goffman, whose implications for "macro" sociological issues have rarely been developed. Giddens's far-reaching theoretical approach is also concerned with grasping the dynamics of modernity, as it touches on issues as diverse as the rise of the nation-state and the transformation of modern intimacy and sexuality. Such a sociological project involves answering some very big questions, including, in his words, "how should we best characterize modernity? What were its origins? What are the major transformations currently influencing the trajectories of development of world history?"[2]

Grand questions, indeed. In his earlier work (prior to about 1990), Giddens contended that the answers involved the systematic reconstruction of social theory, and its replacement by a new, synthetic approach, which he called structuration theory. But that is only half of the Giddens story. After the late 1980s, Giddens moved away from the relatively abstract conceptual issues animating his structuration theory, turning to an in-depth consideration of what he labels "late modernity." In his later work, he has systematically explored the "consequences of modernity," drawing on a wide range of empirical and theoretical materials to construct a theory of the dynamics of late modern societies. In his most recent work, Giddens has become even more concerned with the specific social issues facing modern societies. As he moved from Professor of Sociology at Cambridge University to Director of the London School of Economics in 1997, many of Giddens's writings now address the various questions confronting the Labour Party in Britain.

Giddens's theoretical project has maintained certain continuities, even if he has "changed his spots" over the years. He has consistently criticized the agency/structure, individual/society dualisms that he sees plaguing social theory. He critiques theories that either over-emphasize the deterministic role of social structure in influencing behavior (such as functionalism), or posit a free, decision-making individual relatively unencumbered by social structure (such as symbolic interactionism). Giddens's reconstruction of social theory places an active person at the center of sociological theory *and* modern society, who incorporates social structure into his/her very actions through reflexivity, or "the monitored character of the ongoing flow of social life."[3] Modern social structures are only reproduced by reflexive individuals inhabiting an increasingly "detraditionalized" and globally interdependent world, where old traditions and customs no longer provide signposts for how people should live, and who they should be.

As his concern with modernity demonstrates, Giddens states that a prime objective of social theory must be to "illuminate problems of empirical research."[4] Though often criticized for failing to concretely link theory and research, Giddens ties his rethinking of sociological theory directly to a consideration of the rapidly changing social and cultural conditions of late modernity.[5] Despite appearances to the contrary (as in the seemingly abstract terminology developed in his 1984 book, *The Constitution of Society*), Giddens has always been sensitive to the possibility that intramural sociological debates might lose their link to the real world. Accordingly, even in his most abstruse moments, Giddens has kept in mind the connections of sociological theory and the social world.

According to Giddens, modernity has been misunderstood because of the deficiencies of social theory. Giddens cites Marxism as a most influential interpretive culprit in this context, for it reduces the complexity of the modern world to the economic processes of capitalism. *Contra* Marx's economic reductionism, Giddens introduces four autonomous institutional dimensions of modernity: capitalism, industrialism, administrative surveillance, and the industrialization of warfare.[6] These institutional complexes arise and maintain themselves in a modern culture of incessant change. According to Giddens, "modernity involves the systematic study of social relations as part of the forging and reforging of those relations, something integral to its dynamic character."[7] This creates a modern phenomenon that Giddens labels institutional reflexivity, in which "the regularized use of knowledge about circumstances of social life [is] a constitutive element in its organization and transformation."[8]

Giddens would surely follow the early nineteenth-century social thinker Alexis de Tocqueville in advocating a new social science for a new world.[9] Thus, he introduces a conceptual vocabulary which can illuminate contemporary social changes in late modernity. While I will address his major theoretical concepts at various points throughout the text, here I wish to elucidate his notion of the double hermeneutic, one of the distinguishing features of his critical sociology. Giddens defines the double hermeneutic as the interweaving of the concepts of the social scientist and everyday life, as social scientific ideas are appropriated by laypeople and become part of the new social universe that the researcher studies.[10]

Giddens argues that the double hermeneutic means that social theory is invariably critical theory, in that it tries to grasp the dynamics of a fluid social world, and its concepts become part of the social world, which changes the very nature of society. For example, the sociological concept of role developed by functionalists and symbolic interactionists attempted to systematically explore patterns of social interaction. Yet people reflexively picked up this term, discussing their social world in terms of "role models" and the like. Social theory heavily influences the very conceptual categories that people use to understand their lives, as many of social theory's concepts become part of a society's self-comprehension.

Giddens states that social scientists should recognize this unique intersection of expert and everyday discourses and build it into the very fabric of their theories and research, rather than fetishistically advocating an objective sociology that distances researchers from their impact on social life through a number of quantitative methodological techniques. For Giddens, the double hermeneutic of the social sciences means that social theory is always studying a complex, changing social world. He calls for a "dialogic" sociology in this context, which breaks down rigid divisions between the expert and the layperson when studying social life and formulating social policies. In his most recent work, Giddens supports a new "generative" politics for leftists that transcends the old welfare state model concerned with class issues, such as increasing production, in favor of new concerns dealing with cultural identity, autonomy, and lifestyle.

Thus, Giddens's critical theory is far from Marxism, as he rejects many of Marx's major tenets, from the primacy of class struggle to the viability of socialism. Yet where does one place Giddens on the theoretical and political spectrum? This has always been a problem for commentators on Giddens's work. As Bryant and Jary state, "Sociologists are often unsure what to make of Giddens because he is too big to be ignored, and too singular to be labeled with confidence."[11] For many sociologists, Giddens is a frustrating thinker, as his approach seems to be an almost seamless web, where concepts refer to one another in a private theoretical system that sometimes appears as a conceptual prison whose inmates have developed a somewhat bizarre and self-enclosed linguistic code, rather than pointing the way toward a rehabilitation of social theory.

The impatience with Giddens's work also lies in the catholicity of his interests. He is no doubt an eclectic thinker, drawing from an astoundingly wide range of sociological, philosophical, historical, and anthropological literature (among others), traversing almost the whole of the social sciences in formulating his social theory. This volume situates Giddens within many of these theoretical perspectives, locating his work in various disputes within the social sciences. These debates include the legacy of classical sociological theory for an adequate understanding of modern society, the appropriate methodology for studying the social world, the structure/agency problem in social theory, theories of the transition from non or premodern societies to modern societies, the culture of late modernity and its relationship to postmodernity, the nature of democracy in the modern world, and the impact of feminism and changing definitions of sexuality on conceptions of self-identity.

This is a full, if not overflowing, theoretical plate. But this is why it is necessary to place Giddens in the contexts of theoretical debates. Examining Giddens's theory in isolation from other approaches misses the main contours of his perspective. As Giddens confronts a mammoth number of theoretical approaches, a shifting cast of theoretical characters inhabits the book, many of whom Giddens critically utilizes in developing his theories of structuration and modernity. Giddens engages in debates with almost every school of social theory. He is influenced by Marxism, ethnomethodology, phenomenology, French structuralism, postmodernism, and feminism, among others. I also compare Giddens's work with that of other major social theorists whom he does not discuss in detail, including Alain Touraine, Pierre Bourdieu, Norbert Elias, Robert Bellah, Jeffrey Alexander, and Hannah Arendt. These theorists approach some of the major issues that concern Giddens in ways which are different from his perspective, and can illuminate the distinctiveness, as well as the strengths and weaknesses, of Giddens's social theory.

As the reader peruses this volume, s/he will find many references to Giddens's criticisms of the "orthodox consensus" in sociology, associated with structural functionalism. Giddens contends that the hegemony of functionalism led sociology in some terrible directions, helping to institutionalize the dominance of a naturalistic study of social life and many of the dualities, such as structure/agency, which so exercise him. Two other figures reappear frequently throughout the book. Michel Foucault and Jürgen Habermas, two of the most influential contemporary social theorists of modernity, outline many of the issues that also concern Giddens. While Giddens engages both of them, and particularly criticizes Foucault in many of his works, I compare Giddens and these thinkers not only because they are so influential, but because Foucault and Habermas, too, are rethinking social theory in the wake of changing conceptions of modernity.

Habermas is the most insistent and powerful contemporary defender of the legacy of modernity and rationality for understanding the social world. Giddens, like Habermas, sees much of value in the modernist tradition, though the two agree that this legacy must be critiqued in the light of new social and theoretical developments. Giddens and Habermas also are very sensitive to issues of language when studying society. Both develop a critical theory which points in the direction of participatory, democratic social change.

Yet Giddens is much less confident than Habermas in the legacy of Enlightenment rationality. Giddens argues that history offers no guarantee that progressive social change will occur, and that such beliefs have been at the heart of illusory Marxist dreams which have ended in totalitarianism. Like Foucault, Giddens states that there is no necessary direction in history, as societies abruptly change from one era to another without any overarching logic, such as the Marxist emphasis on class struggle. Moreover, social relations will never be free of power, and positing a conflict-free, classless utopia can lead to dangerous, repressive measures to ensure such a community. Finally, like Foucault, Giddens sees the exclusion and domination of marginalized groups as inherent in the modern project, as a Western rationality concerned with increasing its own power silences some groups while "sequestering" difficult issues, such as death and deviance, beyond the purview of the public.

Giddens develops his own perspective on these various issues, being sure not to cast his theoretical lot exclusively with either the modernist Habermas or the modernist critic Foucault (though Giddens is at base a critic of the postmodern approach). The comparison of Giddens with Habermas and Foucault points to the problems of classifying his theoretical project. Giddens is neither a post-Marxist, as is Habermas, nor is he a poststructuralist, like Foucault. His eclecticism, as well as his maverick politics, has been part of the critical reception of his work.

Giddens and his critics: an overview

The range of Giddens's interests and his critical appropriation of a number of intellectual traditions has guaranteed that he has stepped on many theoretical toes. His work has been subject to a wide variety of criticisms, many collected in the recent four-volume tome of critical essays on his work published by Routledge, entitled *Anthony Giddens: Critical Assessments* (1996).[12] There have also been several books explicating his ideas, including a highly critical and rather idiosyncratic account by Ian Craib, and a more positive analysis by Ira Cohen.[13]

I note three major categories of Giddens criticism: the vagueness of his theory, his inadequate historical approach, and his reliance on an ahistorical notion of subjectivity. Many critics find Giddens's theory of structuration too abstract for a good understanding of the dynamics of the social world. For example, critics argue that Giddens cannot distinguish degrees of freedom and constraint which people face in particular situations, for he offers no criteria for distinguishing between freedom and unfreedom. Giddens does not adequately specify the historical conditions that lead to the emergence of modern institutions (such as industrialized warfare), and he does not adequately grasp the complexity of modern social systems. Even his political position is vague, as Giddens seems to advocate both liberal and socialist policies simultaneously, without placing himself in either camp.[14]

Giddens is also taken to task for his conception of social change. Despite his rejection of evolutionism, he appears to have an implicitly evolutionary and progressive view of history, as he categorizes societies in terms of increasing time-space distanciation (see Chapter 4, pp. 112–14 for a discussion of this concept).[15] His notion of increasing time-space distanciation tends to mimic modernization theory, as social development inevitably advances, and people can do little to resist it.[16] While Giddens adopts a voluntaristic theory that places the free, acting individual at its center, his historical analyses are very deterministic, as people appear to be the playthings of larger forces like the nation-state, modern surveillance, and capitalism.[17] Finally, Giddens's theory of history stresses the discontinuities between eras, downplaying continuities over time. He denies the importance of specifying particular character types in different historical eras, despite his call for a historically sensitive sociology.[18]

This last criticism leads to the most problematic aspect of Giddens's theory. Giddens is accused of having an ahistorical, asocial, and simplistic view of the individual, who has an exaggerated aptitude to remake the world after his/her own imagination. As Bryant argues, Giddens does not develop a notion of the "variations in human capacity for transformative action," but "prefers to assert a noble, almost Promethean" view of the self's capacities.[19] Craib states that Giddens has a simple concept of self-development, for Giddens does not analyze the complexity involved in the internalization of anxiety, and the ambiguities that this creates for self-conceptions and behavior. Giddens also underestimates the complex relationship of the self and the social world, particularly the practical restrictions that people invariably face.[20] Craib joins other critics in arguing that Giddens has difficulty in accounting for how social systems can be imposed on people. In the critics' view, he has an inadequate theory of the complexity of social interdependencies. To paraphrase Bauman, Giddens pays inadequate attention to who can structure social relations, and who is being structured by them.[21]

While Giddens has carefully responded to many of his critics, there is nevertheless much truth to some of these criticisms.[22] In particular,

Giddens tends to develop a view of the individual as almost separated from social structures. This concentration on the self leads Giddens to neglect a precise analysis of how people collectively make and remake social structures through social movements.[23] Thus, he does not adequately address the social and historical circumstances influencing the rise of social movements, nor does he explore issues of social identity and the mobilization of participants in social movements, questions that much of the sociological literature discusses (though Giddens has become more sensitive to these issues in his later work). In addition, a recurring criticism throughout this volume concerns Giddens's lack of a strong concept of culture, as he does not examine people as meaning-seeking creatures whose lives are subtly shaped by their cultural beliefs. Giddens has no strong theory of cultural innovation, of how "different cultural orientations, developed in diverse contexts, can promote or deny capacities for creative social action."[24]

Despite these criticisms, there is much of value in Giddens's reconstruction of sociological theory. As Bryant and Jary state, Giddens's critical appropriation of past and present theories demonstrates both the legacy of the classical tradition of Marx, Weber, and Durkheim for contemporary social theory, and how sociology can borrow from other disciplines in defining its own theoretical agenda. Giddens also challenges the agency/structure dualism that still predominates in much sociological discourse.[25] In addition to these contributions, I feel that Giddens advances sociological theory into the twenty-first century. As he states, "we live in a world . . . for which traditional sources of theory have left us unprepared."[26] Accordingly, he addresses new issues neglected by most social theory, such as the nature of modernity/postmodernity, the rise of a new reflexive, risk society, and the importance of gender and ecological issues in this new social world. Giddens has admirably attempted to take what is best in sociological theory and reformulate it in the context of changing social circumstances.

Part I of this volume explores Giddens's reconstruction of social theory, and his structuration alternative. Chapter 1 examines Giddens's analysis of the strengths and weaknesses of classical sociological theory, which in turn helps to set the agenda for his later theoretical arguments.

For Giddens, classical sociological theory placed the problems of discontinuous capitalism at the center of social scientific discussion, while adopting a critical approach to existing social institutions. However, Giddens believes that it is necessary to break with the classical legacy in many ways. He criticizes the assumptions of industrial society that underlay classical theory, and in particular the evolutionism characteristic of Marxism.

These objections lead him to criticize theories of the convergence of sociological traditions into a new theoretical synthesis, such as Parsons's structural functionalism, Alexander's multidimensional approach, and Habermas's theory of communicative action. I end this chapter by contrasting these latter perspectives with Giddens's understanding of the legacy of classical sociological theory.

Chapter 2 investigates Giddens's methodological perspective through exploring his critique of positivism and interpretive approaches to the study of society. For Giddens, understanding the distinctiveness of modernity cannot rely on the classical legacy of economic reductionism, nor on any other sociological methodology with a deterministic orientation, such as structural functionalism. Nor can sociologists turn to an overly voluntarist understanding of social life, as do symbolic interactionists. This chapter compares Giddens with a wide variety of methodological strategies, from the naturalistic perspective of Parsons and Popper through ethnomethodology and phenomenology, to the critique offered by poststructuralism.

Chapter 3 moves from Giddens's discussion of methodological principles to his actual theoretical work. This chapter outlines Giddens's theory of structuration, developing it in the context of his appropriation of themes from ethnomethodology, Goffman's social psychology, Erikson's analysis of identity, and Heidegger's philosophy.

This chapter compares Giddens, Bourdieu, and Elias on agency and structure. Though these authors emphasize the centrality of reflexivity in contemporary society and the non-discursive and contextual influences on social life (such as Bourdieu's idea of the habitus, and Elias's notion of figuration), they differ in many ways. In particular, Bourdieu and Elias are more sanguine about the possibility of a strong social science than is Giddens, and thus adopt a more deterministic framework than he does. Giddens places much more emphasis on the constituted, creative, and relatively contingent nature of modern social life than do these other sociologists. Further, Bourdieu in particular develops a strategic framework for understanding social action that differs from Giddens's structuration theory.

Part II examines Giddens's analysis of modernity and social change. Chapter 4 explores Giddens's "macro" sociological explanation of social change, including the rise of the nation-state, the modern world-system, and contemporary institutions. I compare Giddens's perspective to modern variants of Marxism, especially Wallerstein's analysis of the world-system. I also contrast his approach to Foucault's discussion of the rise of disciplining institutions and surveillance in the West.

Giddens draws on Marx's theory of capitalism to distinguish class societies from class-divided societies. He introduces his notion of time-space distanciation to capture better than class struggle how societies differ from one another. Giddens also argues that modern nation-states are increasingly part of an interdependent world-system. His theory of modernity ties reflexivity to a sensitivity to intersocial relations like warfare, which are often neglected in sociological analysis.

Chapter 5 explores Giddens's notion of reflexive modernization as the key dimension of the culture of modernity. For Giddens, modernity is a "juggernaut" of constant change. Despite this incessant change, Giddens argues that late modernity is different from what many theorists label postmodernity. He contends that postmodern theorists underestimate the complexity of modernist rationality, which has been radicalized in late modernity. I contrast Giddens's view of modernity to that of Foucault, and I compare his theory to the similar analyses of Habermas and Touraine. Like these latter theorists, Giddens recognizes the importance of new social movements as agents of social change in the modern world.

Chapter 6 examines Giddens's perspective on the prospects for modern democracy, comparing his view to those of the Frankfurt School, Arendt, Lasch, Sennett, and Habermas. Giddens's view of people as reflexively engaging in reconstituting their social lives gives him a much more optimistic view of the possibilities of a vibrant democracy in modern societies than many other theorists, such as Sennett, Lasch, and Habermas. These theorists see democracy as threatened by a capitalist economic and cultural system which promotes the pursuit of wealth, narcissism, and depoliticization at the expense of democratic public participation. Giddens's perspective is much more in line with the cultural studies perspective, which views people as actively reproducing the culture in which they live, rather than being dominated by capitalist commodities.

Chapter 7 explores Giddens's analysis of modern sexuality and self-development. He believes that feminism has greatly influenced contemporary perceptions of these issues. I compare Giddens's analysis to those of many feminists, including Chodorow, Gilligan, and postmodernists such as Butler. I also discuss Freud's and Marcuse's views of sexuality, with which Giddens finds fault. Giddens states that the revolution in gender roles ushered in by feminism has increased both the indeterminacy and possibilities of modern self-development.

I conclude the volume with a discussion of Giddens's critique of the modern welfare state, and an analysis of the overall strengths and weaknesses of his social theory.

Notes

1 Anthony Giddens, *Social Theory and Modern Sociology* (Stanford, Stanford University Press, 1987), p. 42.

2 Ibid., p. 43.

3 Anthony Giddens, *The Constitution of Society: Outline of the Theory of Structuration* (Berkeley, University of California Press, 1984), p. 3.

4 Ibid., p. xxix.

5 For criticisms of Giddens's failure to link theory and practice, see Nicky

Gregson, "On the (Ir)Relevance of Structuration Theory to Empirical Research," in *Social Theory of Modern Societies: Anthony Giddens and His Critics*, ed. David Held and John B. Thompson (New York, Cambridge University Press, 1989), pp. 235–248.

6 Anthony Giddens, *The Consequences of Modernity* (Stanford, Stanford University Press, 1990), p. 59.

7 Giddens, *Social Theory and Modern Sociology*, p. viii.

8 Anthony Giddens, *Modernity and Self-Identity: Self and Society in the Late Modern Age* (Stanford, Stanford University Press, 1991), p. 20.

9 Alexis de Tocqueville, *Democracy in America*, Vol. 1 (New York, Vintage, 1990), p. 7.

10 Giddens, *The Constitution of Society*, p. 374.

11 Christopher G.A. Bryant and David Jary, "Introduction: Coming to Terms with Anthony Giddens," in *Giddens' Theory of Structuration: A Critical Appreciation*, ed. Christopher G.A. Bryant and David Jary (New York, Routledge, 1991), p. 3.

12 *Anthony Giddens: Critical Assessments* 4 vols, ed. David Jary and Christopher G.A. Bryant (London, Routledge, 1996).

13 Ian Craib, *Anthony Giddens* (New York, Routledge, 1992); and Ira Cohen, *Structuration Theory: Anthony Giddens and the Constitution of Social Life* (New York, St. Martin's Press, 1989).

14 Craib, *Anthony Giddens*, pp. 150–151, 158; David Held, "Citizenship and Autonomy," p. 183; Gregson, "On the (Ir)Relevance of Structuration Theory to Empirical Research," p. 213; Martin Shaw, "War and the Nation-State in Social Theory," p. 144, all in *Social Theory of Modern Societies*, ed. Held and Thompson.

15 E.O. Wright, "Models of Historical Trajectory: An Assessment of Giddens's Critique of Marxism," in *Social Theory of Modern Societies*, ed. Held and Thompson, p. 97.

16 John Urry, "Time and Space in Giddens' Social Theory," in *Giddens' Theory of Structuration*, ed. Bryant and Jary, p. 169.

17 Craib, *Anthony Giddens*, p. 149.

18 Richard Kilminster, "Structuration Theory as a World-View," in *Giddens' Theory of Structuration*, ed. Bryant and Jary, p. 87.

19 Christopher G.A. Bryant, "The Dialogical Model of Applied Sociology," ibid., p. 199.

20 Craib, *Anthony Giddens*, pp. 176–177, 188–189.

21 Zygmunt Bauman, "Hermeneutics and Modern Social Theory," in *Social Theory of Modern Societies*, ed. Held and Thompson, p. 46; see also Kilminster, "Structuration Theory as a World-View," p. 97.

22 See Anthony Giddens, "A Reply to My Critics," *Social Theory of Modern Societies*, ed. Held and Thompson, pp. 249–301.

23 Craib, *Anthony Giddens*, p. 151.

24 Kenneth H. Tucker, Jr., "Aesthetics, Play and Cultural Memory: Giddens and Habermas on the Postmodern Challenge," *Sociological Theory* 11 (July 1993), p. 197.

25 Bryant and Jary, "Introduction," pp. 22–23.

26 Giddens, *Social Theory and Modern Sociology*, p. 166. Quoted in David Jary, "'Society as Time-Traveler': Giddens on Historical Change, Historical Materialism and the Nation-State in World Society," ibid., p. 119.

PART ONE

THE RECONSTRUCTION OF SOCIAL THEORY

Giddens states that "social theory stands in need of systematic reconstruction."[1] His theory of structuration aims to overcome the theoretical dualities, such as those of agency/structure, micro/macro, and qualitative/quantitative methodological approaches, which he thinks characterize not only sociology, but the social sciences as a whole. These dualisms prevent the social sciences from attaining a better understanding of the social world.

This necessity for a reconstruction of social theory became particularly acute in the wake of the breakdown of the "orthodox consensus" that ruled sociology from the 1950s until the end of the 1960s. Associated with the structural functionalism of Talcott Parsons, the orthodox consensus consists of three components: functionalism, the notion that a society has its own particular needs apart from its individual members; naturalism, the contention that natural science provides the model for social scientific methodology; and social causation, the idea that social scientists know the cause of an individual's behavior, rather than the person himself/herself.[2] Giddens believes that the orthodox consensus disintegrated for good reasons, as he finds fault with all three of its major elements. Giddens rejects the notion that a society has its own needs apart from those of acting, conscious individuals; he thinks that social science raises distinctive methodological problems that escape the strictures of a natural scientific methodology; and he argues that any explanation of people's actions must take into account their understanding of their behavior.

Giddens does not feel that the breakdown of the orthodox consensus necessarily leads to theoretical pluralism, though that is indeed the case with much modern sociological theory, as schools of thought from ethnomethodology to Marxism to poststructuralism seem to be at odds with one another. He contends that his theory of structuration can lead to a new synthetic sociological orientation, based on a rethinking of such basic sociological concepts as meaning, agency, structure, and power.

Giddens argues that his new interpretation of these concepts can help orient sociological theory to the study of social action in actual space and time. Thus, he states that a perennial debate in sociology, that between micro (agent-centered) and macro (society-centered) approaches should be replaced by a focus on the difference between face-to-face interaction, and interaction with those not physically present. Such a perspective moves sociology from abstract conceptual debates to a focus on real, acting people.[3] Most importantly, Giddens contends that a concentration on people's everyday pragmatic, practical social action can lead sociological theory in a more productive direction than either the deterministic theories of functionalism and Marxism or overly subjective approaches such as symbolic interactionism. He draws on philosophy, especially the linguistic philosopher Wittgenstein, in developing his notions of social practices and practical consciousness. Giddens states that one of the most important aspects of the modern philosophical "linguistic turn" associated with Wittgenstein is the rejection of the dualism of private, subjective experience and an objective culture separated from such experience. In Giddens's words, modern philosophy demonstrates that "personal experience is known to the self as a 'self' only via the public categories of language."[4] He believes that this focus on language leads to a clear appreciation of how the person and society cannot be separated, but must be understood as integrally tied to one another. The individual's practical activities in the course of his/her social life links subjective experience with larger social processes.

Giddens states that these ideas must all be related to one another. Among the bevy of theoretical concepts he introduces, perhaps the notions of the duality of structure and the double hermeneutic best illuminate his theoretical goals. The duality of structure means that people both draw on and create social structures in the course of their everyday social activity. The double hermeneutic refers to the process whereby the different vocabularies of the social scientist and the person acting in society constantly slip into one another, as researchers study the common practices and discourses of laypeople, while social scientific findings become part of everyday language.[5] Giddens's discussion of these two concepts shows that various social phenomena, from the relationship of the individual to social structure to the separation of the findings of the social scientist from the beliefs of everyday people, are not discrete but intertwined.

Giddens devises his approach through a systematic critique of many contemporary social theories. Before explicating the concepts of structuration theory in Chapter 3, we will explore Giddens's foray into the methodological debates in the social sciences and his attempt to derive new rules of sociological method. First, it is necessary to examine Giddens's evaluation of the legacy of Marx, Durkheim, and Weber. His rethinking of classical social theory raises many of the themes addressed in his larger theoretical project.

Notes

1 Anthony Giddens, *Central Problems in Social Theory: Action, Structure, and Contradiction in Social Analysis* (Berkeley, University of California Press, 1979), p. 240.

2 Anthony Giddens, *In Defence of Sociology: Essays, Interpretations, and Rejoinders* (Cambridge, MA, Polity Press, 1996), p. 65.

3 Giddens, *Central Problems in Social Theory*, p. 203.

4 Giddens, *In Defence of Sociology*, p. 205.

5 Giddens, *The Constitution of Society: Outline of the Theory of Structuration* (Berkeley, University of California Press, 1984), p. 374.

1

THE LEGACY OF CLASSICAL
SOCIOLOGICAL THEORY

In most colleges and universities, sociology students who study social theory read texts from Karl Marx, Max Weber, and Emile Durkheim. These three nineteenth-century European social theorists are considered to have formulated the basic theoretical concerns of sociology. Yet the interpretations of these classics have never been straightforward. Debates around the meaning of their writings have fueled sociological theory since its origins. In the wake of the vital social changes affecting the contemporary social world, disputes often now focus on the relevance of these theorists for understanding contemporary societies.

Giddens was introduced to many sociologists through his reinterpretation of the nature and legacy of classical sociological theory which he first developed in his 1971 work, *Capitalism and Modern Social Theory*. Giddens subsequently wrote a number of pieces on the thought of Marx, Weber, and Durkheim.[1] His analysis of the classics challenges the major approaches to the history of sociological theory, such as the perspectives advanced by Parsons, Nisbet, and Zeitlin. Criticizing what he sees as either overly abstract or polemical interpretations of the classical figures, Giddens places Marx, Durkheim, and Weber in the social context of their time. He views each theorist as creating a critical perspective on the nature of modern society, but stresses that these approaches have to be reformulated in fundamental ways in order to make sense of the modern world. Indeed, Giddens's structuration theory cannot be understood apart from his appreciation and critique of both the classical theorists and their sociological interpreters.

This chapter begins with a brief summary of the social theories of Marx, Weber, and Durkheim, followed by a discussion of the most influential sociological interpretations of their work from the 1930s through the 1960s, including those of Parsons, Nisbet, and Zeitlin. I then turn to Giddens's critique of these approaches to the history of social thought, and his own interpretation of the classics. The chapter ends by comparing Giddens's perspective on the history of sociological thought with the approaches of Alexander and Habermas, two of the most important contemporary interpreters of the legacy of classical sociological theory.

Marx, Weber, Durkheim, and the emergence of modernity

Marx's, Weber's, and Durkheim's theories constitute the core of the sociological tradition. They achieved sociology's most distinctive orientations and forceful ideas. Each of these thinkers was contributing to a common intellectual undertaking: what Collins refers to as the discovery of society.[2] They responded in different ways to a shared historical context, which included the rise and transformation of Western society in the nineteenth and early twentieth centuries. The aftermath of the French Revolution, the industrial revolution, and the emergence of the market opened up social, economic, and cultural possibilities and problems previously unthought, from the possibilities of new, more complex types of social organization (capitalism and socialism) to a novel type of culture (based on rationality, social participation, and individualism rather than tradition). Marx, Weber, and Durkheim all see the possibilities for human freedom embodied in the rationality and democracy arising with the modern world, though each also recognizes problems inherent in contemporary societies, exemplified in Marx's discussion of alienation, Weber's view of the loss of meaning in the iron cage of bureaucratic rationality, and Durkheim's analysis of anomie.

Marx's historical materialism emphasizes the rise of capitalism and industry. Though Marx formulates very sophisticated views of ideology and the state, his theory focuses on how people materially produce and reproduce their life in the labor process, which determines their existence. The material reproduction of social life is tied to the existence of classes that are in conflict with one another, for all history is the history of class struggle. Marx believes that modern class conflict arises from the major contradiction of capitalism, namely the social nature of production executed by the proletariat (the working class) versus the private ownership of the fruits of labor, concentrated in the hands of the capitalist class. Socialism, and later communism, means the collective ownership and governing of production, and allows this contradiction to be overcome.

Weber argues that it is the rise of rationality, and not only new forms of class struggle, that distinguishes modern societies from previous forms of social organization. The emergence of capitalism and democracy progressively rationalizes and disenchants everyday life, as the world loses its mysterious and magical qualities in the face of science and reason. From the Protestant ethic associated with the emergence of capitalism to the dominance of bureaucracy in the modern world and the prestige of science, rationality is both institutionally and subjectively anchored in the ways in which modern people live. Despite these rationalizing trends, Weber believes that the complexity of social life ultimately outstrips the ability of the social sciences to fully comprehend it. This respect for complexity extends to the realm of culture, for Weber thinks that science cannot resolve questions of ultimate values; he sees the modern world as ruled by many gods. Such pluralism also informs his understanding of class, status, and party. Though the three intertwine, each has its own independent logic.

Durkheim does not see the modern world as disenchanted à la Weber; rather, he emphasizes the centrality of shared, sacred beliefs in the creation of social solidarity. For Durkheim, society functions like an organism, tending to return to a state of equilibrium when undergoing social changes. But this process does not occur automatically. People's social conduct is based on following rules and beliefs, which they must find convincing and appealing. Social rules provide people with meaning and stability; in order to be effective, these rules must be attached to a sacred core. Society is a sacred, moral universe, whose values need to be respected and periodically revivified. Rituals and ceremonies provide the means for revitalizing social life, which in modern organic solidarity is anchored in the division of labor and in professional and occupational groups. Organic solidarity has to be based on people's democratic and rational participation in the creation of the very groups in which they live. A lack of active participation can lead to a meaningless social existence characterized by anomie and egoism, in which people do not share in the moral benefits of social life.

Parsons, Nisbet, and the interpretation of Weber and Durkheim

Marx, Weber, and Durkheim were important figures in their own time, for they developed powerful theories of society. Yet they became the centerpiece of modern sociological theory through the interpretations of sociologists such as Parsons, Nisbet, and Zeitlin. Parsons, writing in the 1930s, was the most influential interpreter of the sociological tradition. He had virtually nothing to say about Marx, but introduced Weber and Durkheim into the sociological canon. Parsons argues that Weber and Durkheim created the foundations for a truly scientific sociology, for their sophisticated theories decisively broke with those of their often unsystematic predecessors.[3]

Parsons states that Weber and Durkheim were responding to the abstract problem of social order, which he tied to the seventeenth century British philosopher Thomas Hobbes. He argues that Hobbes captures a central dilemma for social theory. In developing the assumptions of utilitarian philosophy, Hobbes states that people are by nature motivated by self-interest; consequently, they must give up some of their selfish desires to a central authority in order to live together in a society. According to Parsons, Hobbes's belief raises the problem of how cooperation in society is even possible. In more sociological parlance, Hobbes's theory questions how social order is possible in an unregulated and competitive system.[4]

Parsons agrees with the Hobbesian emphasis on agents seeking goals and making decisions based on an understanding of their wants and needs. Yet he contends that Weber and Durkheim develop a theory of the normative integration of society that represents a more profound understanding of the social nature of human beings, which differs substantially from Hobbes's theory of self-interest. Parsons argues that Weber and Durkheim realize that people's actions and attitudes are influenced by institutionalized values (such as individual achievement and justice in modern capitalist democracies) as well as by self-interest, heredity, and environment. Parsons states that Weber's discussion of the means–end relationship (that people strive to realize certain goals, utilizing different and/or appropriate means to achieve them) captures an important aspect of social action. People are oriented to situations in terms of motives and values (conceptions about what is appropriate). Like Durkheim, Parsons argues that people's actions often aim to realize ultimate, sacred ends, which are not arbitrary, but are matters of moral obligation.

Thus, Parsons takes from Weber and Durkheim the idea that through living in society people develop norms and values which in turn inform their behavior and attitudes. Modern beliefs in individualism, justice, achievement, and the like, and their institutional embodiments, such as the family, schools, and the law are more influential in determining people's actions than self-interest.[5] Parsons utilizes this interpretation of Weber and Durkheim to develop his theory of structural functionalism, which integrates the needs of society and the individual into a cohesive whole. Parsons is also aware of the shortcomings of these classical figures. He states that Weber does not sufficiently recognize the importance of moral obligation in society, which Durkheim emphasizes. While stressing Durkheim's concern for moral order, Parsons argues that Durkheim is too deterministic in his understanding of human behavior, for society can be changed by people in pursuit of their moral ideals.

After Parsons's analysis of their thought in *The Structure of Social Action* (1937), Durkheim and Weber were firmly entrenched in the sociological canon. Later interpreters developed different dimensions of the classical figures' work. Nisbet in particular formulated an influential interpretation of the sociological tradition, arguing that much of it, especially Durkheim's theory, is a conservative response to the rise of the Enlightenment. Like Parsons, Nisbet believes that sociology represents a reaction against the rationalist individualism of the utilitarians such as Hobbes. Sociology's most characteristic concepts, such as a concern with community, authority, tradition, and the sacred, draw from the conservative tradition of social thought.[6] Thus Durkheim, according to Nisbet, was indebted to French conservatism. Durkheim was predominantly concerned with the preservation of social order; he searched for the enduring bases of social cohesion in the context of the radical changes in social life introduced by the Enlightenment.[7]

Giddens contends that both Nisbet and Parsons misunderstand the impetus behind Weber's and Durkheim's theories. His critique leads to a different understanding of the sociological tradition. Giddens argues that Parsons subsumes the concrete German and European context influencing Weber's sociology under the abstract rubric of the problem of order. Weber attempted to grasp the distinctiveness of capitalism and the modern state in the context of the peculiarities of nineteenth-century German political, economic, and social development. Giddens also states that the problem of order was not the guiding theme of Durkheimian sociology. Rather, Durkheim tried to distinguish between traditional and modern societies. In so doing, he responded to Kantian idealism as much as Hobbesian utilitarianism, for he was concerned with grasping the distinctiveness of modern forms of moral belief.[8] His important distinction between the sacred and the profane and the autonomy of moral sentiments showed the influence of Kantian idealism on his sociology. Moreover, Durkheim did not develop his theory in an abstract confrontation with Hobbes, but in the context of the rise of the Third Republic in France. Durkheim attempted to develop a new form of moral individualism which could provide legitimacy for the Republic in the face of critiques by French conservative Catholics, landowners, and peasants. Finally, attempts to create a science of society have a long history, predating Durkheim and Weber, who did not in any simple sense scientifically break with their predecessors.[9]

Giddens also criticizes Nisbet's perspective for failing to examine the concrete context in which the classical sociologists developed their theories. He is particularly forceful in his critique of Nisbet's interpretation of Durkheim. Giddens argues that Durkheim, like other nineteenth-century thinkers, drew on disparate sources ranging from the conservative Comte to the radical Rousseau, synthesizing them into a new theory of society. Durkheim was not only influenced by the conservative tradition in France, but much more so by his confrontation with the republican and socialist traditions flowing from Rousseau and Saint-Simon (who also influenced Marx), as well as by the German "socialists of the chair," such as A.H.G. Wagner and G. Schmoller, and French neo-Kantians, including Charles Renouvier. Durkheim's theory does not posit the necessity of a conservative form of authority that has to restrain our individualistic inclinations. Rather, the differences between traditional and modern forms of society animate Durkheim's thought. Durkheim argues that modern moral individualism represents a great advance in human freedom. It differs dramatically from the relatively undifferentiated and absolutist form of moral authority characteristic of mechanical solidarity, which cannot be effective under modern conditions. For Durkheim, there is no contradiction between freedom and authority in the modern world, for modern forms of organic solidarity represent a great advance over the often despotic type of social cohesion found in mechanical, premodern societies.[10]

Marx and the history of sociological thought

Though influential in his interpretation of Weber and Durkheim, Parsons virtually ignored Marxist thought. In the context of the ideological ferment of the 1960s, many sociologists argued that Marx played a pivotal role in the history of sociological theory. Zeitlin and Coser in particular state that the perspectives of Durkheim and Weber were a reaction to Marx's historical materialism. Moreover, according to Dahrendorf, Marx helped create a distinctive type of sociology oriented to conflict, which contrasted with Durkheim's functionalist perspective.[11]

Giddens is very uncomfortable with those perspectives which posit that Weber and Durkheim formulated their social theories in response to Marxism. Giddens believes that Weber and Durkheim developed a new type of liberalism that was in part a response to Marx's followers, more than to Marx himself; but more importantly, their theories were an answer to the social challenges raised by conservatives in France and Germany. Despite differences, Weber and Durkheim developed approaches which integrated rationality and democracy into a new form of liberalism that was very different from the types of social order advocated by conservatives. In so doing, their thought actually drew on themes that were similar in many respects to Marxism.

Giddens argues that Weber did not logically refute Marx's materialism with an idealistic reinterpretation of the rise of capitalism in *The Protestant Ethic and the Spirit of Capitalism*, as many commentators have stated. Rather, like Marx, Weber was attempting to understand the nature of modern capitalism. He shares Marx's belief that material forces and social classes are central features of capitalist development. Even more misleading, according to Giddens, is the abstract contrast developed by Dahrendorf of a functionalist Durkheim and a conflict-oriented Marx. Giddens argues that Marx and Durkheim do not have radically different views of human nature and the abstract requirements of society, for both see human needs and constraints as socially generated. Both are intrigued by the problem of social change, and each attempts to understand the particular dynamics of modern societies. Durkheim, in Giddens's words, is concerned with achieving change rather than maintaining order.[12] Durkheim's main theoretical puzzle does not concern clarifying the conditions favoring social integration vs. social breakdown, but involves specifying differences between traditional and modern societies. This latter opposition accounts for differences between Marx and Durkheim, which arise from differing analyses of the transition from traditional to modern societies. In particular, they disagree regarding the origins and significance of class conflict in this transition.[13]

In sum, Giddens contends that most commentators on the classical sociological tradition misinterpret its legacy. They do not realize that Marx, Weber, and Durkheim developed theories about the distinctiveness of the modern world, and the ways in which Western society of the late nineteenth and early twentieth centuries differed dramatically from previous forms of social organization. For Giddens, the classical thinkers grasped the problems and prospects of a new type of capitalist society that was very different ("discontinuous," in Giddens's word) from traditional societies. This "great transformation" caused by the rise of capitalism and modern forms of the state and culture is the central drama that the classical theorists attempted to understand, as each developed a critical approach to modern institutions.[14] Moreover, Giddens argues that the great transformation, as it was played out in France, England, and Germany, provided the context for these thinkers' reflections on the nature and dynamics of modern societies. These theorists were not primarily concerned with creating an abstract sociological theory, but they were responding to specific problems that they faced within their own societies.

Giddens believes that a sound analysis of the nature and legacy of classical sociological theory must begin by placing the thinkers in the concrete context of their time and societies. Such historical specification not only illuminates their ideas, but also problematizes Parsons's notion that modern sociological theory is some sort of convergence of the ideas originally formulated by the classical founders, and Zeitlin's idea that Durkheim's and Weber's theories were conservative responses to Marx. For Giddens, no grand sociological narrative that seamlessly ties modern and classical theory emerges from an examination of Marx, Weber, and Durkheim.

Giddens argues that each classical theorist's perspective is incomplete. Weber's theory of rationalization does not satisfactorily grasp possibilities for meaningful change in the modern world, for he is unable to fully comprehend the moral bases of modernity. Because his perspective is tied to aristocratic values of heroism and manliness, Weber cannot recognize that modern societies might develop forms of solidarity that are more than expressions of bourgeois mediocrity.[15] While Durkheim develops a theory of moral order based on active, democratic participation in occupational groups and a republican government, his analysis of the state is faulty. Giddens argues that Durkheim's concern with the collective conscience associated with moral individualism leads him to neglect the systematic treatment of how political power is generated, especially in parliament and political parties. Nor does Durkheim account for the generation of socially diverse interests which create much conflict in modern societies.[16] Finally, Giddens sees Marx's emphasis on the organization of production as the generator of conflict, and the source of social progress, as the major problem with Marxist analysis. Marx, like many nineteenth-century thinkers, uncritically celebrates the "Promethean attitude" that the expansion of productive forces is unproblematically tied to social progress. Moreover, he develops an instrumental understanding of nature. Marx's concept of labor is not sufficiently differentiated to grasp the complexity of people's relationship to nature. Thus, Marx has no theory of the possibility of environmental degradation as a result of the expansion of industry.[17]

Giddens argues that it is necessary to break with the classical legacy in many ways. In particular, he criticizes the assumptions of an invariant industrial society and the evolutionary theory of history that underlie classical approaches. Giddens states that classical sociological theory is based on economic and industrial reductionism, whether it be in the form of Marx's criticisms of capitalism or Weber's analysis of bureaucracy. These classical accounts neglect the autonomy of other institutional changes, including the rise of administrative power, the growth of military power and war, the importance of the nation-state and its regionalization in the world-system, and the distinctive cultural dimension of modernity. They do not see that history is a contingent process, often characterized by ruptures and breaks rather than progressing in any sort of linear fashion.[18] Finally, Giddens argues that classical sociological accounts tend to be too deterministic, and do not adequately theorize the role of agents' reflexivity in the reproduction of social life. People skillfully and actively make and remake their social world, and can change society accordingly.

Giddens differs from the major interpreters of the classical sociological tradition, who developed their analyses from the 1930s through the 1960s. His view of the origins and legacy of sociological theory has not remained unchallenged. In the 1980s two influential sociologists reinterpreted the sociological canon in ways very different from Giddens's contextual perspective. Often animated by a sympathetic interpretation of Parsons, Alexander has rethought the premises of functionalism, while Habermas has reworked the Marxist tradition. They argue that, though Marx, Weber, and Durkheim raise issues of action and order, or system and lifeworld, they do not sufficiently link them together in a coherent, systematic theory of society. Accordingly, the still valuable classical theories must be supplemented by a new multidimensional theory, in Alexander's lexicon, or a new theory of communicative action, for Habermas.

Alexander and multidimensionality

A recent reaffirmation of the importance of the classical theorists, and a corresponding reinterpretation of their significance, has been formulated by Alexander. He argues that Marx, Weber, and Durkheim, and their American interpreter Parsons, raised central issues that still inform the social sciences. Each classical theorist recognizes, if only implicitly, that any social theory contains voluntarist and determinist elements, for a sociological perspective must advance a theory of human freedom and the conditions under which such freedom is influenced and/or constrained. According to Alexander, Marx and Durkheim waver between freedom and determinism in their analyses, never fashioning a clear synthesis that integrates these disparate orientations into a coherent whole. Weber and Parsons self-consciously attempt such a theoretical synthesis of voluntarist and determinist moments, but are unable to do so satisfactorily. Alexander argues that his multidimensional approach captures the distinctive contributions of the classical theorists, and provides a synthetic sociological theory.

A full understanding of Alexander's interpretation of the classics must examine his own sociological theory, which critiques positivism while building on the non-positivist achievements of Marx, Weber, Durkheim, and Parsons. Alexander contends that his multidimensional theoretical logic breaks with the positivist persuasion in social science, while also surmounting the problems of classical sociological theory. Positivism consists of the belief in a clear difference between metaphysical beliefs and empirical observations, the indifference of metaphysical beliefs to any true science, and the notion that the social sciences must assume a scientific orientation along the lines of natural science. Further, for the positivist persuasion, empirical observations are unproblematic, theory must be analyzed and/or tested in terms of such empirical observations, and scientific knowledge is progressive and cumulative. According to Alexander, positivism continues to rule the social sciences.[19]

Alexander argues for a "postpositivist" theoretical model, criticizing several positivist postulates in advancing his alternative. For Alexander, all empirical data are informed by theory; scientific commitments are based on the principled rejection of data as well as on empirical evidence; general theoretical elaboration tends to be dogmatic and ad hoc rather than skeptical and progressive; and shifts in scientific belief occur when empirical changes are matched by theoretical shifts, which often are unclear because they are not explicitly stated.[20]

According to Alexander, scientific development is a two-tiered process, propelled by theoretical as much as empirical argument. He attempts to develop a theoretical methodology to capture this logic. Alexander contends that often social sciences appear to be lacking such a theoretical logic, as well as empirical rigor, because of their relative lack of consensus relative to the natural sciences.[21] He argues that the conditions of social science make agreement on the precise nature of empirical knowledge problematic. Unlike the natural sciences, changes in social scientific knowledge often have direct implications for social life. Yet foremost in Alexander's critique of positivism is the independent logic that characterizes theoretical argument in the social sciences. Persuasive theoretical discourse is often based on its logical coherence, interpretive insight, value relevance, and expansiveness of scope, rather than simply fitting the available facts. Moreover, explanation in the social sciences is hampered by the difficulty of successfully and sufficiently operationalizing complex social variables into testable hypotheses.[22]

Like Parsons, Alexander believes that voluntarism and determinism are basic issues that have been characteristic of theoretical reasoning in the Western philosophical tradition since its inception. These issues, in sociological and more specifically Parsonian language, include that of action, or subjective motivation; and that of order, or how people are interrelated in society. This distinction corresponds to that between sociological idealism (action) and sociological determinism (order).[23] Alexander believes that every theory must adopt a stance toward the order question as well as a theory of motivation.[24] He argues that action is both instrumental and normative, ordered through internal and external structures. Multidimensionality preserves voluntarism while also recognizing the external conditions and barriers to its realization. His multidimensional approach not only attempts to disclose reality, but extends a particular interpretation of it.[25]

This theoretical perspective informs Alexander's view of the classics. For Alexander, the classics play several roles for sociological thinking. First, they allow sociological discourse to maintain boundaries by providing a common frame of reference, a common set of issues arising from the classics' work. More importantly, the writings of the classical theorists, like the works of great artists, stand on their own merits. Classical social science remains powerful because of the extraordinary sensitivity and insight into the social world produced by Marx, Weber, and Durkheim, their understanding of the issues and problems involved in reconstructing and changing the social world, and their elaboration of an effective ideology that continues to inspire modern social scientists (seen especially in the work of Marx).[26]

Revision of views about the classical theorists does not occur because of new discoveries about their lives and/or work, but because of the changing interests and intentions of contemporary theorists. Thus, the debate over the conflict and functionalist alternatives in sociology involved rethinking the nature of classical theory. Moreover, in no sense did Parsons discover the classics. His theoretical intentions informed his analysis of Weber and Durkheim.[27]

Alexander's reconstruction of classical sociological theory brings all of these issues to bear. He focuses on the classical theorists' orientations to order and action, seeing each theorist as developing internal tensions between sociological materialism and idealism. He examines the pre-suppositions of their thought, and relates their theories to empirical and ideological issues. For Alexander, Marx's early work was strongly voluntarist, but for empirical, ideological, and epistemological reasons he moved toward a more instrumental type of reasoning. Durkheim, on the other hand, showed a determinist and materialist orientation in his early work. Later, in such books as *The Elementary Forms of the Religious Life* (1965[1912]), Durkheim turned toward a more voluntaristic socio-logical theory. According to Alexander, the strains in each theorist's perspective help account for the vastly different interpretations of their work formulated by followers of Durkheim and Marx.[28]

Alexander sees Weber as the only classical theorist consciously attempting to surmount the dualisms of idealism and materialism so dominant in the history of social thought. Influenced by the idealist and materialist strands of the German intellectual tradition, Weber realizes that every act has an instrumental component of calculation and is affected by material circumstances. Yet acts also take place in a cultural context which supplies them with meaning. In fact, modern rationality owes much of its power to its moral origins in the Protestant ethic. So, for Weber, instrumental rationality is always bounded by normative considerations; his thought is multidimensional because "rational action is mediated by normative order."[29]

Weber's synthetic sociology ultimately took an instrumental direction. Like other German liberals, he accepted the reality of the relatively unchanging instrumental interests of classes and nations associated with class conflict and *realpolitik*, while also paying homage to the more idealist strands of German romanticism. Weber drifted toward a cultural pessimism characteristic of many German intellectuals because he did not believe that an ethical orientation could survive in a "disenchanted" modern world devoid of a strong religious foundation. Unable to bridge the epistemological gap between religious and non-religious thought, Weber saw the decline of the sacredness of the Protestant ethic as producing a modern world rife with meaninglessness, an "iron cage" in his unforgettable image.[30]

Giddens would not necessarily disagree with all the aspects of Alexander's sophisticated analyses of classical theorists. Like Giddens, Alexander ties the thought of the classical figures to their social and intellectual context. He grasps tensions in their theoretical edifice which lead to problematic positions. Alexander recognizes Weber's inability to develop a non-religious moral basis for modern societies, which informs his view of modernity as an iron cage. Finally, Giddens concurs with Alexander that sociology must break with positivist assumptions. Yet Giddens believes that, like Parsons, many of Alexander's arguments are misguided. For Giddens, abstract problems of order and action should not be the subject matter of sociology, for they give the illusion of more continuity than really exists in the history of social thought. Moreover, the classical theorists tried to explain the distinctiveness of modernity, rather than address these purely theoretical issues.

Habermas and communicative action

Giddens faces another formidable opponent in Habermas, who understands the legacy of the classics in a way different from structuration theory. Habermas is the most prominent current representative of the neo-Marxist Frankfurt School of critical theory established by German scholars such as Max Horkheimer and Theodor Adorno in the 1930s. These authors criticized the emerging one-dimensionality of modern society, in which corporate capitalism, technology, and the mass culture industry such as television reduced the scope of human freedom and critical thinking. As modern society arose, alternatives for a better and/ or different society were reduced to one based on instrumentally rational categories.[31]

Though in the Marxist tradition, the theorists of the Frankfurt School reject economic determinism, arguing that cultural and political processes have an existence independent of the realm of production. An emphasis on the autonomy of philosophy and reflection informs their critique of instrumental rationality, which they see as broader than industrial capitalism. In *The Eclipse of Reason* (1974[1947]), Horkheimer defines instrumental reason as consisting of examining the means–end relationship of social action in terms of calculation and probability; the reduction of reality to formalized, ahistorical, mathematical categories which result in technical recommendations rather than reflection on the meanings of people's actions; and a lack of concern about the ethical implications of scientific practice.[32] Critical theorists believe that this instrumental rationality has run rampant in the modern world. They trace its origins not solely to capitalism, but to the Enlightenment project itself. For these theorists, Enlightenment assumptions about the ties between science and inevitable progress helped usher in the reign of instrumental rationality, which inhibits the possibilities of mutuality, happiness, autonomy, and democracy.[33]

Habermas follows in this Frankfurt School tradition, but reformulates and critiques it in several significant ways. A good entry-point into Habermas's complex social theory is in terms of his relationship to the rationalization theory of Weber. For Weber, like the early Frankfurt School, rationalization is the overarching master trend in the West, tied to the decline of traditional forms of authority. Weber links the rise of rationalization to the Protestant ethic, the emergence of capitalism and bureaucracy, rational bookkeeping, and a scientific worldview.[34] Like Horkheimer, Weber sees the rationality of the modern world as defined largely by the most coherent, calculable, and efficient means to reach a predetermined end.

Habermas believes that Weber's definition, like that of the Frankfurt School, unduly restricts the concept of rationality. For Habermas, rationalization means more than simply the development of more efficient, calculable ways of ordering the world. Habermas also contends that rationalization consists of the development of greater moral insight, an enhanced ability to think critically about ethical life, and the universalization of moral values. This "communicative" form of rationality can contribute to a type of moral solidarity developing apart from taken-for-granted traditions. Because many moral norms now have to be justified and legitimized publicly, communication and argument rather than ostensibly "natural" traditions form the best means of achieving social consensus.

This turn toward argument and principled reasoning can be seen in the contemporary importance of the ideas of democracy, the universal foundations of morality, equal rights, and procedural law. All are based on rational attachment to universal principles, such as justice, freedom, and equality, which can provide a basis for social solidarity other than taken-for-granted tradition. For solidarity to be generated requires an egalitarian social situation, where unconstrained mutual understanding is possible. According to Habermas, such communicative action involves the creation of consensus formulated by participating equals, which allows people to be free from unnecessary social, natural, and psychological constraints.[35]

Habermas believes that instrumental reason cannot simply be discarded or overcome, for the modern world has become too complex to allow full democratization at all institutional levels. Accordingly, Habermas grounds his distinctions between instrumental and communicative rationality in two different realms of social life, the system and the lifeworld. Habermas argues that the system corresponds to the economic and bureaucratic sphere of modern life responsible for the material reproduction of society, which is informed predominantly by instrumental rationality and its criteria of efficiency and calculability. The lifeworld consists of those realms of interaction, such as family, friends, and voluntary associations, which are oriented toward communicative action and the development of shared values. Both the lifeworld and system can become more rational, though in two different senses – more efficient in the system, more consensual and participatory in the lifeworld.[36]

Habermas contends that the spheres of system and lifeworld can only be balanced in a less class-divided society that is informed and guided by a lively public sphere, which mediates between the system and the lifeworld. Consisting of a number of overlapping institutions from associations and social movements in civil society to the legislative and legal systems, the public sphere means more than the simply formal argument about public issues that is undertaken by political parties. A truly vital public sphere, dispersed through diverse realms and places, allows public opinion to be formed through debate and discussion, where individuals can come together to confer rationally on matters of general interest. Such issues as how best to use expertise and production in the context of the overall goals and values of society should be subjects of debate in this realm.[37]

Yet Habermas sees the rational and universal characteristics of the public sphere threatened in modern societies by the "colonization of the lifeworld." For Habermas, colonization occurs when the system criteria associated with instrumental reason become part of everyday life, as corporations take over more of people's leisure time, consumerism runs rampant, and the state intervenes and controls more of the lifeworld. In such a context, there are fewer capacities and places for the cultivation of democracy.[38] One hopeful sign that Habermas sees in the modern world concerns the rise of new social movements, such as the women's and environmental movements, which open up new avenues for participation.[39]

Given these major themes, Habermas's relationship to classical social theory can be addressed. Indeed, he develops his arguments through a reinterpretation of the classical sociological tradition. Like Alexander, Habermas believes that Weber unnecessarily narrows the concept of rationality in an instrumental direction. Weber thinks that an ethical viewpoint can only be maintained in a religious context; hence, he ends his discussion of the rise and decline of the Protestant ethic with his famous metaphor of the iron cage, an ethically diminished world in which the moral moment dissolves into, in Weber's words, "the polar night of icy darkness."[40] Habermas contends that other possibilities for an ethical position exist outside of religion, from the humanistic ethics that arose in the Renaissance to Durkheim's famous discussion in *The Division of Labor in Society* (1984[1893]) of organic solidarity as exemplified in the non-contractual bases of contract. Durkheim's arguments show that principles such as justice, individual responsibility, and competence underlie people's social relations with one another; such a "post-conventional" morality is based on attachment to universal, secular, yet still sacred principles rather than religiously anchored ones.[41]

Weber's narrow view of rationality also does not allow him to fully understand the class-based and historically specific problems associated with the rise of instrumental rationality and capitalism. Habermas interprets the Marxist tradition (which includes not only Marx, but Lukács and the Frankfurt School), as implicitly recognizing the problems associated with the colonization of the lifeworld, as seen, for example, in Marx's theory of alienation. Such colonization is responsible for many of our social ills, from alcohol and drug addiction to crime, as possibilities to lead a meaningful life are undermined by the bureaucratic and instrumental invasion of the lifeworld. Yet Marx concentrated exclusively on the production process, and his theory proved unable to grasp the problems and possibilities of modern society tied to the cultural and political realms.[42]

Moreover, according to Habermas, many Marxists (curiously similar to Weber), overemphasize the problems associated with the rise of modern rationality. To develop a more complete and optimistic picture of the rationalization processes of modernity, Habermas turns to Durkheim and Mead. These theorists implicitly outline the contours of the theory of communicative action *avant la lettre*, for they see that interaction between people is the basis of the development of the self and the rise of social solidarity within the lifeworld. In particular, Habermas argues that Durkheim's theory of the transformation of the collective consciousness from mechanical to organic solidarity, first developed in *The Division of Labor*, provides a basis for communicative action. The rationalization of archaic worldviews grounded in mechanical solidarity allows the freeing of the rational potential of communicative action, leading to modern notions of individualism and the universalism of law and morality. Such a "linguistification of the sacred," as Habermas puts it, facilitates the understanding of modern organic solidarity in a sophisticated manner. For Habermas, as the rituals of non-modern societies are transformed with the rise of organic solidarity, the authority of the holy is replaced by the "authority of an achieved consensus." The disenchantment of the sacred does not result in a meaningless world *à la* Weber, but releases the linguistic basis of communicative action from its embeddedness in religion. The sacred is thus transferred into the binding power of argument and agreement.[43] Such a consensus can be realized in a democratic public sphere, where morality becomes tied to the sacred basis of law and the belief in the sanctity of the person, the "cult of the individual," in Durkheim's famous phrase.[44]

In many ways, Giddens agrees with Habermas's assessment of the classical social theorists. He too contends that Marx has an overly instrumental understanding of production and its relationship to culture. He also argues that Weber does not have a sufficient appreciation of the ways that social life is reproduced through skilled interaction; like Habermas, Giddens sees Durkheim's theory of moral individualism as providing a meaningful rationale for modern social action, avoiding the perspective of Weber's iron cage, though Durkheim too has no adequate conception of the role of the skilled individual in reproducing society.

Yet Giddens argues that Habermas's vision of the classics replicates many of the problems of Alexander and Parsons. The classical theorists were not confusedly discussing an inadequate theory of communicative action, just as they were not concerned with the problems of action and order. Marx, Weber, and Durkheim do not predate Habermas's theory in any simple way. According to Giddens, the classical sociological theorists do not converge in any contemporary sociological perspective, whether it be Parsonian structural functionalism or Habermasian communicative action. The classical sociologists' thought is inextricably tied to their own historical era.

These misinterpretations of classical sociological theory have had baneful consequences for contemporary practitioners, according to Giddens. Alexander and Habermas, though sophisticated theorists, are absorbed in abstract controversies which do not lend themselves to clear discussions of the accomplishments of skilled agents in concrete social situations. For more unsophisticated sociologists, the misunderstanding of the classics raises two other problems. First, especially those sociologists influenced by Parsons tend to see Weber and Durkheim as inaugurators of a new scientific sociology which breaks decisively with its predecessors. This misinterpretation often provides the impetus for the misguided scientistic program of much modern sociology. Second, and more importantly, many contemporary sociologists uncritically adopt the reductionist economic and/or industrial models developed by Durkheim, Marx, and to a lesser extent Weber. By accepting the reductionist consequences of these classical theories, sociologists do not sufficiently analyze the distinctive military, cultural, and administrative dimensions of modernity.

Giddens believes that Alexander and Habermas, like many sociologists, are still fascinated with epistemological questions, concerning how we know the world and how best to grasp social action, order, and the like. Giddens argues that these concerns need to be replaced by what he calls an ontological orientation. Rather than debating abstract theoretical issues of determinism and freedom, social theory should reconstruct the view of the agent, the individual in the full complexity of his/her social relations. Giddens does not defend this notion of an ontology in great detail, but seems to think that social theorists waste a lot of energy in fruitless debates about the nature of reality. In Bryant and Jary's words, Giddens is a "naive realist; there is a world out there and the ease with which one can bump against it is for him, as for Durkheim, confirmation of its facticity."[45]

Giddens advocates reconceptualizing the agent as neither a passive follower of rules nor an entirely free person, but as a reflexive, knowledgeable actor, bound by particular circumstances. Thus, for Giddens, the subjectivism/objectivism dualism can be rethought as the duality of structure, in which social structure and individual conduct presuppose one another, and which characterizes all social behavior.[46] Each contributes to the ongoing reconstitution of society. Giddens also contends that his approach can lead to a more empirically sensitive approach to behavior, which is clouded by the epistemological disputes of much sociological theory.

We will return to a more complete discussion of Giddens's relationship to contemporary functionalism and critical theory in later chapters. Giddens's critique of classical social theory foreshadows several of the themes that characterize his structuration theory. In particular, he emphasizes the importance of rejecting many of the assumptions shared by the classical theorists regarding the modern social world, especially the predominance of the industrial society model and its concomitant economic and industrial reductionism. Giddens argues for a reflexive sociology that breaks decisively with these models, and develops a more complex and variegated view of the dynamics of the modern social world.

It is important to point out at this juncture that Giddens's criticisms of Habermas, Alexander, and the legacy of the classics raise some difficult issues for his own social theory. All of these theorists share the view that the triumvirate of Marx, Weber, and Durkheim constitutes the core of classical sociology, neglecting other figures who could conceivably achieve canonical status, such as W.E.B. DuBois and Charlotte Perkins Gilman. The latter authors raise issues of race and gender that the classical theorists did not substantively address. Giddens, Habermas, and Alexander, though sensitive to the social context in which the theorists wrote, focus on internal European developments when analyzing the classics. They do not consider the influence of the European Empires and imperialism on each author, and thus do not explore in detail the possibility that Eurocentric biases might have substantially influenced these authors' work.[47]

Giddens does reject the evolutionism of the classical tradition in his structuration theory. Yet his approach to the intricacies of rationalization, both as a historical process and as a characteristic of contemporary societies, is not clearly spelled out. This lack of clarity points to some problematic features in Giddens's approach to history. His emphasis on the discontinuity of history makes it difficult to understand how people can build on and learn from the past, and draw on "collective learning processes," in Habermas's terms. This accent on historical ruptures does not clarify what contemporary social theory can take from the classics. Finally, Giddens's replacement of epistemological with ontological concerns raises many questions. His attempt to bypass the action/order issue (in Alexander's lexicon) by moving to another level of analysis may mean that he simply ignores the problem rather than reflecting on and resolving it in terms of his own theoretical perspective.

These complicated theoretical issues involve how we can know and study the social world, which necessarily leads to questions of methodology. The next chapter will examine Giddens's methodological position in detail.

Notes

1 *Capitalism and Modern Social Theory: An Analysis of the Writings of Marx, Durkheim, and Max Weber* (New York, Cambridge University Press, 1971).

Giddens's other work on the classical theorists include *Politics and Sociology in the Thought of Max Weber* (London, Macmillan, 1972); *Emile Durkheim* (New York, Viking Press, 1979); *A Contemporary Critique of Historical Materialism, Vol. 1, Power, Property, and the State* (Berkeley, University of California Press, 1981); *The Nation-State and Violence, Vol. 2 of A Contemporary Critique of Historical Materialism* (Berkeley, University of California Press, 1985). Giddens has also written on the classical theorists in his collections of essays, *Studies in Social and Political Theory* (New York, Basic Books, 1977), and *Profiles and Critiques in Social Theory* (Berkeley, University of California Press, 1982). See also his Introductions to *Emile Durkheim: Selected Writings* (New York, Cambridge University Press, 1972), and *Durkheim on Politics and the State* (Stanford, Stanford University Press, 1986).

2 See Randall Collins and Michael Makowsky, *The Discovery of Society* (New York, Random House, 1998).

3 Talcott Parsons, *The Structure of Social Action* (2 vols) (New York, McGraw-Hill, 1937).

4 Ibid., *Vol. 1*, p. 307; see also Jonathan Turner, *The Structure of Sociological Theory* (Belmont, CA, Wadsworth, 1991), p. 53.

5 Ibid., pp. 53–54.

6 Robert Nisbet, *The Sociological Tradition* (New York, Basic Books, 1966), pp. 8–9, 18.

7 Ibid., p. 13.

8 Giddens, *Studies in Social and Political Theory*, p. 211.

9 *The Giddens Reader*, ed. Philip Cassell (Stanford, Stanford University Press, 1993), pp. 50–72. See also Giddens, *Politics and Sociology in the Thought of Max Weber*, and *Studies in Social and Political Theory*, pp. 236–240.

10 Giddens, *Studies in Social and Political Theory*, pp. 214–218.

11 Irving Zeitlin, *Ideology and the Development of Sociological Theory* (Englewood Cliffs, NJ, Prentice Hall, 1968); Lewis Coser, *Masters of Sociological Thought* (New York, Harcourt-Brace Jovanovich, 1977); Ralph Dahrendorf, *Class and Class Conflict in Industrial Society* (Stanford, Stanford Univerity Press, 1958). See also Alvin Gouldner, *The Coming Crisis of Western Sociology* (New York, Basic Books, 1970).

12 Giddens, *Studies in Social and Political Theory*, p. 250.

13 Ibid., pp. 221–224.

14 Karl Polanyi, *The Great Transformation* (Boston, Beacon Press, 1957).

15 Anthony Giddens, *Beyond Left and Right: The Future of Radical Politics* (Stanford, Stanford University Press, 1994), pp. 105, 109.

16 Giddens, *Studies in Social and Political Theory*, pp. 263–272.

17 *The Giddens Reader*, pp. 38–40. See also Giddens, *A Contemporary Critique of Historical Materialism, Vol. 1.*

18 Giddens, *The Consequences of Modernity* (Stanford, Stanford University Press, 1990) pp. 55ff.

19 Jeffrey Alexander, *Theoretical Logic in Sociology, Vol. 1, Positivism, Presuppositions, and Current Controversies* (Berkeley, University of California Press, 1982), pp. 5–9.

20 Jeffrey Alexander, "The Centrality of the Classics," in *Social Theory Today,* ed. Anthony Giddens and Jonathan Turner (Stanford, Stanford University Press, 1987), p. 17.

21 Alexander, *Theoretical Logic in Sociology, Vol. 1*, pp. 30–34.

22 Alexander, "The Centrality of the Classics," pp. 20–23.

23 Alexander, *Theoretical Logic in Sociology, Vol. 1*, pp. 68–70.

24 Ibid., p. 92.

25 Ibid., pp. 123–124.

26 Alexander, "The Centrality of the Classics," pp. 28–31. On Marx and Durkheim, see Alexander, *Theoretical Logic in Sociology, Vol. 2, The Antinomies of Classical Thought: Marx and Durkheim* (Berkeley, University of California Press, 1982).

27 Alexander, "The Centrality of the Classics," pp. 42–46.

28 Alexander, *Theoretical Logic in Sociology, Vol. 2, The Antinomies of Classical Thought*.

29 Alexander, *Theoretical Logic in Sociology, Vol. 3, The Classical Attempt at Theoretical Synthesis: Max Weber* (Berkeley, University of California Press, 1983), p. 55.

30 Ibid., pp. 123–126.

31 On the history of the Frankfurt School, see Martin Jay, *The Dialectical Imagination* (Boston, Little, Brown, 1972).

32 Max Horkheimer, *Eclipse of Reason* (New York, Seabury Press, 1974[1947]), pp. 3–57.

33 Max Horkheimer and Theodor Adorno, *Dialectic of Enlightenment* (London, Verso, 1979).

34 Max Weber, *The Protestant Ethic and the Spirit of Capitalism* (New York, Scribner, 1976).

35 Jürgen Habermas, *Theory of Communicative Action, Vol. 1, Reason and the Rationalization of Society* (Boston, Beacon Press, 1984); *Theory of Communicative Action, Vol. 2, Lifeworld and System: A Critique of Functionalist Reason* (Boston, Beacon Press, 1987). See also Jeffrey Alexander, "Habermas's New Critical Theory: Its Promise and Problems," *American Journal of Sociology* 91 (1985–1986), pp. 400–424.

36 Habermas develops these arguments in *Theory of Communicative Action, Vol. 1* and *Vol. 2*.

37 See Habermas, *The Structural Transformation of the Public Sphere: An Inquiry into a Category of Bourgeois Society* (Cambridge, MA, MIT Press, 1989). See also Kenneth Baynes, "Communicative Ethics, the Public Sphere, and Communication Media," *Critical Studies in Mass Communication* 11 (December 1994), pp. 322–323.

38 Habermas, *Theory of Communicative Action, Vol. 2*, pp. 318ff.

39 Ibid., pp. 391–396.

40 Weber's quote is taken from George Ritzer, *The McDonaldization of Society: An Investigation into the Changing Character of Contemporary Social Life* (Thousand Oaks, CA, Sage, 1993), p. 162. Weber's reference to modernity as an iron cage can be found in *The Protestant Ethic and the Spirit of Capitalism*, p. 181. For Habermas's critique of Weber, see *Theory of Communicative Action, Vol. 1*, pp. 143ff.

41 Habermas, *Theory of Communicative Action, Vol. 2*, pp. 43ff. On Durkheim's discussion of the non-contractual bases of contract, see *The Division of Labor in Society* (New York, Free Press, 1984[1893]), pp. 149ff.

42 Habermas, *Theory of Communicative Action, Vol. 1*, pp. 339ff.

43 Habermas, *Theory of Communicative Action, Vol. 2*, p. 77.

44 Ibid., pp. 81–84. Durkheim discusses the cult of the individual in *The Division of Labor in Society*, pp. 338–339.

45 Christopher G.A. Bryant and David Jary, "Introduction," *Giddens' Theory of*

Structuration: A Critical Appreciation, ed. Bryant and Jary (New York, Routledge, 1991), p. 27.

46 Giddens, *The Constitution of Society*, p. xx.

47 On the issue of Empire and classical sociological theory, see R.W. Connell, "Why is Classical Theory Classical?," *American Journal of Sociology* 102 (May 1997), pp. 1511–1557.

2

NEW RULES OF SOCIOLOGICAL METHOD: POSITIVISM, INTERPRETIVE SOCIOLOGY, AND STRUCTURATION THEORY

Any perusal of sociological journals demonstrates that sociologists use a wide variety of methodologies, from complex statistics based on probability theory to in-depth observations of particular groups. Despite their variability, these different types of methodological strategies are conducted in the context of specific social and/or intellectual problems. For instance, Durkheim's 1898 book *Suicide* attempts not only to understand the conditions leading to different suicide rates among various countries, but also advances a general theory of the nature and dynamics of modern society. Durkheim uses differences in suicide rates to illustrate his theory that a new type of rational, secular organic solidarity based on the division of labor is replacing the highly traditional, anti-individualistic mechanical solidarity of premodern societies.

Durkheim is often considered the founder of the quantitative approach to sociological research, which attempts to understand social life in terms of causal relationships between clearly defined, measurable variables. From this perspective, for example, a sociologist interested in analyzing the relationship between class and voting behavior will collect representative, statistically significant data on the groups in question, as well as examine past voting patterns. The sociologist will present the results in quantitative form, defining class in terms of specific, measurable indices (such as income and educational level), and, if the data warrant it, posit a direct relationship between class position and typical voting behavior. This type of quantitative research is very popular in sociology and the other social sciences.

But there are also other ways to study social life. For example, if a researcher is interested in the impact of relocated refugees on a particular community, this research might not be amenable to precise quantitative measures, in part because it is a new phenomenon about which research has not yet accumulated. To get at the root of this process, a researcher would have to familiarize himself/herself with the community under study by visiting it and getting to know the residents, and investigating the histories of the community and the refugees. The social scientist would try to observe the processes by which the townspeople understand the refugees, and vice versa. In this type of qualitative research, the sociologist attempts to comprehend the social context of the people's lives that s/he is studying, exploring how the group(s) under study comes to define itself and the world around it. Research procedures characteristic of this type of social science include observing and/or interviewing the people one is studying. This qualitative research is oriented toward an in-depth understanding of particular situations and an understanding of the processes by which people develop meaning in their lives, while quantitative research is aimed at the explanation and prediction of social behavior and attitudes in numerical form.

These two methodological approaches are often at loggerheads, as practitioners on each side of the divide devalue the results of the other. Proponents of qualitative sociology often argue that their quantitative colleagues reduce the complexity of social life to a finite number of variables, presenting an inaccurate picture of society in the process. Quantitative researchers accuse qualitative sociologists of a subjective, idiosyncratic portrayal of social life that should be subjected to the rigors of scientific method.

Giddens finds the quantitative/qualitative split in sociology an example of the unhelpful dualisms that he thinks characterizes much of the social sciences. He contends that a practical and critical sociology must move beyond such dualities in order to accurately grasp the dynamics of social life. Accordingly, he calls for new rules of sociological method, which not only problematize the quantitative/qualitative duality, but also encourage a rethinking of the sociologists' relationship to their research, and a sensitivity to the interplay of social science and the social life which sociologists study. Giddens believes that only a thoroughgoing reconsideration of such sociological conceptual staples as agency, structure, and objectivity can furnish the tools for a new approach. Giddens formulates some of his most innovative theoretical concepts in this context, for he argues that the reproduction of social structure cannot be separated from the activities of skilled social agents, and vice versa. For Giddens, the quantitative/qualitative methodological dualism unfortunately mirrors and reinforces the micro/macro separation which has led sociologists down so many unfruitful paths. He advocates sociological study which builds reflexivity into its very core.

As is his custom, Giddens develops his methodological approach through a critique and synthesis of a wide range of sociological and philosophical approaches. This chapter examines many varieties of scientific and interpretive social science, from structural functionalism to phenomenology and poststructuralism, and Giddens's critique of these perspectives. It introduces some of Giddens's major themes, which will be developed more fully in the next chapter. Before moving to the theoretical context of Giddens's analysis, some historical background on the quantitative/qualitative split within sociology is necessary. The roots of the conflicts between quantitative and qualitative approaches extend to the origins of sociology and the larger cultural and philosophical controversy over positivism in the late nineteenth century.

The controversy over nineteenth-century positivism and the romantic reaction

A positivistic philosophical climate permeated late nineteenth-century European culture, and left its marks on the emerging discipline of sociology. Comte's mid-nineteenth-century advocacy of a sociological positivism, combined with the power and persuasiveness of Charles Darwin's biological theories of natural selection in the 1860s, encouraged a scientific ferment which contributed to the desire for a natural science of society. This theoretical quest for a science of society could be seen in theories as diverse as Herbert Spencer's emphasis on heredity and environment as determinants of human behavior and Durkheimian sociology.

The growth of positivism was aided by a new type of corporate, large-scale capitalism that came to prominence throughout Europe in the early twentieth century. Reformist governments were part of this new economic and social order, as they attempted to solve social problems scientifically. The Liberal Party in Britain, the Radical Party in France, the American Progressive movement, and Wilhelm II in Germany all looked to social science for guidance in social policy.

Yet the 1890s also saw a reaction to the philosophical hegemony of positivism. Theorists and artists such as Freud and Dostoevsky stressed the irrational or non-rational sources of human behavior, embedded in the unconscious. In France, the philosopher Henri Bergson and the novelist Marcel Proust emphasized the uniqueness of the human spirit, as the person's inner life escaped rational categories. They contended that the subjective sense of time and experience was very different from the mechanical time of the clock. Aesthetic modernism, especially the Cubism of Picasso and Braque, saw the human world as fragmented, not subject to uniform, predictable laws.

Methodologically, this emphasis on the uniqueness of the human spirit led the philosophers William Dilthey and Benedetto Croce to posit a clear distinction between the "human" and the natural sciences. They argued that the human sciences were invariably historical, as they studied an ever-changing social reality which required sympathetic, hermeneutic understanding of the past and of others. The uniqueness of

positivism by incorporating much of Weber's emphasis on the importance of values in various phases of research.

Nevertheless, functionalists believe that a science of society, akin to a natural science, is both desirable and possible. Sociologists sympathetic to this endeavor contend that sociology is not yet a mature science, for it is still searching for a total, unified theory like Newton's laws of gravity or Einstein's theory of relativity. Merton in particular suggests some avenues that an emerging scientific sociology should follow, and the type of sociological theory appropriate to such a task. For Merton, sociology can progress by better empirical investigation of testable theoretical propositions which clearly formulate relationships between variables. Such "middle range" theorizing analyzes delimited research problems; its findings can then be consolidated into an ever larger theoretical edifice.[3]

Parsons develops the functionalist approach on a much grander scale than Merton. Parsons is one of the most influential advocates of the notion that social science should strive to achieve the theoretical scope and empirical methods characteristic of the natural sciences. While Parsons discusses such issues at a general theoretical level, Popper formulates a concrete theory of generating empirical social science with his theory of falsifiability. The work of Parsons and Popper makes several presuppositions that are characteristic of the scientific model. These include the following:

1   An objective world of facts exists apart from the observer.
2   One understands the world through observations which can then be tested empirically.
3   The concepts of scientific knowledge are internally consistent and stable over time.
4   The truth of a proposition is distinct from its origins.[4]

Though Parsons composes a theory of social action while Popper is more concerned with the nature of scientific explanation, they share these epistemological assumptions. These presuppositions and their implications are the focal point of attack by the interpretive approaches.

Parsons

Building on his interpretation of Weber and Durkheim, Parsons argues that a scientific, objective study of society is possible. Like Weber, Parsons is interested in generating a theory of social action, or meaningful subjective behavior. While Weber concentrates on the intentions of people acting in social life, Parsons contends that a theory of social action has to take into account the material, physical, and normative constraints on people's actions. Thus, while Parsons is concerned with the subjective decision-making of people, he thinks that their decisions are influenced by normative and situational factors beyond their control.[5]

In Parsonian language, such normative and situational elements consolidate into "systems" which influence personal behavior. Parsons argues that individual action develops in the context of four types of action systems (cultural, social, personality, behavioral), which consist of different types of social roles. These roles cluster into institutions, such as schools, families, and the like, within these systems. Within the social system, schools teach the skills necessary for people to function adequately in occupations, while the economy organizes jobs in order to facilitate production. The cultural system is composed of patterns of ideas, expressive symbolization, and standards of evaluation, such as scientific method. It is organized around the meaning of objects and the expression of meaning through symbols and signs, including ideals of beauty and artistic merit.[6] The cultural system also provides the values which regulate and inform behavior, such as economic success and individual achievement. Religious and other institutions embody symbols and values. For the personality system to function effectively, the family must socialize children to give them the proper motivation for fulfilling social roles. To achieve adulthood, children learn the most important and appropriate cultural values that will enable them competently and happily to fulfill occupational roles in the social system. While these different systems must interpenetrate in order to be effective, they also function according to their own internal rules, often outside of the conscious intentions of people. Their smooth interaction is necessary for a well-ordered society.

One of Parsons's major contributions to a science of society lies in the relationship of the social to the cultural system. Problems relating to knowledge arise when the cultural and social systems of action are improperly integrated. When this disjunction occurs, the values of society impinge on the scientific process, becoming particularly acute when there is a "discrepancy between what is believed and what can be scientifically correct."[7] Objective science becomes subordinate to ideological or political ends. Parsons believes that it is of utmost importance to specify and delimit the boundaries between institutionalized values and empirical evaluation.

For Parsons, the criteria for empirical evaluation are not problematic. He contends that the study of society can explicitly follow the logic of the natural sciences. There are universal standards of empirical validity. The natural and social sciences differ only in their respective object of study and their degree of sophistication. Because the structure of explanation is similar in all scientific study, *Verstehen*, or the understanding of other people and cultures, is merely a prelude to scientific study, a means of formulating hypotheses that can be scientifically verified or refuted. Particular systems of meaning and evaluation are important in the selection of scientific problems and the determination of the significance of scientific knowledge for a particular society, but the criteria for determining scientific empirical knowledge are universal.[8]

In sum, Parsons does not think that social conditions directly influence the structure of scientific explanation. The relationship of knowledge to interest is an external one; values can only affect the growth of science through determining scientific problems and the status of science in society. Ultimately, scientific knowledge is best served by institutions guaranteeing the autonomy and progress of science. Parsons does not develop his methodological perspective in great depth. In order to better grasp the assumptions of the scientific perspective, it is necessary to turn to the work of Popper.

Popper

Like Parsons, Popper believes that there is no essential difference between the study of nature and the study of society. However, Popper argues that social scientists have often misinterpreted the logic of natural science while attempting to emulate it, resulting in a pseudo-science ranging from theories based on pure induction to grand historical overviews that claim to have deciphered the laws of history and society.[9] For Popper, there is no possibility of a purely inductive or observational science; all of our observations are "theory impregnated," and knowledge only results from confronting scientific problems. Popper writes: "Knowledge does not start from perceptions or observations or the collection of data or facts, but it starts, rather, from problems."[10] Despite this seemingly interpretive approach to scientific analysis, Popper postulates an objective world of facts that cannot be denied, and to which all scientific theories aspire.[11]

This tension between interpretations of reality and objective truth is the basis of Popper's theory of "critical rationalism." In order to progress toward the truth, scientific theories must be testable empirically; they must be falsifiable. Since any theory can find evidence to support it, it is essential that theories be severely tested and refutations attempted. Theories which do not meet the above criterion are unscientific.

In order to be falsifiable, a theory must follow the mode of "deductive causal explanation," which has prediction and testability as essential components. This is the universal basis of scientific method, true of both social and natural science. Popper describes this form of explanation as follows:

> From the hypothesis to be tested – for example, a universal law – together with some other statements which for this purpose are not considered as problematic – for example, some initial conditions – we deduce some prognosis.[12]

Popper not only applies this explanatory approach to the social sciences, but he also develops a theory of methodological individualism. Popper devoted *The Open Society and Its Enemies* (1996) and *The Poverty of Historicism* (1964) to an analysis and attempted refutation of the "essentialism" that characterizes much philosophy and social science from Plato to Marx and beyond, which tries to grasp the universal essence of the natural and social worlds. Popper would like to substitute a nominalistic model of social analysis for the essentialist position. He desires a description of social life "in terms of individuals, of their attitudes, expectations, relations, etc."[13] Individuals and not institutions act. Yet, according to Popper, individuals act in situations, and an objective understanding of the situation in which action occurs, in which individuals' goals become explicable, is possible. For Popper, such an approach can lead to a comprehension of the action appropriate to the situation observed, utilizing a rational and theoretical construction against which to compare actual cases. This theoretical procedure also could lead to an analysis of intended and unintended consequences for the individual.[14]

While the actual process leading to the formulation of hypotheses about human behavior is haphazard and unpredictable, the testing of hypotheses is not. Thus Popper, like Parsons, sees the process of *Verstehen* as leading to potentially interesting hypotheses about human action, but the empathy characteristic of *Verstehen* as a method is unscientific and cannot be falsified.[15]

In the last analysis, the basis for and guarantee of the growth of knowledge for Popper is the existence of a community of scientists who freely and rationally criticize one another's theories. Like Parsons, Popper separates the truth of a theory from its origins; the connection of knowledge to interest is external. Because scientific analysis and methodology are universal and neutral, institutions must be set up to allow the expansion of the dialogue crucial for the advancement of science, the basis of an open society.

Giddens praises Popper's skeptical attitude toward scientific findings and his version of scientific progress as bold and innovative. He also shares Popper's recognition of the importance of theory in scientific work and his break with empiricism. But Popper's perspective does not escape the difficulties associated with the natural science model. Drawing on Kuhn's analysis of the historical development of science in *The Structure of Scientific Revolutions* (1962), Giddens argues that Popper does not investigate the cultural assumptions underlying his philosophy of critical rationalism. As Giddens states, "There is *no way* of justifying a commitment to scientific rationality rather than, say, to Zande sorcery, apart from premises and values which science itself presupposes, and indeed has drawn from historically in its evolution within Western culture."[16] Moreover, Giddens believes that falsification is not as simple a procedure as Popper suggests, for "what 'counts' as a falsifying observation thus depends in some way upon the theoretical system or paradigm within which the description of what is observed is couched." Theories also have various ways of incorporating seemingly "falsifying instances" that can be explained without discarding the underlying theoretical approach.[17]

Giddens also criticizes Popper's and Parsons's ignorance of the extent to which the reproduction of society results from the actions of skilled, reflexive agents. Popper and Parsons alike do not explicate subjectivity adequately, taking the existence of the individual for granted. This lack of attention to the problem of agency overlaps with their indifference to the complex connections of the researcher and everyday life that is invariably a part of social scientific analysis. Because the sociologist studies a human world rich in meaning, the issue of meaning is at the core of social scientific research, not merely an addendum that can be got rid of through methodological fiat. The complex interplay of the researcher and the social world is best captured in Giddens's notion of the double hermeneutic. For Giddens, social science consists of both "the meaningful social world" created in everyday life, and "the metalanguages invented by social scientists," which often overlap as social scientific concepts become part of everyday public discourse, and social science necessarily draws on the meanings created by people in the course of their daily lives.[18] Thus, the study of the social world cannot be approached using a simple model of objectivity, since the positions of the researcher and the layperson cannot be easily separated.

The interpretive approach

Hermeneutics, the centrality of interpretation in all human activity, is in one form or other a central concept for qualitative sociological perspectives. Despite the diversity of the interpretive approaches which will be discussed below, all share certain features which distinguish them from the scientific perspective. The shared distinctiveness of the interpretive approaches can be illustrated by considering an example presented by Winch. Winch writes:

> Was the Pharisee who said, "God, I thank Thee that I am not as other men are" doing the same kind of thing as the Publican who prayed "God be merciful unto me a sinner?" To answer this one would have to start by considering what is involved in the idea of a prayer; and that is a *religious* question. In other words, the appropriate criteria for deciding whether the actions of these two men were of the same kind or not belongs to religion itself.[19]

The criteria by which one interprets the above two actions cannot rest merely on methodological conventions. The standards for deciding that the two acts belong to the same class of phenomena arise from an understanding of the subject studied, and a comprehension of the observer's relationship to the subject, rather than from a general methodological postulate. These have the following closely related implications for an interpretive study of society:

1   The strict separation of observer and observed cannot be maintained. Explanation is not achieved through a process analogous to physical or natural processes, but is concerned instead with the explication of meaning. The imagery characteristic of an interpretive science is one of *participation* in/with the object of study.
2   The creation of meaning has an *intersubjective* basis. Meanings are created and reproduced through the *interaction* of individuals in daily life; subjective understanding is constituted in an intersubjective context which varies between cultures and historical eras.
3   Knowledge cannot be severed from the social context in which it originates. All knowledge, whether scientific or commonsensical, derives from the intersubjective nature of social life.

Though all of the interpretive approaches share these criticisms of the natural science model, their respective analyses proceed along different paths. Symbolic interactionism focuses on the interpretive processes that people use to construct a meaningful social world. Phenomenological theory, represented by Schutz, attempts to construct an objective, replicable social science similar to that desired by Weber. Schutz undertakes this task in part through criticizing Weber's understanding of subjective meaning, the ideal type, and *Verstehen*. The subject matter of sociology is reconstituted by this school on the basis of common-sense intersubjective understanding. The philosophers Winch and Taylor follow a similar analysis, but they stress the primacy of linguistic forms rather than everyday "typicalities" in the constitution of social life. Winch, Taylor, and the sociologist Bellah depart from Schutz in denying the universality of a scientific mode of understanding. A critique of science is also integral to the postmodernist understanding of social inquiry. But poststructuralists such as Foucault problematize not only natural scientific approaches to society, but interpretive ones as well.

Symbolic interactionism

The symbolic interactionist perspective, associated with the early twentieth-century social psychologist George Herbert Mead and popularized in the 1940s and 1950s by Herbert Blumer, emphasizes that processes of interpretation should be at the center of any conception

of society. From the symbolic interactionist perspective, social interaction invariably means that people define and interpret one another's
actions. People respond to others based on interpretations of their
conduct, gestures, and language. As Blumer states, "human interaction
is mediated by the use of symbols, by interpretation, or by ascertaining
the meaning of one another's actions."[20]

Blumer's approach extends Mead's conception of the self. For Mead,
the self is reflexive, in that a person can become the object of his/her
own thought and actions. He/she can become angry with himself/
herself, take pride in himself/herself, and the like. This active process of
understanding and acting on oneself also applies to other contexts, in
that people continually make all of reality meaningful by interpreting
events and actions. People do not respond to social life in a mechanistic,
predetermined way.

The human self is constructed through the interpretations of events,
objects, other people, and oneself. Individuals develop their sense of self
in the context of family, peers, and the media, among many other
factors. Thus, people bring many assumptions and beliefs into any
situation. The interpretive process is invariably a social one, accomplished through sympathetically taking the role of others. This process
of role-taking shows that the individual is a social product, and that
"group or collective action consists of the aligning of individual actions,
brought about by the individuals' interpreting or taking into account
each other's actions."[21]

For Blumer, Mead's analysis has different implications for the study of
society than does structural functionalism. Blumer was particularly
exercised by the power of functionalism in sociology in the 1950s and
early 1960s. According to Blumer, functionalism ignores the active role
of people in reproducing their own social lives. For example, Blumer
states that socialization is not the passive internalization of values, as
functionalists would have it, but the "cultivated capacity to take the
roles of others effectively."[22] Quantitative perspectives that reduce social
life to a statistically formulated causal relationship between an independent and dependent variable cannot penetrate the complexity of the
social context surrounding any social act. Variables are historically
bound, and often have no fixed or uniform indicators. Quantitative
analysis does not explore how people interpret their world, the particular experiential dimension of their social life. Social scientists also
seldom reflect on their own premises. They often forget that they are
studying a world of meaning, and that they must immerse themselves in
the social world of the people they are studying.

In sum, Blumer contends that quantitative sociologists develop an
inaccurate picture of the social world. As Blumer states, "when con-
verted into the actual group activity for which it stands, a sociological
variable turns out to be an intricate and inner-moving complex."[23] For
example, social change is a process that results from historically specific

interactions in group life; it is not imposed on people in an exogenous manner. To study such processes, the researcher must become familiar with the experience of the people under study, and see the group through their own eyes.

Schutz and phenomenology

While symbolic interactionism holds many of the major tenets of the interpretive approach, other perspectives develop these themes in different ways. Though critical of many aspects of the self-understanding of the social sciences, Schutz believes that a universal logic characterizes all empirical sciences. Like the natural sciences, social science should attempt to construct objective "theoretical systems embodying testable general hypotheses."[24] Schutz also argues that empirical knowledge can be discovered through controlled inference, that it is intersubjectively verifiable by observation, and that it can be expressed in terms of regularities or variables. "Sympathetic understanding" in Dilthey's sense of replicating emotionally and psychically the experience of another is impossible.[25] Furthermore, Schutz agrees with Popper's notion that all observations are "theory impregnated," in that pure induction is a fiction. But Schutz draws radically different conclusions from this approach than does Popper. For Schutz, the observer does not merely impute meaning to what s/he studies, but confronts a world already rich in meaning, intentionality, symbolism, and interpretation. The social science observer not only studies a pre-interpreted reality, but his/her very forms of thought derive from common sense.

Schutz's analysis of common-sense meanings is brought out most clearly in his critique of Weber's ideas about subjective meaning. Weber sees the creation of meaning in terms of the isolated actions of individuals. According to Schutz, such a conception of meaning construction is both primitive and solipsistic – it neglects the complexity and richness of meaning that is inherent in the *social* and *intersubjective* nature of society. Weber also fails to distinguish between scientific and common-sense understanding. The distinction between our own experience of the other person and the other person's experience, which Weber does not elaborate, is fundamental to an understanding of science and its relationship to social life.[26]

This distinction is illustrated in Schutz's reinterpretation of the Weberian ideal type. Scientific understanding is indeed characterized by the use of the ideal type that follows the canons of established scientific procedure, such as logical consistency, testability, etc. However, this scientific form of understanding derives from a more fundamental source – the ideal types and "typicalities" of common-sense understanding. The pre-scientific, experiential form of the common-sense world is based on the taken-for-granted knowledges by which people interpret and understand others in their everyday interaction. Such under-standing draws on life experiences or "biographical relevances" and the common interests of the individuals involved in interaction, through which they interpret their world. Schutz outlines three aspects of the socialization of knowledge that are integral to the intersubjective and typical character of common-sense knowledge:

1   The reciprocity of perspectives. Though people have different per-spectives, they understand one another by using typifications that allow them to interchange standpoints.
2   The social origin of knowledge. Knowledge is created through the influence of socialization patterns (teachers, parents, etc.). Perhaps the best example of the social origin of knowledge and corre-sponding typifications is everyday language, made up of "pre-constituted types."
3   The social distribution of knowledge. Knowledge varies from individual to individual, not only in degree, but in distinctiveness, clarity, and the like.[27]

Because sociology studies an intersubjective, pre-interpreted world, it is necessarily concerned with the nature of *Verstehen*. Schutz defines *Verstehen* differently than the natural science theorists. For Schutz, *Verstehen* is "the particular experiential form in which common-sense thinking takes cognizance of the social-cultural world."[28] *Verstehen* underlies all of social life, and thus social analysis and natural scientific study as well. It is the hermeneutic basis for all communication. Phenomenology posits that *Verstehen* is as necessary to a comprehension of science as to an understanding of the social world. A science which realizes this centrality of understanding will critically investigate its philosophical presuppositions and reflect on its philosophical founda-tion. *Verstehen* is therefore not a method "providing empirical criteria for determining the validity of hypotheses; as a philosophically directed method it is concerned rather with the conceptual framework within which social reality may be comprehended."[29] *Verstehen* in the context of phenomenology provides a means for critical self-appraisal that is lacking in the natural sciences.

Schutz argues that all knowledge begins with common sense and cannot be separated from the social context in which it arises. Knowledge is intimately related to social interests, but in a manner that remains undifferentiated by Schutz. Berger and Luckmann extend this thesis in *The Social Construction of Reality* (1967), stating that not only is all knowledge socially constructed, but that the world consists of socially constructed multiple realities. Furthermore, people with objective power in society, those who control dominant institutions, can impose their definition of reality on others.[30] They investigate more precisely than Schutz the relation of knowledge to specific interests. Their theory does not tie knowledge to interest in an external manner, but in a direct and integral way – society structures what we take to be knowledge. However, this issue is obscured in their analysis because Berger and Luckmann consciously avoid the epistemological questions raised by the sociology of knowledge and addressed by Schutz.

In sum, Schutz connects knowledge and society, but he still subscribes to the ideal of an objective social science, though one which must establish continuity between everyday life and scientific constructs. This ideal of a universal science becomes problematic in the work of the ethnomethodologists.

Ethnomethodology

One of the implications of the interpretive approaches delineated above is that multiple realities exist side by side in social life. First developed by Harold Garfinkel, ethnomethodology is a sociological perspective that takes this idea of multiple realities seriously. From this approach, any conception of reality is fragile and subject to change. Ethnomethodologists problematize the assumption, prevalent among interpretive approaches, that people share a pre-existing social world. They are concerned with how people actively constitute such a common world. According to ethnomethodologists, social integration does not result from a consensus on shared values or interests, but from explicit and implicit practices that people use to create social order. Shared meaning arises from the mutual recognition of a social rule. In Garfinkel's words, common understandings are best understood as "an operation rather than a common intersection of overlapping sets."[31] These researchers believe that people are skilled social agents who work very hard to produce a sense of a shared social and/or objective world, composed of values, rules, and the like.

Ethnomethodologists utilize the notions of reflexive action and indexicality to grasp how people make sense of the world. Reflexive action is the idea that people consciously try to maintain a consistent vision of reality, even in the face of problems and conflicts; it concerns the gestures and words that people use to develop and sustain this reality. Social reality is not something that exists prior to the reflexive actions that people engage in to create this social order. Ethnomethodologists contend that social actions cannot be understood apart from the social context in which they occur. They state that actions are "indexical," in that all meanings are tied to particular contexts.[32] Sociologists and social scientists should not impose their sense of reality on the social world, for their concepts are intimately tied to their own institutional context, which is very different from those of the subjects that they study.

For ethnomethodologists, much of our social life is taken up with convincing each other that we indeed share a social world. Garfinkel discusses "doing a reciprocity of perspectives," whereby people use gestures to assure one another that they understand each other. People also use an etcetera principle to facilitate interaction, as they assume unstated understandings and wait for others in a conversation to supply information which makes sense of their preceding statements.[33] Ethnomethodologists study how the pre-existing assumptions about newsworthiness influence journalists' decisions about what to report as news; how teachers develop expectations about students which maintain classroom order; and the ways in which fragmentary and contradictory client records are combined by social welfare agents into a consistent narrative that conforms to their assumptions and official policy about welfare recipients. From an ethnomethodological perspective, sociologists should not only examine the rules and values that characterize social groups, but explore how such rules and values are negotiated, maintained, and accomplished.

The symbolic interactionist, phenomenological, and ethnomethodological perspectives concentrate on micro-processes of social interaction. In sensitive studies of particular social contexts, they explore the myriad ways in which individuals make sense of their social life. But these approaches have a deficient analysis of larger social and cultural processes that affect individual interpretive activity. They do not examine in detail Marx's and Weber's contentions that people's class position affects their behaviors and beliefs and their capacity to exercise power. Nor do they explore the ways that collective symbols, rituals, and beliefs shape group life. This latter approach, like the work of the later Durkheim on religion, views culture as a public system of beliefs that supplies people with a conceptual vocabulary of meanings and symbols by which they can understand the social world. The next section investigates some of the major perspectives, represented by Winch, Taylor, and Bellah, within this cultural persuasion.[34]

The linguistic and cultural turn

Winch, Taylor, and Bellah develop many of the themes that are addressed by phenomenology and ethnomethodology, but in a direction that is different from the phenomenological analysis of consciousness and the ethnomethodological account of indexicality. All three turn to the study of language and cultural traditions and their integral relation to social practices and moral considerations. The linguistic turn is a specifically Wittgensteinian one for Winch, in that he elaborates ideas developed by Wittgenstein in his later work. In so doing, not only Winch but also Taylor and Bellah relativize and radicalize some of the main threads of phenomenological and symbolic interactionist analysis.

However, the understanding of these authors converges with phenomenology and symbolic interactionism in many ways. They emphasize the intersubjective basis of society and knowledge. Taylor writes that intersubjective meanings structure subjective meanings; they are "constitutive of the social matrix in which individuals find themselves and act."[35] Understanding meaning is more important than comprehending function in social analysis. Further, Blumer, Schutz, and the cultural analysts agree that all sociological understanding must take into account the participants' understanding of their situation. These perspectives contend that the self-understanding of scientists must be reflexively examined, and its role in social research and public discourse clarified. Schutz, Blumer, Winch, and Taylor also concur that *Verstehen* is not primarily a means of establishing testable hypotheses, but is essential to the nature of communication and a prerequisite for engaging in social life.

Winch

Despite these similarities, there are many differences between the linguistic philosophy of Winch and these other approaches. For example, the common-sense typifications of phenomenology are replaced by Winch's emphasis on linguistically structured rules of social life. Central to Winch's analysis is the idea that people are rule-following creatures, whose nature is exemplified in and in part constituted by language. Indeed, reality cannot be understood apart from linguistic categories. Further, language is embedded in a network of social practices that give it meaning. Winch writes: "To give an account of the meaning of a word is to describe how it is used; and to describe how it is used is to describe the social intercourse into which it enters."[36]

For Winch, the natural science model is unable to grasp this complex of rules and meanings that characterize social life. Winch states that one should not view culture as if it consisted of isolated individuals held together by physical forces; insisted social interaction should be comprehended as the exchange of internally related ideas and social relations. The concept of understanding that emerges from Winch is one of participation in a culture rather than observation of a culture. The criterion for correct understanding is analogous to success in conversation or interaction: ultimately, it is based on common understandings between the observer and the observed. In Winch's words:

> Whereas in natural science it is your theoretical knowledge which enables you to explain occurrences you have not previously met, a knowledge of logical theory on the other hand will not enable you to understand a piece of reasoning in an unknown language; you will have to learn that language.[37]

For Winch, *Verstehen* is the method *par excellence* of the social sciences, as well as characteristic of the nature of social life. Understanding the internal grammar of a particular society, its rules and social practices, is the task of a social science.

The relativistic implications of this approach are accepted by Winch. Like Berger and Luckmann, Winch sees a multiplicity of realities, but these are structured linguistically rather than socially through consciousness. However, Winch draws out the radical ramifications of this position, and it is this that separates him from the phenomenological school. He takes the existence of multiple realities to mean that scientific rationality is characteristic of a specific culture. Science is embedded in language and social practices that have no exclusive claim to reality, and in fact construct reality in a particular way. Thus, the Azande of central Africa have different conceptions of rationality and intelligibility than the corresponding ideas in the West; neither their language nor their social practices demonstrates a concern with scientific action in the Western sense.[38]

Winch criticizes the illegitimate extension of Western rationality to all forms of understanding as a type of cultural imperialism. He dismisses attempts to create an objective social scientific model following that of the natural sciences, accepting the relativistic implications of his participatory approach to the study of culture.

Taylor and Bellah

While also sympathetic to the notion that social life embodies particular linguistic rules, Taylor and Bellah develop a specifically cultural sociology and philosophy, in contrast to Winch's exclusive emphasis on the role of language and social practices in the construction of social reality. For Taylor, self-identities are created and sustained in the context of a cultural community which supplies us with ways of feeling, speaking, and understanding. Our interpretations substantially shape our experience, which is dependent on the cultural and linguistic traditions that we have available to us. Our public experience thus intersects with our private world and sense of self. As Taylor states, "the individual's particular projects and plans are drawn from the sum of what has been handed down by the linguistic community of which s/he is a member."[39] Individuals are always situated in a moral universe which provides meaning for their lives; they must always struggle with the moral definition of "what we as humans *are*."[40]

Moral considerations and motivations are intrinsically tied to one another. Human identities are formed through interactions in the context of a larger culture. Only in the modern world has identity become problematic. The radical individualism which pervades Western, and especially American, culture does not enable people to sufficiently grasp the role of cultural traditions in shaping their social identities. According to Taylor, selves exist only intersubjectively, and must be articulated in public language and symbols. Modern identity "is deeper and more many-sided than any of our possible articulations of it."[41]

Bellah and his colleagues have engaged in sociological studies which apply interpretive methods akin to those of Taylor to the study of contemporary American individualism. In *Habits of the Heart* (1985) and *The Good Society* (1992), Bellah et al. explore the ways in which cultural traditions – "symbols, ideals, and ways of feeling" – influence American conceptions of individualism, commitment, and institutions.[42] Bellah's work emphasizes social science as a form of social and self-understanding, promoting ethical and philosophical reflection on the ends of individual and societal existence. The best versions of interpretive social science juxtapose the traditions, aspirations, and ideals of a society with its present realities, encouraging reflection on its goals and moral practices.

Like Taylor, Bellah believes that there are significant differences between the natural and social sciences, for the study of history and ethics is constitutive of the social sciences in ways that it is not in the natural sciences. Unlike natural science, each generation of social science practitioners can learn much from the founders of their respective disciplines. Social science studies the manner in which the major components of a society fit together, and how individual character is affected by society and vice versa. Finally, Bellah et al. argue that social science investigates the moral and political meaning of democracy, citizenship, and the like.[43]

Because of these differences between natural and social sciences, the objective, value-neutral study of society advocated by scientific sociologists is not possible when examining the social world. Studying the possibilities and limitations of a society cannot be value-free. Social scientists are involved in the very society that they analyze. Their interpretations of social life depend on the various traditions and institutions in which they are enmeshed. The social scientist, to have any effect on social life, must be part of a living cultural tradition, which is a conversation about the meaning and value of a common life. The goal of a social science should be to engage the public in dialogue, and clarify and promote reflection on the sources and implications of the languages and beliefs that people use to understand their self and society.

Bellah and Taylor see ethical issues as central to social scientific inquiry. They believe that researchers should engage in a type of what the anthropologist Clifford Geertz calls "thick description," investigating the richness and depth of the moral traditions and cultural idioms which inform people's behaviors and attitudes. Social science should not engage in a search for social laws. Rather, it should enrich people's lives by making public the cultural and moral traditions at their disposal, while also prompting them to become aware of the importance of their obligations to one another.

Despite the dizzying variety of approaches within the interpretive persuasion, Giddens finds some problems common to all of them. He contends that interpretive perspectives, while concentrating on the production of society, have not sufficiently concerned themselves with its systematic reproduction. For example, Schutz, while interested in clarifying the conditions of social action, does not adequately study the relationship between its intended and unintended consequences. This neglect translates into a failure to satisfactorily theorize the structural dimension of social life. Winch neglects issues of institutional and social change and the mediation of different cultures, topics that are central to sociology. He also does not examine the role of social power in determining who makes the rules of society. The context and conventions of social life do not appear to be negotiated by people in Winch's analysis. Finally, Winch does not distinguish between lay and technical concepts in his approach, thus leaving untheorized the relationship between expert knowledge and everyday life.[44]

Similar problems arise in ethnomethodology. According to Giddens, ethnomethodologists do not explore issues of power or conflicting social and economic interests. They do not address how the purposive pursuit of interests often structures individual behavior. They need to complement their concentration on agency with an account of structural change and stability. Finally, the reflexivity of the social scientist himself/herself is not explicated by ethnomethodologists.

Like Bellah and Taylor, Giddens believes that the social scientist must reflexively examine his/her research, and its potential contribution to the enrichment of everyday life, if social science is to maintain a critical edge.[45] However, Giddens contends that the Bellah and Taylor approach is too oriented toward cultural continuity and consensus, as they emphasize the integrative aspects of a shared culture to the detriment of an analysis of the conflicting social and economic interests in social life. Giddens also argues that modernity's rapid pace of change breaks apart and recombines cultures to such an extent that no cultural system can remain homogeneous and stable over time.

The postmodern challenge

Bellah and Taylor advocate an historically informed mutual understanding across diverse disciplines and historical eras. Poststructuralism rejects such a hermeneutics. For poststructuralists, the interpretive and scientific methods and perspectives discussed above are both part of the modernist tradition. None of the social sciences subtly examine the role of power in structuring social inquiry, critically reflect upon their assumptions about the social world, or sufficiently analyze the ways in which social knowledge inherently marginalizes and excludes versions of truth that do not accord with these assumptions. For example,

Foucault contends that an interpretive approach to history narcissisti-cally relates the present to the past. The interpretive social scientist wishes to tailor history to his/her own purposes and identity. Foucault renounces such a historiography, which searches for the silenced voices of the past embodied in texts pregnant with meaning. His archaeological approach examines historical texts as strange artifacts which inevitably escape the historian's attempts to derive meaning from them. A Foucauldian and poststructuralist historical consciousness explores historical and social ruptures rather than continuities; gaps rather than wholes. History has no overriding meaning and continuity, as historical eras arbitrarily appear to the Foucauldian historian as a kind of kaleido-scope in which one period dissolves into another, with no consistent logic tying them together.

Foucault's critique of social scientific and historical disciplines accords with poststructuralist critiques of rationality, foundationalism, and the like. Foucault argues that social science developed a Promethean view of the relationship of knowledge to people's activities, exemplified in examples as diverse as Marx's theory that the organization of social labor determines the constitution of societies and Blumer's view that people define the situations that they are in, and act on the basis of those definitions. This desire to comprehend society forms the basis of social scientific truth, as social scientists try ever harder to understand social reality in the face of social problems and social changes.

For Foucault, this attempt to discover truth masks the social scientist's will to cognitive self-mastery and power. The very identity of social science is based on increasing knowledge, which translates into the control of some people over others. Social theorists, from Marx to Parsons, attempt to make the incomprehensible subject to rational categories, believing that rationality can achieve a true knowledge of the world. Universal theories of society are good examples of this tendency. Parsons, like Marx, argues that we are most free when we are most knowledgeable and divorced from local, parochial ties. This knowledge allows people to feel secure in their identities, to feel that they grasp the truth. Yet this universal knowledge is tied intimately to power, as social science turns people into objects of scientific investigation in its quest for universal truth, and attempts to control all of social life. The desire for power underlies the claims to truth and identity that inform the social sciences.[46]

A good example of a poststructuralist approach to social scientific study is Edward Said's influential 1978 book, *Orientalism*. Said states that the very notion of the Orient is a Western invention: it was imagined as an exotic place of romance and danger. Western scholars systematized their assumptions under the guise of the humanities and social sciences, as they "scientifically" demonstrated that the Orient was a barbaric land whose values were different from, and inferior to, Western rationality, progress, and logic. For Said, such conceptions allowed the West to

dominate the Orient. Scholarly disciplines focusing on the Orient justified the West's incorporation and definition of the inferiority of non-
Western peoples. Orientalism is essentially an imperialist view of the
world.[42]

Said's critique of Orientalism can be applied to the role that men have
played in defining women, or the ways that whites define people of
color. Such identities and power differentials are not objective, natural
categories. Knowledge cannot be separated from the workings of power;
all dominant identities are founded by subjugating and denying the
humanness of others.

The poststructuralist approach sensitizes the researcher to his/her
role in structuring and, indeed, dominating the very groups that s/he
studies. From this postmodern perspective, almost any sort of research
involves a power imbalance, and is therefore suspect. Poststructuralism
takes the critique of the tenets of objective social science to an extreme,
problematizing the possibility of any type of empirical social science.

Giddens's new rules of sociological method

Giddens is very involved in these debates about the nature of social
scientific inquiry. He argues that social science should attempt to be
theoretically engaged and empirically grounded. Giddens develops his
structuration theory through a critique of the various approaches discussed in this chapter, as he tries to form an alternative conception of
social science that overcomes the problems of these disparate theoretical
and methodological perspectives. He views social science as beset by
dualities which need to be integrated into a new sociological theory.
Before moving on to some of Giddens's arguments about how such a
synthesis can be achieved, it is necessary to explore his critiques of
interpretive and scientific sociologies in more detail.

Giddens and poststructuralism

Giddens contends that many poststructuralist claims make sense, such
as the argument that rationality and power are tied to one another.
Yet he believes that poststructuralism's fascination with textual and
literary analysis misrepresents fundamental aspects of social interaction.
Society is not simply a network of power which structures people's self-
understanding. Poststructuralism does not examine people as knowledgeable, skilled agents. It cannot grasp the intersubjectivity of everyday
life, and thus cannot effectively explain the social world. Giddens advocates a pragmatic and hermeneutic theoretical perspective over a poststructuralist one, drawing on Winch's and Wittgenstein's practical
analysis of social interaction, which is the pragmatic accomplishment of
"that which has to be done."[48] For Giddens, people pragmatically attempt

to solve the social problems that they confront. Poststructuralists cannot account for this complexity of social practice, or comprehend the centrality of reflexivity in this practice. People are active social agents who reproduce society, which has a structure that influences their behavior and beliefs. This duality of structure is ignored in postmodern analyses.

Giddens rejects many of the themes of poststructuralism. In doing so, he turns to some of the tenets of the natural science model of social scientific research. He contends that any sociology must examine the ways in which social structures are reproduced. However, Giddens rejects many of the assumptions implicit in the functionalist approaches that have characterized the attempts to develop a scientific sociology.

Giddens and functionalism

Giddens criticizes the contention that society functions like a natural organism. Parsons, like Durkheim, tended to see changes in societies as endogenous and naturally unfolding. Giddens states that this theoretical perspective cannot account for "purposive, reflexively monitored action."[49] Parsons, like Durkheim, has no sense that society is based on the skilled abilities of participants, who must creatively coordinate their actions. As Giddens writes, "There is no action in Parsons's 'action frame of reference,' only behaviour which is propelled by need-dispositions or role-expectations."[50] Because this inadequate function-alist theory of agency was based on the internalization of values, it was unable to see social life as actively constituted by its members.

Functionalists also neglect complex levels of social organization that are rationally and consciously monitored (as are most bureaucracies), and not simply unconsciously and automatically reproduced. Indeed, Giddens rejects any notion of an independent social system functioning outside the actions and consciousness of its members. Such an approach misses the significance of power in structuring social relations. Functionalists do not tie social action to the power of different groups in society, in large part because of their imagery of integration. They also do not grasp the negotiated character of norms, which are often based on compromises of conflicting and divergent interests.[51]

Functionalism, like positivism, lacks a satisfactory understanding of the complexity of institutions and history. Moreover, functionalism's view of natural scientific explanation is misguided, for it is based on the belief that language unproblematically reflects reality. *Contra* function-alism, Giddens contends that interpretation is a central part of all sciences. Metaphor and metonymy are not just literary devices, for they structure the vocabularies of the natural sciences, just as they do the social sciences. Language is a constitutive part of the social world.[52]

In sum, Giddens believes that the functionalist perspective does not sufficiently take into account the creative element of human action. For example, Parsons's theory of the internalization of values as the key factor in the formation of personality relates motivation to a consensus of values. Against this Parsonian determinism, Giddens argues that society is a skilled accomplishment. Giddens thinks that sociological analysis should focus on acting humans, while recognizing that actions have unintended consequences which "can involve homeostatic processes that promote social integration."[53] The reflexivity of people is not a nuisance to be avoided in the quest for objectivity (as in the self-fulfilling prophecy, for example), but a defining aspect of the human experience which gives social science its unique interpretive character.

Giddens and the interpretive perspectives

Giddens is sympathetic to many of the themes of the interpretive social scientific approaches. Phenomenology, linguistic social science, and ethnomethodology demonstrate that everyday social action involves complex processes of reasoning akin to theorizing. For example, Schutz and Winch recognize, in different ways, the importance of reflexivity in human behavior. Schutz's phenomenology identifies the active role of consciousness in interpreting versions of social reality. He also realizes that people's knowledge of the social world is often tacit and unspoken, based on a kind of learned cultural competency. Winch, like Wittgenstein, believes that people formulate knowledge of themselves and their society only through using publicly available linguistic categories. Moreover, the reflexivity inherent in social life means that all social norms and routines are fragile.

   In many ways, Giddens is most attracted to the ethnomethodological perspective. Like Garfinkel, he contends that sociology should concentrate on the taken-for-granted aspects of social interaction (what Giddens terms practical consciousness). Giddens also believes that ethnomethodology captures the centrality of reflexivity in social life in a more profound way than do other interpretive perspectives. Because reflexivity is the way in which people actively make social reality, it cannot be separated from the social context in which it occurs. Indeed, it is an integral part of this social reality. People draw on stocks of knowledge that are used in the reproduction of their social action. For Giddens, as for ethnomethodologists, people's reflexive knowledge of a social situation fundamentally alters that situation, becoming a constituent part of it.[54] Finally, ethnomethodologists grasp that much of the order in society stems from recognizing and following implicit rules of social conduct.

   Yet Giddens finds fault with the interpretive persuasion. For Giddens, none of the interpretive approaches sufficiently theorizes the centrality of power and the struggle over interests in social life. They do not address the historical transformation of institutions. Their analysis of subjectivity is also often strangely undertheorized, as they assume too great a harmony between the individual and society. Further, while functionalists have a faulty view of scientific explanation when collapsing distinctions between natural and social scientific types of explanation, Giddens believes that the interpretive perspectives draw too large a distinction between the natural and social sciences. They do not realize that all science has a hermeneutic moment, for social *and* natural reality must be interpreted by the scientist.[55]

Giddens's conception of social scientific study

Giddens argues that social science raises general issues about understanding that go to the core of human societies. For Giddens, mutual understanding is not a methodological postulate, but "the very ontological condition of human life in society as such." The researcher must grasp the culture of a society and be able to participate in it in principle, if s/he is to understand that society.[56] Understanding or *Verstehen* involves "publicly accessible" meanings articulated in language and embedded in tacit rules. Like Winch, Taylor, and Bellah, Giddens contends that because language is a public medium, standards of meaning deriving from a particular community can be understood by a sensitive outside observer. Social science is unavoidably interpretive because it studies people who are "concept-bearing and concept-inventing agents" who theorize about their lives.[57] Moreover, self-understanding is tied to our understandings of others. Reflexivity is a part of social scientific and everyday activity, as it is a social phenomenon. Neither social scientists nor laypeople exist outside of it, as people constantly react to new information about their world, which in turn changes it.

This study of people's active reconstitution of their social world must be tied to an understanding of the "impersonal" processes of history and social structure. As Giddens writes, "All social science depends upon grasping, in specific historical circumstances, the relation between knowledgeable activity in the light of convention and social reproduction brought about in an unintended fashion."[58] Grasping the interplay of structure and action is the key to social research. Giddens does not write a manifesto that advocates a specific step-by-step methodology, but develops concepts that can sensitize researchers to important issues in all social research, and makes them aware of the pitfalls of received approaches.

For Giddens, the methodological complexity involved in understanding meaning is central to the "postpositivist" phase of science that characterizes our time. Natural and social sciences alike recognize that all "theories are underdetermined by facts," and that "all observation statements are 'theory-impregnated'."[59] He states that "the social sciences share with natural science a respect for logical clarity in the formulation of theories and for disciplined empirical investigation."[60]

Moving between theories involves "hermeneutic tasks," for the observer must be able to grasp the different contexts which he/she studies.

Yet Giddens contends that the relation between natural science and its field of study is not mediated by mutual knowledge, as is the relationship between social science and its public. Giddens states that there are no methodological distinctions between history and social science, as all social laws are historical. They can be altered by social action, and they also require particular conditions in order to be effective. Because everyday beliefs are constitutive of people's worlds, social science has a more complex relation to its subject matter than does natural science. The claims of social science have to be defended *vis-à-vis* the agents whose activities they claim to explain. He argues that social science deals with social relations between subjects, rather than the relationship between a social subject and external nature. Thus, social science investigates a pre-interpreted social world that is lacking in natural science. This hermeneutic experience makes social scientific generalizations more cautious and context-dependent than in the natural sciences.[61]

Giddens recognizes two types of generalization of law-like behavior in the social sciences. The first concerns generalizations based on the social conventions of a given culture (most North Americans brush their teeth in the morning, for example). The second is more akin to a natural science law, based on the unintended consequences of social action. Giddens views the poverty cycle occurring in many Western societies as such a type of generalization. Within poverty areas, poor schools ensure that students are not motivated toward academic values, teachers have difficulty controlling the classroom, young people are ill qualified after leaving school, they get low-income jobs, live in poor areas, and their children repeat the cycle. However, people can change this pattern as they become more reflexive about it.[62] Generalizations are dependent on a particular historical and social context. Explanation in the social sciences is not a search for invariant laws, but can be better understood as "the clearing up of puzzles or queries." This approach problematizes the explanation/description dichotomy used by most sociologists. When a description helps clarify a problem, it is explanatory; yet an explanation can never be completed, because it invariably involves the unstated assumptions of etcetera clauses, in ethnomethodological parlance.[63]

Giddens finds perhaps the most prominent difference between the social and natural sciences in the double hermeneutic of the social sciences. Because the social theorist studies other people, s/he interprets a social reality rich in meaning. Social scientists' findings can become available to the public and part of their everyday life, circulating "in and out of the social world they are coined to analyze," further problematizing any simple separation of the scientist and his/her public.[64] For example, concepts such as citizenship and political sovereignty,

developed by political theorists from the Renaissance to the Enlightenment, became part of public discourse, thus helping to shape the very
world they attempted to describe. Because of the double hermeneutic,
there can be no objective accumulation of knowledge apart from its
social use, as in natural science. Yet because social science cannot remain
insulated from the social world and social scientific concepts become
part of everyday life and discourse, it is in many ways more influential
than natural science. In fact, the greatest contribution of sociology is not
the manufacture of generalizations which can be technically applied to
society, but the "absorption of concepts and theories" into the social
world that is studied, reflexively remaking the very subject matter of the
social sciences.[65]

An example of the double hermeneutic can be seen in Giddens's
recent works, *Modernity and Self-Identity* (1991) and *The Transformation
of Intimacy* (1992) in which he argues that feminism and gay and
lesbian movements have transformed everyday life. Self-identity is now
a reflexive, negotiated project, and relations between the genders have
become more democratic and open to change than ever before. Giddens
shows that these changes in intimacy resulted in part from the influence
of popular social scientific treatises on therapy and self-help that
were incorporated into people's lives, encouraging a more open, less
repressed understanding of personal experience. This democratization
of gender relations has consequences beyond the intimate sphere. As
practices of intimacy change, legal and social structures are necessarily
transformed. These changes range from new rights for children to the
necessity of a viable, participatory public life which allows personal
autonomy to flourish. Everyday and social scientific discourses interpenetrate, creating new types of social structure and personal identity.

This continual interaction of the individual and society makes any
methodological distinction between structure and action, micro and
macro, inadequate for social theory. Structure derives from routines and
patterned social practices, which become regularized in institutions.
Accordingly, empirical sociological work should analyze "recurring
social practices."[66] Giddens's reflexive sociology posits that people are
skilled agents involved in producing their social lives. Institutions
should not be seen as separate from people, as they always derive from
social interaction. For instance, the changes often remarked upon
concerning the contemporary family are inseparable from the actions of
the people within them, who create and remake families. Families do not
change simply because of structural forces working upon them; rather,
people themselves, drawing on the rules and resources available to them
in particular historical circumstances, change families, and this in turn
changes the individuals involved. Structuration theory is based on these
"generative rules and resources drawn upon by actors in the production
and reproduction of systems of interaction." Giddens conceptualizes the
production and reproduction of social life as the duality of structure,

where structure both generates interaction and is reproduced by it. (These concepts will be more fully explored in Chapter 3.)[67]

If the duality of structure and the double hermeneutic differentiate social science from the natural sciences, they show the affinities of social science with the arts. Social science and the arts draw on mutual knowledge to develop dialogue between subjects, and both creatively mediate between forms of life. One of the greatest contributions of social science is to help mediate between cultures, i.e. to let people know what it is like to live in a different society. Giddens places this hermeneutic moment at the center of his approach to sociological study and its applications. He advocates a dialogical model of research and policy implementation rather than an instrumental, technical version. In his dialogical paradigm, connections are forged between researchers, policy-makers, and those people affected by potential social policies. Research cannot simply be applied in an instrumental manner, but must have the persuasive power to modify people's knowledge about their social world, so that they can change their behavior accordingly.[68]

Giddens realizes that his social scientific agenda is somewhat vague and can only supply sensitizing concepts which can point researchers in some methodological and substantive directions. Yet he believes that his structuration theory adequately combines the scientific and artistic elements of social investigation. He also contends that his theory of structuration fulfills the criteria for a critical theory of society, for it ties intended to unintended consequences of social action, and regards the potential for change in power differentials as inherent in every social interaction.[69] Giddens's version of structuration theory builds the reflexivity of the layperson and researcher into its very organization, overcoming many of the dualities that have characterized social science, and especially sociology. For Giddens, social scientific research is not amenable to formulaic statements, as it requires a sensitive approach to social context and individual action. Giddens links his research agenda to his larger theory of structuration. It is to a more thorough consideration of structuration theory that we now turn.

Notes

1 H. Stuart Hughes, *Consciousness and Society* (New York, Vintage, 1958).

2 Max Weber, *The Methodology of the Social Sciences* (New York, Free Press, 1968).

3 Robert Merton, *On Theoretical Sociology: Five Essays, Old and New* (New York, Free Press, 1967), pp. 51–52, 63.

4 Paul K. Feyerabend, "Against Method: Outlines of an Anarchistic Theory of Knowledge," *Minnesota Studies in Philosophy* 4 (1964).

5 Jonathan Turner, *The Structure of Sociological Theory* (Belmont, CA, Wadsworth, 1991), p. 60; Talcott Parsons, "The Action Frame of Reference," in

Talcott Parsons on Institutions and Social Evolution, ed. Leon Mayhew (Chicago, University of Chicago Press, 1982), pp. 94–95.

6 Talcott Parsons, "An Approach to the Sociology of Knowledge," *Transactions of the Fourth World Congress of Sociology* 4 (1959), pp. 26–27.

7 Ibid., p. 38.

8 Ibid., pp. 25, 32, 35. See also Talcott Parsons, "Value-Freedom and Objectivity," pp. 56–65 in *Understanding and Social Inquiry*, ed. Fred Dallmayr and Thomas McCarthy (Notre Dame, University of Notre Dame Press, 1977).

9 Karl Popper, *The Poverty of Historicism* (New York, Harper and Row, 1964).

10 Karl Popper, "The Logic of the Social Sciences," in *The Positivist Dispute in German Sociology*, ed. Theodor Adorno et al. (New York, Harper and Row, 1976), p. 88.

11 Karl Popper, *Conjectures and Refutations* (New York, Basic Books, 1962), pp. 223–228; *The Philosophy of Karl Popper*, ed. Paul Arthur Schilpp (LaSalle, IL, Open Court, 1974), pp. 987–1111.

12 Popper, *The Poverty of Historicism*, p. 132.

13 Ibid., p. 136.

14 Popper, "The Logic of the Social Sciences," pp. 102–104.

15 Karl Popper, *The Open Society and Its Enemies*, Vol. 1 (Princeton, Princeton University Press, 1966), pp. 59–64.

16 Anthony Giddens, *New Rules of Sociological Method: A Positive Critique of Interpretative Sociologies* (Stanford, Stanford University Press, 1993), p. 146.

17 Ibid., pp. 147–148.

18 Anthony Giddens, *The Constitution of Society: Outline of a Theory of Structuration* (Berkeley, University of California Press, 1984), p. 374; *Central Problems in Social Theory: Action, Structure, and Contradiction in Social Analysis* (Berkeley, University of California Press, 1979), p. 95.

19 Peter Winch, "The Idea of a Social Science," *Rationality*, ed. Bryan Wilson (New York, Harper and Row, 1970), p. 4.

20 Herbert Blumer, *Society as Symbolic Interaction* (Berkeley, University of California Press, 1969), p. 139.

21 Ibid., p. 142.

22 Ibid., p. 77.

23 Ibid., p. 74.

24 Alfred Schutz, "Concept and Theory Formation in the Social Sciences," in *Philosophy of the Social Sciences, a Reader*, ed. Maurice Natanson (New York, Random House, 1963), p. 246.

25 Ibid., p. 235.

26 Alfred Schutz, *The Phenomenology of the Social World* (Evanston, IL, Northwestern University Press, 1967), pp. 9–14.

27 Alfred Schutz, "Common-Sense and Scientific Interpretations of Human Action," in *Philosophy of the Social Sciences*, ed. Natanson, pp. 311–315.

28 Schutz, "Concept and Theory Formation in the Social Sciences," p. 239.

29 Maurice Natanson, "A Study in Philosophy and the Social Sciences," *Philosophy of the Social Sciences*, ed. Natanson, p. 281.

30 Peter Berger and Thomas Luckmann, *The Social Construction of Reality* (New York, Doubleday, 1967), pp. 21, 121–125.

31 Harold Garfinkel, *Studies in Ethnomethodology* (Englewood Cliffs, NJ, Prentice-Hall, 1967), p. 30.

32 Ibid., pp. 1–3.

33 Ibid., p. 3.

34 For a good comparison of Weber's and Durkheim's views of culture, see Ann Swidler, "Cultural Power and Social Movements," in *Social Movements and Culture*, ed. Hank Johnston and Bert Klandermans (Minneapolis, University of Minnesota Press, 1995), pp. 25–27.

35 Charles Taylor, "Interpretation and the Sciences of Man," *Understanding and Social Inquiry*, ed. Dallmayr and McCarthy, p. 119.

36 Winch, "The Idea of a Social Science," p. 9.

37 Ibid., p. 16. See also Taylor, "Interpretation and the Sciences of Man," p. 103.

38 Peter Winch, "Understanding a Primitive Society," in *Rationality*, ed. Wilson, pp. 81–82, 93–94.

39 Charles Taylor, "Language and Society," in *Communicative Action: Essays on Jürgen Habermas's The Theory of Communicative Action*, ed. Axel Honneth and Hans Joas (Cambridge, MA, MIT Press, 1991), p. 24.

40 Ibid., p. 33.

41 Charles Taylor, *Sources of the Self: The Making of Modern Identity* (Cambridge, MA, Harvard University Press, 1989), p. 29.

42 Robert N. Bellah, Richard Madsen, William M. Sullivan, Ann Swidler, and Steven M. Tipton, *Habits of the Heart: Individualism and Commitment in American Life* (Berkeley, University of California Press, 1985), p. 27.

43 Ibid., pp. 300–302.

44 Anthony Giddens, *Studies in Social and Political Theory* (New York, Basic Books, 1977), p. 123; *New Rules of Sociological Method*, pp. 23, 38–39, 54–57.

45 *New Rules of Sociological Method*, p. 46; see also *Studies in Social and Political Theory*, pp. 175–178.

46 On Foucault's critique of social science, see *Discipline and Punish: The Birth of the Prison* (New York, Vintage, 1977).

47 Edward Said, *Orientalism* (New York, Vintage, 1978).

48 Giddens, *Central Problems in Social Theory*, p. 4; italics in the original.

49 Giddens, *Studies in Social and Political Theory*, p. 12; see also "A Reply to My Critics," in *Social Theory of Modern Societies: Anthony Giddens and His Critics*, ed. David Held and John B. Thompson (New York, Cambridge Univerity Press, 1989), pp. 250–251.

50 Giddens, *New Rules of Sociological Method*, p. 21.

51 Ibid., p. 26; *Studies in Social and Political Theory*, p. 14.

52 Ibid., pp. 44, 104, 108, 245; *In Defence of Sociology*, p. 68.

53 Giddens, *Studies in Social and Political Theory*, p. 111.

54 Giddens, *Central Problems in Social Theory*, pp. 57–58; *New Rules of Sociological Method*, pp. 6, 22.

55 *New Rules of Sociological Method*, p. 60; *Central Problems in Social Theory*, pp. 121, 254; "A Reply to My Critics," p. 251.

56 Giddens, *New Rules of Sociological Method*, p. 24; *Central Problems in Social Theory*, pp. 5–6.

57 Giddens, *Social Theory and Modern Sociology* (Stanford, Stanford University Press, 1987), p. 70; *Studies in Social and Political Theory*, pp. 174–175.

58 Giddens, *In Defence of Sociology*, p. 72.

59 Giddens, *Studies in Social and Political Theory*, p. 11.

60 Giddens, *Social Theory and Modern Sociology*, p. 149.

61 Giddens, *New Rules of Sociological Method*, pp. 14–15, 154; *Central Problems in Social Theory*, pp. 230–231; *Studies in Social and Political Theory*, p. 166.

62 Giddens, *In Defence of Sociology*, pp. 70–71.

63 Giddens, *Central Problems in Social Theory*, p. 258.

64 *The Giddens Reader*, ed. Philip Cassell (Stanford, Stanford University Press, 1993), p. 149; see also *New Rules of Sociological Method*, p. 9.

65 Giddens, *Social Theory and Modern Sociology*, p. 48.

66 Giddens, "A Reply to My Critics," p. 252; see also *New Rules of Sociological Method*, p. 7.

67 Giddens, *Studies in Social and Political Theory*, p. 14; see also *New Rules of Sociological Method*, pp. 165–169.

68 *New Rules of Sociological Method*, p. 156; *Social Theory and Modern Sociology*, p. 47.

69 Giddens, *Studies in Social and Political Theory*, p. 123.

3

STRUCTURATION THEORY: RECONCEPTUALIZING AGENCY AND STRUCTURE

Sociology has frequently been described as in a state of crisis. Given sociology's roots in theorists as disparate as Durkheim, Comte, Weber, and Marx, and their different approaches to the study of society, such a sense of continual crisis within the discipline is not surprising. Frequently this takes the form of conflicts between a belief in the importance of actively promoting social change (often from the Marxist heritage) and an advocacy of disinterested, value-free scholarship (inspired by Weber). Accordingly, crises in sociology often intersect with larger social crises, from the "great transformation" of Western industrialization that provided the context for classical social theory to the anti-colonial struggles, student movements, civil rights movements, and anti-war demonstrations of the 1960s and 1970s that have shaped much recent social theory.

These social crises helped inform more rarefied theoretical disputes within sociology concerning how best to understand a rapidly changing social world. The positivist/interpretive controversy within the discipline discussed in Chapter 2 is one indicator of these conflicts. This methodological debate points to other dualisms, from agency/ structure to subject/object, which constantly recur and fuel the sense of crisis within sociology. In his work on structuration theory, Giddens does not address in great detail the social environment's influence on sociology as much as the discipline's internal theoretical deficiencies which inhibit its understanding of social life. He attempts to overcome the theoretical impasse of sociology by reformulating the subject/object and agency/structure dualities. This chapter explores Giddens's theoretical arguments. It investigates Giddens's structuration theory through a close examination of his notions of agency, social practices, ontological security, unintended consequences, and time-space issues. Goffman's work on social interaction will be discussed, as it is especially important to Giddens in this context. Giddens shares the problematic of transcending the duality of structure and agency with the theorists Elias and Bourdieu, who will be compared to Giddens in this chapter.

Sociology and crisis

Alvin Gouldner captured the mood of turmoil within the discipline in his important book, *The Coming Crisis of Western Sociology* (1970). He argues that the orthodox consensus in sociology, based on Parsonian-inspired structural functionalism, was breaking down in the face of the profound social changes of the 1960s. Orthodox sociology, according to Gouldner, could not grasp these social changes, and demonstrated its conservatism by dismissing the significance of these new social trends. By the 1960s, sociology had lost the critical spirit that had informed the work of its founders, especially Marx and Weber.

Gouldner contends that as a university professor, Parsons was isolated to some degree from the real world, and that this was illustrated in his sociology. He took the abstract problem of social order as the starting point of sociological research, rather than problems developing in the real world. He reinterpreted European sociology, especially the work of Durkheim and Weber, in the context of American optimism. Parsons did not confront Marxism in any substantive way, while implicitly developing sociology as an alternative to Marxism.

In dismissing Marxism, Parsons instead turned to the German tradition of idealism and to French social science. Gouldner states that Parsons synthesized the romantic tradition of the importance of subjective values and feelings in his voluntarist theory of action, which drew heavily on Weber, with the French emphasis on the ways in which the social system influences and constrains human action, exemplified in Durkheim. Yet Parsons never completely overcame this split between the active subject and the external influence of institutions, wavering in his work between a strong emphasis on the autonomy of moral values and the freedom of personal choice, on the one hand, and the functional requirements of a social system that demanded that people act a particular way, on the other.[1] Interestingly, in this context Gouldner's Marxist orientation merges with Alexander's more sympathetic interpretation of Parsonian sociology. Both Gouldner and Alexander state that Parsons's theoretical incoherence, demonstrated in the split between an active subject and a deterministic social system, foreshadowed the functionalist inability to respond adequately to the social changes of the 1960s and early 1970s.

Gouldner contends that the Marxist revival occurring within and outside of sociology in this era provided Parsonian sociology with a true competitor for intellectual dominance. Yet by the mid-1970s, the theoretical split between an active subject and a deterministic social system was replicated within Marxist thought. Alexander shows that this split was inherent in Marx's original thought, but it arose forcefully in the 1970s in the internecine disputes between Althusserian Marxists who believed that people were destined to act out the logic of their class positions, and more humanistically inclined Marxists, from E.P. Thompson to the Frankfurt School, who placed much more emphasis on the autonomy of agency and cultural values and the possibility of people consciously creating social change. In fact, by the late 1970s Marxist and functionalist sociologies both had often-antagonistic structural and voluntarist camps. This micro/macro duality is an abiding concern in sociology.

Giddens's early sociology, while not overtly responding to the social crisis occasioned by the 1960s and 1970s social movements, nevertheless addresses the prevailing attitude of crisis and stasis within sociology. For Giddens, the crisis is largely a theoretical one, for sociological theories are characterized by dualisms which inhibit a clear understanding of social life. Giddens shares Gouldner's and Alexander's criticisms of Marxism and functionalism, as he sees these theoretical traditions suffering from two similar conceptual problems. First, either the voluntarist or determinist side of the individual/society dichotomy is emphasized, as people are seen as either free agents or as following norms or class interests with little choice, as their actions are determined by the functional requirements or the class arrangements of society. Second, the notion of the self within functionalism and Marxism is not very complex. The agent him/herself is not conceived of as a subjective world toward which people can reflexively act. Giddens contends that a more fruitful sociological theory must engage issues of agency, structure, and social reflexivity in a new key. He argues that social structures are both the condition and the outcome of people's activities; one cannot exist without the other. Before moving to a discussion of Giddens's structuration theory, Bourdieu's and Elias's similar attempts to overcome the various dualisms characteristic of most sociology will be addressed.

Bourdieu

Like Giddens, the French sociologist Bourdieu argues that any satisfactory social theory must challenge the opposition of structure and individual action, as the one cannot be understood without the other. Bourdieu states that social science can only advance through overcoming subject/object dualisms. He contends that his notions of cultural capital, habitus, and distinctive fields can capture the complexity of social action, and move social theory in a progressive direction.

Much like Weber and Giddens, Bourdieu believes that sociology is primarily concerned with the ways in which power pervades all realms of society. As Craig Calhoun succinctly states, "Bourdieu's sociology is aimed largely at an account of power relations, and especially of the many ways in which power is culturally produced, reproduced, and manipulated."[2] Bourdieu develops a theory of symbolic power and its relationship to economic and political power, emphasizing the pursuit of symbolic profit and the accumulation of symbolic capital as a complementary activity to the amassing of economic capital. As Bourdieu demonstrates in his investigations of phenomena as disparate as culture, schools, and sports, no social practices are disinterested; all are riddled with power differentials which affect occupational and class outcomes. He especially investigates the ways in which subtle class differences and class power are played out in symbolic and cultural realms.

In Bourdieu's view, people develop social strategies with the intention of increasing their "cultural capital," which is inscribed in their very type of personality, ways of bearing, voice, grace, linguistic competence, and the like. Many of these advantages subtly accrue to those born in the upper classes. Much of Bourdieu's work shows how cultural capital is unevenly distributed among different classes, and the ways in which cultural capital helps reproduce the class structures of modern societies. Class mobility is difficult not only because of the lack of material resources, but also because of the difficulties that individuals in the working and poorer classes face of assimilating the cultural capital associated with the upper classes. Accordingly, Bourdieu argues that sports are one of the few means of upward mobility for people in the poorer classes. Sports represent for boys (and increasingly for girls) what beauty has always represented for girls: a market of cultural capital based on physical capital.[3]

Bourdieu's analysis of cultural power is part of a larger project that attempts to grasp how individuals, though attempting to achieve their goals, reproduce the social structures that surround and inform their actions. For Bourdieu, people experience a particularly comfortable sense of place, what he calls "le sens du jeu," through sharing a habitus, which he defines as a "system of durable, transposable dispositions."[4] Calhoun's elaboration on the meaning of habitus is especially well put: he calls it "the embodied sensibility that makes possible structured improvisation." The habitus can be compared to the sense and cohesiveness that jazz musicians develop while playing together, which does not depend on formal rules.[5] The habitus is embodied in movements, facial gestures, posture, etc. It cannot be reduced to linguistic acts, or mathematically plotted; as Bourdieu states, "Where one sees an algebra, I believe that it is necessary to see a dance or a gymnastic."[6] For Bourdieu, habitus cuts through subject/object dichotomies, and allows social reality to be understood in terms of practical social relations. The habitus gives people a strong pragmatic, non-discursive sense of social competence, of how to act in particular situations.

Bourdieu's discussion of intellectuals, cultural distinctions, gift-giving, and the like demonstrates the complex relationships between the habitus and the contests over social power in autonomous yet interdependent fields. Following Weber, Bourdieu sees modernity as complexly differentiated; aesthetics, morality, and science compose the major dimensions of modern life, as they represent distinctive fields which follow their own independent logics of practice and evaluation. These fields are not simply economically determined; rather, in each one, participants grasp its implicit rules, and struggle to augment its particular symbolic capital (whether it be profit, honor, or prestige). Often at stake in these contests is the right to speak, a linguistic hegemony which privileges some manners of speaking over others. Bourdieu argues that language is pragmatically based: its functioning cannot be grasped apart from its institutional context. Language expresses class distinctions through different vocabularies and accents. Words can be used as a means of restraint and control. Through language, competence and authority are demonstrated. Much of Bourdieu's work on education shows that school systems help to standardize cultural and linguistic differences among people, as native peoples feel compelled to abandon their own language in favor of the dominant one. Those who lack facility in the official language are effectively silenced, while the categories of the dominant symbolic system can be used to evaluate practices, such as schoolwork.[7]

But social relations are not merely linguistic; they are structured dispositions which are realized through social practices. The recognition of an official language becomes inscribed in people's very inclinations, and thus becomes almost imperceptible. As Bourdieu states, "what exist in the social world are relations, not interactions between agents or intersubjective ties between individuals, but objective relations which exist independently of individual consciousness and will, as Marx said."[8] Still, these relations do not mechanically determine social action. In his analysis of gift exchange, Bourdieu stresses the interval between gift and counter-gift. It is during this interval that different orientations and strategies can be played out. He writes, "To substitute *strategy* for the *rule* is to reintroduce time, with its rhythm, its orientation, its irreversibility."[9] Thus, even the seemingly altruistic practice of gift-giving displays elements of strategies that allow one to accumulate cultural capital and social prestige.

Fields and the habitus structure not only everyday life, but intellectual pursuits and strategies as well. Bourdieu categorizes the German philosopher Martin Heidegger as someone who existed in social and philosophical fields that, unknown to him, shaped his thought and allowed him to augment his particular type of cultural capital. Inhabiting a philosophical field structured by a habitus, carrying out the requirements of his social space, the "thinker is less the subject than the object of his most fundamental rhetorical strategies."[10]

Bourdieu situates Heidegger's philosophy in the general social crises faced by post-World War I Germany, which affected all sectors of society. World War I, the failed German revolution of 1918 and the 1917 Bolshevik Revolution, political assassinations in post-World War I Germany, the 1919 Treaty of Versailles, the occupation of the Ruhr, and the Depression provided the context for Heidegger's approach. These events not only helped create an "ideological mood" among the educated bourgeoisie, they also provoked a crisis in the German university. For many intellectuals on the fringe of academia, such as Spengler and Junger, these events were the catalyst for a critique of the meaningless-ness engendered by industrialism, mathematical rationalism, and demo-cracy, and a corresponding turn inward, an emphasis on spontaneity over rationality, and the search for a specifically German principle of freedom. These themes crystallized in a call for a new intellectual aristocracy to carry out a conservative revolution. According to Bourdieu, those most attracted to this perspective included a new generation of academic proletarians frozen out of university positions and humanities professors who saw the status of their disciplines declining in favor of the natural and social sciences.[11]

Heidegger reproduced these general themes in philosophical discourse. Given the requirements of intellectual distance and the precise language of the philosophical habitus, Heidegger's philosophy recast many of the themes of the conservative revolution while simul-taneously appearing to transcend them by dealing with more funda-mental concerns. By claiming that issues such as nihilism could only be correctly expressed through a philosophical discourse of authenticity and concerned with such existential questions as the confrontation with death, Heidegger was able to persuade many that "the solitary search of the authentic thinker seems to have nothing in common with the opportunistic theorizing of the warrior bored with lesser combats."[12]

Bourdieu recognizes that Heidegger was quite adept at "playing" the philosophical field. Heidegger expertly related his position to those of German canonical authors, to disguise the political dimension of his elusive and ambiguous perspective. He situated himself in the context of the Kantian philosophy prevalent at the time; this philosophical space shaped the options that he could pursue. Heidegger not only tried to increase his cultural capital as a philosopher by moving beyond the Kantian legacy, but also attempted to advance the social status of philosophy by raising it to a new level of autonomy that would augment the social power of philosophers. By philosophically formalizing the ferment of the conservative revolution, Heidegger created a new posi-tion so powerful that all other philosophers would have to rethink their positions in relation to his. Further, Nazism provided the opportunity for Heidegger to become the philosophical *Führer* of the regime.

Heidegger could not reflect on these considerations, for to do so would have meant questioning his belief in the possibility of pure philosophy. This rethinking would necessarily have involved "taking into account the process of the empirical constitution of the cognitive subject," the role of history in constituting time, and the impossibility of converting social questions into philosophical ontology.[13]

Bourdieu's study of Heidegger shows how fields structure thought, and that even the most abstract philosophy cannot be separated from issues of social power. Situating Heidegger in his social and philosophical context is a concrete demonstration of how to overcome the individual/society dualism that confounds so much social theory. Bourdieu contends that this agency/structure dichotomy characteristic of most sociology must be theoretically rethought if social science is to advance. He states that his notion of habitus allows a more sensitive understanding of the intersection and inseparability of agency and social structure than is found in most sociological theories. Bourdieu argues that the habitus imbues people with a tacit sense of how to become competent social agents, which is realized in practices that are constitutive of social life.

Giddens's sociological theory is in many respects similar to that of Bourdieu. Giddens joins Bourdieu in arguing that the structure/action duality characteristic of most social theory is a false dichotomy, for social action and social structures presuppose and require one another. Like Bourdieu, Giddens states that social practices are central to the ongoing reproduction of societies. Giddens and Bourdieu share a practical view of language, which is a key means through which people address social problems together. These theorists view the issue of time as a primary aspect of social processes that has not been sufficiently recognized by sociological theories. Placing time at the center of social analysis moves theory away from a view of individuals as separated from the social structures that they actively reproduce. Bourdieu and Giddens also see power as inseparable from any social interaction.

However, Giddens's approach emphasizes more than Bourdieu's the intelligence of people in the context of a modern, reflexive world. People's behaviors and beliefs, even those of philosophers such as Heidegger, are not simply structured by fields. Individuals are very knowledgeable about the conditions influencing them. For Giddens, modernity and rationalization demand the increasingly reflexive coordination of social action and the corresponding diminution of taken-forgranted structures, such as tradition. Bourdieu would probably dispute this claim, for he argues that social relations are still opaque in the modern world, and not as amenable to change as Giddens believes. Giddens's theory is different from Bourdieu's in part because he draws on ethnomethodology and Goffman's interaction theory in much more detail than does Bourdieu in constructing his notion of people as knowledgeable, reflexive agents.

Elias and figuration theory

The sociologist Elias also argues that social theory is beset by dualities that inhibit a satisfactory account of the dynamics of social life. Best known for his work on the "civilizing process" in the West, Elias contends that his notion of "figuration theory," which stresses the interdependence of people, can overcome the pernicious theoretical divisions within sociology.

According to Elias, sociology has a distinctive subject matter, for the reality of society cannot be reduced to the qualities of the individuals who compose it. Because many laypeople and social scientists do not recognize the independence of society and the contribution made by sociology to studying it, they engage in reductive and dualistic approaches to social life. The duality that most disturbs Elias is the contemporary emphasis on the separation of the individual from society. He recognizes that many people now feel that a gulf exists between the individual and social life, in the wake of the rise of modern individualism and the concomitant privatization of much of the social world. Elias finds this belief to be misguided, as he argues that the individual and society are simply two different sides of the same coin, for the person has no "inside" that can be separated from his/her "outside." In fact, the psyche of the individual is best understood as a social relation, tied to a "specific, historically determined inner life."[14] Thus, the individual was very different in the twelfth century compared to the twentieth century, to the extent that twelfth-century children had a different "structure of instincts."[15]

Elias contends that many recurring philosophical disputes surrounding the issue of meaning are due to this individualistic approach, which does not take into account that the person must be understood in an historical and social context. Individuals do not create meaning in isolation, for it is the social context which influences individual actions and provides the cultural and social resources which inform meaningful behavior. Elias shares Bourdieu's contention that the habitus, the person's dispositions that are shared with others of that society, links the individual and society. The development of different notions of the individual are due to changes in the habitus, which in turn is tied to the larger dynamics of communities, such as the nation or the state.[16]

Elias believes that his theory of figuration can capture the dynamics of groups, societies, and individuals. Individuals can only be truly comprehended in terms of "their interdependence, the structure of their societies, in short . . . the figurations they form with each other."[17] Figurations are the "webs of interdependence . . . characterized by power balances of many sorts," including schools, families, and the like.[18] People are not interdependent only by nature (in order to survive, for example), but also by culturally learned, "socially generated reciprocal needs," which involve education and socialization. Because people have a variety of ties with one another, from the family to education, they form particular configurations. Elias compares figurational social processes to a dance at one point in his work, to games in another. To Elias, dances are not mental constructs, though they are relatively independent of specific individuals (there are general dance steps which characterize different types of dances). However, dances can only be realized by people's specific dancing. Dances change over time due to people's innovations. The figurations of society share these dance-like qualities, as they generate general rules for behavior which are actualized only in specific actions.[19]

Elias emphasizes that changing balances of power are an integral part of all figurations. In Elias's view, power is based on the individual's scope for action within specific, hierarchically arranged social positions, which often arise from characteristics such as class and gender. Power cannot be understood apart from relationships. The dynamics of figurations also escape the intentions of the individuals involved, as people's actions invariably involve consequences which are "unplanned and not immediately controllable," though they can be rationally understood.[20] Though rationalization processes in the West have made social change somewhat more controllable, unintended consequences still invariably occur. Elias contends that the analysis of unintended consequences is particularly applicable to long-term social changes, where "social sequences proceed blindly, without guidance." These processes have no end or goal in sight. Elias points to the reduction of inequality throughout the last two centuries as an example of such a trend, along with the increasing specialization of occupational tasks.[21]

Elias's work on the civilizing process best demonstrates unintended and influential social changes occurring over a long time span. In his two-volume work, *The Civilizing Process* (1978), a study that moves from the Middle Ages to the nineteenth century, Elias argues that there is a long-term trend in a civilizing direction in European people's psychological make-up. An important component of this civilizing process is the shift of many social acts, from defecation to sexuality, "behind the scenes of social life." Contemporary peoples are now much more easily embarrassed and disgusted by such acts, as their manners have become more refined.[22]

Elias does not believe that changes in manners and in the threshold of embarrassment and shame over the centuries were a "natural" development, nor were they due to a recognition of the health benefits of particular types of behavior. Rather, like Bourdieu, Elias states that the elaboration of the everyday conduct of manners was due in large part to efforts to maintain social distinctions. Standards of control over impulses were first developed by social superiors, gradually diffusing to those of equal status or below. Such changes occurred as people of different social status interacted. From the sixteenth century onward, as the European population grew and trade brought more countries into contact, people of diverse social origins increasingly formed a new social hierarchy. They were forced to develop a uniform code of conduct, resulting in a more open and competitive society. In France, for example, this change was largely due to the gradual centralization of social power in the monarchy and the rise of court society, as standards of conduct associated with the court of the King gradually spread to other sectors of society.[23]

Such courtly behavior was much more controlled than conduct in the Middle Ages. In medieval society, there were few restraints on emotions, due in part to the lack of internalized social conventions. Further, there was no social center which could dictate behavior. Much social behavior was still public. In fact, elites seemed to delight in public displays. The medieval lord did not demand that social inferiors act in a particular way as he mingled with them. The contrast between the lord's behavior and that of peasants only heightened the lord's pleasure, confirming his difference from the peasant.[24]

The nobles' sense of mastery and contempt for social inferiors was strong, in large part because nobles were not over-dependent on peasants to maintain their lifestyle. The social world centered around the noble knight. Elias's vivid description of medieval life is worth quoting: "Hungry dogs, begging women, rotting horses, servants crouching against the ramparts, villages in flames, peasants being plundered and killed – all this was as much a part of the landscape of these people as are tournaments and hunts. So God made the world: some are rulers, others are bondsmen."[25] In such a world there is little embarrassment regarding public behavior, just as there is little need to control emotions. Knights took pleasure in violence and battle; people generally were very volatile emotionally, swinging from one extreme to another.[26]

The social changes involved in the decline of this medieval figuration included the rise of the nation-state, which consolidated power in a social center and promoted uniform standards of conduct, and a new, emerging capitalist economy. Elias states that by the end of the Middle Ages, money had become more decisive than manners in maintaining social distinctions, as "what people actually achieve and produce becomes more important than their manners."[27] Such social changes involved a new conception of linear time as well. Elias argues that people learn their culture's specific sense of time over many generations. Time is not an abstract, uniform flow that influences social life from without, but is integrally tied to society. Time is the "social activity of timing," which differs from culture to culture.[28]

Elias contends that his figuration theory overcomes the dualisms characteristic of much social theory. It demonstrates the intersection of the individual and society, as the development of the individual (psychogenesis) is inextricably tied to changes in society (sociogenesis). As he argues in *The Civilizing Process*, changing figurations from medieval times to the present account for our different concepts of the individual, manners, shame, embarrassment, and the entire range of emotional controls that exist in different societies.

Giddens shares Elias's goal of overcoming theoretical dichotomies in social theory, especially the individual/society dualism. Both are searching for a theoretical language that can express the inseparable interconnections between individuals and the social relations in which they are embedded. Giddens and Elias recognize that much of what is considered shameful in the contemporary world is the result of an historical process, as behaviors relating to manners, sexuality, and the like are kept at a distance from public life (sequestered, in Giddens's vocabulary). Giddens also shares Elias's contention that all social action involves power and unintended consequences, which must be rationally analyzed for a satisfactory account of the reproduction of societies.

Giddens has many differences from Elias, however. Giddens defines sociology's distinctive subject matter as the analysis of the institutions of modernity, rather than the study of an abstract version of society or social figurations. As Giddens states, sociology is not "a generic discipline to do with the study of human societies as a whole, but that branch of social science which focuses particularly upon the 'advanced' or modern societies."[29] Giddens rejects Elias's postulate of a close connection between psychogenesis and sociogenesis, as he feels that this approach underestimates the complexity of non-modern cultures. Giddens cites anthropological studies of the complexity of non-modern languages to dispute Elias's claim that medieval European people's emotional lives were in some sense less complicated than ours.[30] For Giddens, Elias's approach downplays the reflexive capacities of all peoples, no matter their cultural ambience. Elias, like Bourdieu, has an undeveloped notion of agency, for Elias does not grant sufficient weight to the autonomous actions of the reflexive individual, who actively reproduces society through social practices.

Giddens and structuration theory

Giddens, like Bourdieu and Elias, rejects the Parsonian functionalist theory that socialization and interaction are based on the relatively passive internalization and acting out of values. These theorists argue, *contra* Parsons, that the reproduction of society results from people's practical, creative activity. Bourdieu, Elias, and Giddens all stress that an adequate social theory must place the specific analysis of cultural time and space at its center. They also argue that social reproduction is dependent upon a kind of public culture embodied in social rules and language. Giddens differs from Bourdieu and Elias in discussing links between agency and structure in Wittgensteinian terms, as he sees the reproduction of society as a practical activity concerning the ongoing accomplishment of what needs to be done in order for social life to continue. Giddens's pragmatic view of the intersection of agency and structure also draws on French structuralism, Goffman's social psychology, and ethnomethodology, which gives his approach more complexity than that found in Elias or Bourdieu.

According to Giddens, a major problem with most sociology is its inability to theoretically formulate a conception of the reflexive, acting person. In Giddens's view, the person must be conceptualized as a knowledgeable agent who can justify his/her actions. Moreover, agency involves a notion of practical consciousness, which is "all the things that we know as social actors, and must know, to make social life happen, but to which we cannot necessarily give discursive form."[31] Giddens states that this conception of the agent must be integrated with an account of the conditions and consequences of social action. For Giddens, social structure is both enabling and constraining.

Giddens conceives this relationship of agency and structure as the duality of structure, in which people reflexively produce and reproduce their social life.[32] His analysis of societies turns on the importance of social practices (the enactment of everyday activities which reproduce society) and ontological security (a belief in the reliability and durability of social life). In developing these concepts, Giddens draws on Goffman's social psychology. In Giddens's view, Goffman shows the importance for social interaction of the maintenance of trust and tact across different social situations. Following Goffman and the ethnomethodologists, Giddens argues that sociologists must study what people take for granted, and how they are able to act consistently in different contexts.

Goffman helps supply Giddens with a more complex social psychology than that of Bourdieu or Elias. Indeed, one of the most innovative aspects of Giddens's social theory is his use of these microsociological perspectives in his theory of structuration. Giddens's notions of ontological security, the importance of social routines, and the centrality of social practices in the reproduction of social life owes much to these sociologists. While we discussed ethnomethodology in Chapter 2, some discussion of Goffman is necessary to better understand Giddens's sociology, especially his conception of agency.

Goffman and dramaturgical theory

Goffman is the most important sociological exponent of dramaturgical theory, which Giddens believes has been underused as a resource for social theory. Goffman is concerned with the ways in which people constitute a public for one another, and how they mutually disclose their subjectivities in so doing. He contends that this publicly viewed disclosure process is not spontaneous, for people can monitor what the public sees of their actions, and reflect upon their own performances. In sum, Goffman views people as role-playing creatures in a scripted social world.

Much like the ethnomethodologists, Goffman states that the impression of reality that people develop "is a delicate, fragile thing that can be shattered by very minor mishaps."[33] He is not concerned with whether or not a given impression is true in some ultimate sense, but rather with how an impression is managed, and the ways in which it might be disrupted or criticized. Goffman argues that all performers must "enliven their performances with appropriate expressions," excluding those impressions that might be misinterpreted or could discredit the performer.[34]

Goffman contends that people expend much energy in performing and reinforcing a sense of a shared social reality, based on mutual expectations. He states that societies are organized according to the principle that "any individual who possesses certain social characteristics has a moral right to expect that others will value and treat him in an appropriate way."[35] This notion of social status is related to the idea that the individual should be who he or she claims to be. Accordingly, people spend much of their time avoiding and repairing problems arising from the necessity of reciprocally defining situations.

Social status must be enacted. Status, and the prestige accruing to certain social positions, are not material things. Status is "a pattern of appropriate conduct, coherent, embellished, and well articulated."[36] Goffman argues that to be a given type of person embodying a particular social status, one must sustain the standards and appearances that are attached to the social group to which one belongs or aspires. Everyday performances in social roles must pass a standard of propriety, decorum, aptness, and fitness. Our sense of self is a product of the public roles that we play, not a cause of them. Though we impute our sense of self to an unchanging core personality, it is in reality a dramatic effect. This is increasingly obvious in the ways in which the media and politics have become intertwined, so that we believe that we grasp a candidate's personality when we are actually observing his/her dramatic performance on television.

Status and public performances are integral to the credibility of institutions and public life. This credibility is maintained in various ways, from the possession of expertise to the "right" appearance for the job. Goffman states that labor unions, universities, and other licensing bodies require training to suggest that the practitioner has learned something which sets him/her apart from non-experts. Moreover, one learns to look and dress a certain way to maintain status. A corporate executive holds a job partly because s/he learns to appear and act like a corporate executive.[37]

These performances are always fraught with peril. The ways in which a person may convey impressions might differ dramatically from what s/he wishes to convey. Loss of muscular control, acting too much or too little concerned with the interaction, and suffering from inadequate dramaturgical direction are all pitfalls that confront the role-player. The audience can also question whether the person giving the performance is actually authorized to do so.

To manage our precarious social existence, Goffman states that we distinguish between front and back stages. The front region is the place where the performance takes place; it usually requires that activities live up to certain socially defined standards. Goffman believes that there is also a back region, where the illusions that are played out on the front stage are constructed. Intruders must be prevented from entering the back region if we are to maintain the appearance of social order we enact in the public realm.[38]

Giddens believes that Goffman captures the central sociological fact that people are skilled agents who engage in very complex social interactions. Goffman shows the fragility and complexity of the tacit and informal rules and norms that govern social life. These norms are sanctioned through subtle, everyday social cues, such as laughing, rolling of the eyes, yawning, and the like. Giddens contends that Goffman demonstrates how norms and rules supply the rights, obligations, interpretations, and taken-for-granted knowledge necessary for communication. Giddens also follows Goffman's distinction between front- and backstage behavior in his discussion of ontological security. Giddens argues that the back stage is a place where self-conceptions can be repaired, and people can engage in criticism of and resistance to front-stage demands and conventions.[39]

Giddens criticizes Goffman's strategic view of the performance of social roles on the front stage. According to Giddens, in order to sustain ontological security, front regions must be more than mere façades, for social life would then be characterized by extreme anxiety. The public world is maintained by the stability of social routines, the majority of which must be almost habitually enacted without deep skepticism or cynicism. As Giddens writes, "It is precisely because there is generally a deep, although generalized, affective involvement in the routines of daily life that actors (agents) do not ordinarily feel themselves to be actors (players)." Routines create social integration, and social encounters must be formed and reformed in everyday life, through mutual talk and actions in particular contexts.[40]

Giddens also argues that Goffman, like the ethnomethodologists and other social psychologists, does not adequately theorize the nature of social structure and social power. Yet Goffman clearly sees the importance of rule-following in social interaction. Giddens contends that Goffman's sociology, focused on the complexity involved in obeying and enacting social rules, shows the need for a new conception of meaning, agency, and structure in social theory. He complements Goffman's notion of rule-following behavior with some insights from French structuralism.

Giddens on meaning

Giddens reformulates the structuralist insight that language structures social reality, and that the shape of a culture is determined by its language. In doing so, he rethinks the Swiss linguist Ferdinand de Saussure's distinction between *langue* (the abstract rules that inform all language use) and *parole* (or the language that people actually use). Saussure argues that linguistic meaning arises only in the context of a system of language in which words convey differences from one another. In spoken language, as Hawkes points out in his summary of Saussure's linguistics, "what makes any single item [word] 'meaningful' is not its own particular individual quality, but the *difference* between this quality and that of other sounds." The different meanings of the English words *tin* and *kin* can only be understood because of the differences in their initial consonants. As Hawkes states, the meaning of a word "resides in a structural sense in the difference between its own sounds and those of other words."[41]

Thus, the meaning of words does not reflect objects in the real world, but derives from the conventions of a language. Accordingly, linguistic signs are arbitrary, as they have no intrinsic relationship to the world they purport to represent. As Giddens comments in his summary of Saussure's linguistics, "the utterance 'tree' is no more or less appropriate to a tree as an object than 'arbre' is."[42] For Giddens, the significance of Saussure's linguistics is that it demonstrates the ways in which our linguistic categories structure our sense of reality, rather than merely reflecting it. Language is a self-enclosed reality, from this perspective.

Giddens is not satisfied with this semiotic turn toward understanding meaning. According to Giddens, social meaning does not simply derive from differences in an enclosed linguistic system, as many in the Saussurean tradition argue. Like Goffman, Giddens contends that meaning is bound up with practical activity in the real world. Giddens states that an adequate understanding of meaning must be tied to the ethnomethodological "use of methods" embedded in practical consciousness. The meaning of words is not solely due to the differences in basic linguistic codes. More fundamentally, word meanings derive "from the 'procedures' which agents use in the course of practical action to reach 'interpretations' of what they and others do."[43] Language cannot be understood apart from social practices, which allow social life to go on, even if the full complexity of these practices cannot be expressed verbally. A culture's largely non-discursive mutual knowledge informs the "methods used by lay actors to generate the practices which are constitutive of the tissue of everyday life."[44] For example, ethnomethodologists have shown that in everyday life people are able to follow and participate in conversations due to a variety of social conventions, such as etcetera clauses, without the explicit, discursive articulation of meaning.

Social conventions are very important in the reproduction of social life. Social conventions are the taken-for-granted norms and beliefs of a particular society, such as the custom of pausing at stoplights in Western nations. According to Giddens, such conventions may seem simple, but in reality they are extremely complex. They require an enormous amount of culturally specific knowledge. Moreover, in contemporary philosophy in the wake of Wittgenstein's emphasis on social practices, matters concerning the nature of reality that were debated in abstract philosophical languages are now seen to rest on social conventions. Much of the knowledge that people have of social conventions is non-discursive, grounded in the practical activities of social life.

Giddens on agency

Giddens argues that his conception of social meaning requires a new theory of agency, or people's capacities to act in the social world. In micro-sociological approaches, such as symbolic interactionism, ironically agency and subjectivity are not closely examined, for they are the taken-for-granted assumptions of the theory. Conversely, the functionalist model of individual social action, based on the person acting out internalized values, and the disappearance of the subject posited by postmodernism, are equally fallacious. Giddens states that an adequate conception of the agent must involve an active subject situated in time and space.[45] Such a conception of agency links it to social structure.

Giddens's notion of agency posits the person as reflexive, able to monitor his/her experience and give reasons for his/her actions. Agency should be identified with reasoning and knowledge, rather than simply willing, as personal experience invariably involves social learning, and applying such knowledge in particular contexts. Agency includes the capacity to act otherwise, because people are "concept-bearing" creatures who can imagine different courses of action.[46] Giddens believes that people are rational, but distances himself from Weberian notions of a universal instrumental rationality. He prefers the ethnomethodological conception of rationality. Like the ethnomethodologists, Giddens believes that the rationalization of social action is a skilled accomplishment tied to particular social contexts. Through reflexive monitoring, people rationalize their social conduct. Their accounts of their behavior draw on shared cultural stocks of knowledge that are also used in the reproduction of their actions. There is no universal rationality which operates independently of people's activities in all times and places. Because Giddens sees social activities as continually recreated by people's actions which then serve as the very means by which they express themselves, he argues that people invariably develop knowledge about why they engage in particular practices. Thus, for Giddens, there are different types of rationality that vary from society to society, given the different stocks of knowledge available in different societies – and no one type of rationality is necessarily "superior" to another.[47]

According to Giddens, the capacity to express reasons for one's actions is but one aspect of agency. Agency is composed of three levels. Discursive consciousness refers to the conscious reasons that people give to explain their behaviors and motivations. Practical consciousness is the unarticulated beliefs and knowledges that people use to orient themselves to situations and interpret the actions of others. Giddens believes that only ethnomethodology, phenomenology, and Goffman's sociology have sufficiently articulated this level. The unconscious, discussed by Freud, is the third component of agency. The unconscious is that which cannot easily be put into words and resides beneath our conscious existence. Giddens ties the unconscious to memory, which is always implicated in our day-to-day actions. People have unconscious motivations for trust and security, but the unconscious rarely motivates their behavior directly.[48]

In Giddens's view, practical consciousness is the most important dimension of this triad, for much of the time people act tacitly in social life, and monitor their actions as "a *continuous flow of conduct*" rather than as discrete acts.[49] Practical consciousness mediates between the dualisms of conscious/unconscious and voluntarism/determinism. Giddens's definition of agency distances him from psychologistic theories of human motivation that do not sufficiently take into account social context, nor do they emphasize the pragmatic side of human action. Giddens believes that people's understanding of the world lies in practical rather than discursive consciousness, for it is contextually bound, not abstract. We understand something by applying the right formula, which in turn allows for the methodical continuation of a sequence of actions, akin to following a rule.

Rules

Giddens contends that people follow rules patterned in social structure; collective knowledge of social rules is the condition of social interaction. He states that people are both rule-following and rule-creating creatures who are knowledgeable about their actions. Giddens follows Wittgenstein's dictum that following rules and the constitution of social life are inseparable from one another. Like Wittgenstein, Giddens argues that rules are not an abstract *langue* informing social life from the outside, but are only constituted through social action. Thus, rules are never fixed. In Giddens's words, "all social rules (codes and norms) are transformational."[50]

To know a rule is to implicitly know what one is supposed to do in particular situations; rules are widely used and sanctioned. Rules can be used in contexts other than those in which they originated. As Sewell states regarding Giddens's structuration theory, "rules of etiquette, or aesthetic norms," no matter what their origin, can be "generalized to new situations."[51] Rules vary between societies and historical eras, and are closely tied to social practices, which make them concrete.

Resources and power

While Giddens believes that rule-following behavior is inseparable from meaningful social action, he also thinks that the rules of social life serve other purposes. Rules are inseparable from the exercise of social power. Giddens writes of the two dimensions of rules: "that relating to the *constitution of meaning*, and that relating to *sanctions* involved in social conduct."[52] Rules are bound up with penalties for improper social behavior, which in turn "draw upon modes of domination structured into social systems."[53]

Social interaction is more than rule-following conduct, for its outcome is also shaped by differences in power and the resources which people have at their disposal. "Resources" refers to the material equipment and organizational capacities that people possess which allow them to get things done. Rules and resources are not distributed randomly through-out society, for they are differentially coordinated with one another according to differences in social power.

Giddens contends that the recreation of rules and structures involves the communication of meaning (modes of typification), the exercise of power (based in part on access to power), and the evaluation of conduct through moral rules and norms. Power for Giddens has a dual sense, in that it refers to the transformational capacity to get things done char-acteristic of all social action, and to the ability to achieve one's wishes, even against the desires of others. The exercise of power is not just dependent on material resources, but also involves verbal skill and other forms of "cultural capital," in Bourdieu's terms. People always contest power, however. Garfinkel's well-known dictum that people are not cultural dopes is indeed true. But people do more than strategically resist hegemonic power. They attempt to understand meaning based on their practical consciousness, and they use power to allocate resources and authority.[54] A more extensive discussion of power can be found in Chapter 4.

In sum, rules and resources can be combined in different ways, and provide the medium through which social interaction takes place. Rules and resources are inseparable from the texture of everyday life. This orientation toward the "material levers" of social action distances Giddens from the more idealistic implications of French structuralism.[55] But Giddens's notion of the centrality of practical activity involves more than rule-following behavior and the exercise of power, as it also includes an appreciation of the role of the unconscious in at least partially influencing social life.

Ontological security and trust

For Giddens, the reproduction of society is based primarily on practical activity. The unconscious never influences our conscious existence directly, as unconscious desires are invariably mediated by social interaction. According to Giddens, the most important feature of the role of the unconscious in everyday life is through the development of trust and what the psychoanalyst R.D. Laing calls ontological security. Giddens believes that people must develop a notion of trust in order for stable and continuous social relations to exist. Trust is tied to ontological security, which refers to a belief in the continuity of self-identity over space and time, and the reliability of social life. This sense of security, rooted in the infant's relationship to his/her caretakers, is emotional rather than cognitive, and grounded in the unconscious.[56]

Social order is not a given; it must be continually reconstituted. Social conditions generate anxiety which must be overcome with a sense of trust. Giddens draws on the psychologist Erikson for his notion of trust, which is a fundamental trait for a stable sense of self. Like Erikson, Giddens argues that, though the self has an integrity which allows it some distance from social life, it must submit to social interaction. The self must have a tactful recognition of the needs of others. Such a recognition is dependent on the stability of social routines, which, following Goffman, Giddens sees as central to the continuity of personality and institutions. As Giddens states, day-to-day life involves "an ontological security expressing an autonomy of bodily control within predictable routines."[57] Giddens, following the ethnomethodologists and Goffman, examines opening and closing rituals, turn-taking in conversation, tact, and body position in this context. Such activities sustain routines over time and space. They allow the creation and recreation of routines, of rules and resources. Routinization ties the basic security system of the self to the reflexively monitored, episodic character of social life.

Giddens develops a complex view of agency, grounded in ontological security, practical consciousness, rules, resources, and social routines. Yet as people produce and reproduce these social phenomena, they take on the reality of social structures that are to some degree "external" to social interaction. Giddens contends that most sociology has reified the idea of social structure, effectively severing it from everyday activities. He attempts to conceptualize how social interaction produces such structures, and how these structures in turn influence social action. For Giddens, agency and structure are inseparable, for all social activities are recursive, in that they are continually recreated by people as the very means by which they express themselves. Social action is therefore dependent on the intersection of motive and possibility.

Social practices

Giddens states that the most important task of modern social theory is the recovery of a theory of the subject which does not lapse into solipsistic subjectivism, and which is tied to a notion of social structure. He contends that this theoretical innovation requires a notion of "what cannot be said (or thought) *as practice*," which concretely links the person and social structure.[58] Social practices develop through the transformations of rules over time and in different physical spaces. Social practices are the behavioral and institutional dimensions of the practical consciousness of reflexive people, who draw on shared cultural beliefs and stocks of knowledge. Deeply layered social practices form institutions, "which have the greatest time-space extension" within societies.[59]

Giddens replaces the functionalist notion of roles with that of practices, which are the "'points of articulation' between actors and structures."[60] The notion of social practices also is superior to the postmodern view of society as structured like a text. As Giddens states, following Wittgenstein, society is not akin to an abstract language. Rather, "the constitution of language as 'meaningful' is inseparable from the constitution of forms of social life as continuing practices." Language is a social practice, inseparable from *"that which has to be done."*[61] Actions are *"situated practices"* which connect the person and social structure.[62] Social acts and language must be studied in context, as social practices are the "outcome of a process of production."[63]

Structures

Giddens conceptualizes the formation and reformation of social practices as the duality of structure, in which social structure is both the facilitator and the result of people's conduct. For Giddens, structure is much like the abstract *langue* of Saussure. Structures organize social action, but they do not exist outside of social practices, which are "chronically implicated" in the production and reproduction of structure. Structures are better conceived as "structuring properties" which exist only in actual social practices, only in their "instantiations in such practices as memory traces orienting the conduct of knowledgeable human agents."[64] In Saussurean language, Giddens refers to structures as "an absent set of differences."[65] Structures do not exist as patterns in time and space, as do social routines; they are rather "relations of absences and presences" that only become concrete through human action. For example, understanding a sentence presumes comprehending an entire system of linguistic syntax, though the latter is not "present" in every sentence.[66]

Giddens is attempting to distance sociological theory from the notion that social structure is a thing-like, constraining social fact (in

Durkheimian language), which has an essence that can be measured. Giddens believes that structures are not external to human action, but are integrally involved in the everyday practices which bind time and space together in ever new combinations. This is the basis of Giddens's argument about the duality of structure, in which rules and resources are drawn upon but also constituted by the social activities of people.

Giddens contends that the structures which people create, such as language and social conventions, open up new possibilities, yet they also limit them, to some degree. Constraint for Giddens means placing limits on the number of paths which people can pursue in a given social situation. *Contra* structuralists, Giddens argues that there are few situations in which behavior is determined completely. Sociological explanations must dispense with all forms of determinism, and should refer to purposive agents and their interaction with the constraining and enabling aspects of the social contexts in which they are embedded.

Giddens does see some restrictions on the reflexive agent. The individual requires an unconscious sense of trust in order to be able to act. Agency is also limited in many other ways. People cannot linguistically formulate all that they know, and much knowledge remains tacit. The time-space stretch of modern institutions means that many people's activities occur within the context of broad institutions which they cannot control. The capacity of some with more power to sanction others limits the agent's freedom of action. Finally, people may have a distorted or blocked understanding of social relations.[67]

Another important obstacle to the agent's freedom concerns unintended consequences. Giddens states that social reproduction "occurs under conditions of 'mixed intentionality,'" which involve both intended and unintended elements of social action.[68] An understanding of the unintended consequences of social action is an integral part of Giddens's sociology. People's knowledge is limited, as they live in a restricted social area in an increasingly globalized and culturally diverse world. In such a context, neither people nor governments can fathom all the outcomes of their social activity. For example, Western urban renewal projects set up in the 1960s and 1970s to increase housing for low-income people sometimes had the opposite effect. These projects often destroyed neighborhoods and created desolate, uninhabited regions, as landlords left an area rather than complying with governmental housing standards, or responded to this government program by turning residential housing into non-residential buildings.[69]

In Giddens's view, social interaction and the reproduction of society only succeed through "the knowledgeable application and reapplication of rules and resources by actors in situated social contexts."[70] However, the manifold dimensions of these social contexts cannot but elude some of the knowledge capabilities of people. Accordingly, Giddens calls for an analysis of those elements of social structure that reach beyond individual understanding, which he ties to the time-space problematic.

The time-space problematic

The establishment and maintenance of social interaction takes place in social time and space. Functionalists identify time with social change, assuming that social stability and timelessness go together. However, in Giddens's view, time is integral to all social action. Parsons attempted to eliminate time from the analysis of social structure by asserting that the fundamental problem of social theory was the problem of order – how could a cohesive society result from the uncoordinated actions of self-interested individuals? Giddens believes that this orientation to understanding social life underplays both the history and the concrete context in which people act. He contends that the fundamental problem of social theory concerns the interrelationship of individual actions which are embedded in social relations which stretch across space and time. The micro/macro distinction in sociology should be abandoned in favor of an analysis of differences between face-to-face interaction (social integration) and interaction with those not physically present (system integration).[71] For Giddens, the timing and spacing of everyday life are central to all aspects of social systems.

According to Giddens, time and space are integral to the very nature of objects – they are not outside the object, merely influencing it. As he states, "Most social analysts treat time and space as mere environments of action and accept unthinkingly the conception of time, as measurable clock time, characteristic of modern Western culture."[72] In developing the centrality of time-space relations for social theory, Giddens follows in part the philosophy of Heidegger. Like Heidegger, Giddens argues that time and space are not external to our social lives, as they are more than simply frameworks for interaction. Time cannot be separated into past and present in any simple way, as temporal intervals are not standardized moments which simply pass on, but are structured differences which give form to content, as in a musical rhythm. Time is always present, which means that it is not an empty continuum, as evolutionists posit, but dynamic and ever-changing. Our experience of time associated with minutes, hours, etc. is not "natural," but is socially created. Giddens believes that time can be broken down into the time of everyday life, the life-cycle of the organism, and the *longue-durée* of social change over centuries. None of these conceptions of time can be reduced to the other, and the understanding of the interpenetration of all three is necessary for an adequate theory of social interaction and social change. Time-space relations operate in different ways on the level of the individual, as unconscious processes link past and present, and the routinization of our everyday interactions becomes necessary for our ontological security.[73]

For Giddens, social time is a major component of a society's internal composition, for it structures "the temporal ordering of social reproduction."[74] People in different cultures experience time differently.

haunted social science since its origins. It bursts into a disciplinary crisis when social changes outstrip available theoretical categories for understanding them, as occurred in the 1960s and 1970s and is now happening in our late modern era. Giddens's structuration theory attempts to rethink what he considers to be outmoded social theories beset by agency/structure dualisms, placing social practices, practical consciousness, and the reflexive individual at the forefront of theoretical concern.

Giddens believes that his notion of the duality of structure effectively captures the dynamics of the reconstitution of society. He argues that reflexive individuals actively reproduce the social world around them. In opposition to Parsonian functionalism, Giddens states that social systems do not have goals; only individuals have teleologies. Yet individuals reproduce their social ties in the context of specific cultural time and space which necessarily escapes their understanding. These issues of time and space are central to Giddens's social theory, especially his theory of social change.

Giddens's theory of social change is superior to that of Bourdieu and Elias in many ways. As many critics point out, it is difficult to envision, given Bourdieu's and Elias's theories, how people can reflexively and collectively change social conditions and reconstitute their identities.[85] Bourdieu in particular has trouble accounting for the emergence of new cultural forms in the context of social change, as he sees all social relations as bound up with strategies tied to power. The role of social science in social change is also not well explicated in these theories. They have no analysis akin to Giddens's notion of the double hermeneutic, which complicates the social scientist's relationship to his/her subject matter. Because of the double hermeneutic, the social scientist's findings can become available to the public and integrated into everyday life, further problematizing any simple separation of the scientist and his/her public. Historically, the findings and vocabulary of social science have played an integral role in changing the self-understanding of different cultures, from early modern notions of state sovereignty to contemporary treatises on therapy and the self.

Thus, Elias and Bourdieu have difficulty accounting for how the interpenetration of structure and agency can result in new, emergent cultural forms. Yet Giddens also does not develop a strong conception of culture in his theory of structuration. Like Bourdieu, and to a lesser extent Elias, Giddens tends to see culture "only as an environment of action in relation to which actors [have] a radical reflexivity," rather than a fundamental shaping aspect of our social experience.[86]

This lack of attention is in part due to Giddens's theory of the self-reflexive individual who is not determined by his/her social circumstances. Social structure is conceived to a great degree in terms of social routines, necessary for the ongoing reproduction of society, but which can be changed by people in the course of their everyday social action. Yet Giddens does not discuss these social routines as culturally defined systems of belief which influence behavior. He has no strong concept of cultural hegemony, or culture as a form of social power.

Giddens does turn to explicitly cultural issues in his recent discussion of modernity, feminism, and the self, which will be addressed in Part II of this volume. He prefaces this discussion of the culture of modernity with an analysis of large-scale institutions such as the nation-state. These institutions also include industrialism and capitalism, which tie space and time together in distinctive ways. An exploration of these modern institutions is inseparable from Giddens's theory of social change, as they are also examples of the unintended consequences of behavior so important to understanding societies. The rise of the nation-state, modern industry, and the city involved novel types of time-space regionalization, as new public–private constellations appeared, such as the separation of work from the home. Particular social experiences, including death and sexuality, were sequestered outside of the purview of public life. The next chapter examines these issues in depth, in the context of Giddens's critique of Marxism.

Notes

1 Alvin Gouldner, *The Coming Crisis of Western Sociology* (New York, Basic Books, 1970).

2 Craig Calhoun, *Critical Social Theory: Culture, History, and the Challenge of Difference* (Cambridge, MA, Blackwell, 1995), p. 305.

3 Pierre Bourdieu, "Sport and Social Class," in *Rethinking Popular Culture: Contemporary Perspectives in Cultural Studies*, ed. Chandra Mukerji and Michael Schudson (Berkeley, University of California Press, 1991), p. 366.

4 Pierre Bourdieu, *Outline of a Theory of Practice* (New York, Cambridge University Press, 1977), p. 72.

5 Calhoun, *Critical Social Theory*, p. 304.

6 Pierre Bourdieu, *Choses dites* (Paris, Les Éditions de Minuit, 1987), p. 90.

7 See Pierre Bourdieu, *Language and Symbolic Power* (Cambridge, MA, Harvard University Press, 1991).

8 Pierre Bourdieu, "From the Sociology of Academics to the Sociology of the Sociological Eye," *Sociological Theory* 7 (1989), p. 29.

9 Bourdieu, *Outline of a Theory of Practice*, p. 9.

10 Pierre Bourdieu, *The Political Ontology of Martin Heidegger* (Stanford, Stanford University Press, 1991), p. 105.

11 Ibid., pp. 8–14.

12 Ibid., p. 34.

13 Ibid., p. 63.

14 Norbert Elias, *The Society of Individuals* (Cambridge, MA, Basil Blackwell, 1991), pp. 55, 28; Norbert Elias, *What is Sociology?* (New York, Columbia University Press, 1978), p. 106.

15 Elias, *The Society of Individuals*, p. 23.

16 Ibid., pp. 159–160, 182, 200–201; Elias, *What is Sociology?*, p. 127

17 Ibid., p. 72.

18 Ibid., p. 15.

19 Norbert Elias, *The History of Manners. The Civilizing Process, Vol. 1* (New York, Pantheon, 1978), pp. 261–262.

20 Elias, *What is Sociology?*, pp. 116, 146.

21 Ibid., pp. 153, 155.

22 Stephen Mennell, *Norbert Elias: An Introduction* (Cambridge, MA, Blackwell, 1992), pp. 31, 43–44.

23 Elias, *The History of Manners, Vol. 1*, pp. 36, 106, 223; see also Mennell, *Norbert Elias*, pp. 47–49.

24 Elias, *The History of Manners, Vol. 1*, pp. 106, 117, 210.

25 Ibid., p. 212.

26 Ibid, p. 214; see also Mennell, *Norbert Elias*, pp. 57–58.

27 Elias, *The History of Manners, Vol. 1*, p. 106.

28 Mennell, *Norbert Elias*, pp. 211–212.

29 Anthony Giddens, *The Constitution of Society: Outline of a Theory of Structuration* (Berkeley, University of California Press, 1984), p. xvii.

30 Ibid., p. 241.

31 Anthony Giddens, *In Defence of Sociology: Essays, Interpretations, and Rejoinders* (Cambridge, MA, Polity Press, 1996), p. 69.

32 Anthony Giddens, *Central Problems in Social Theory: Action, Structure and Contradiction in Social Analysis* (Berkeley, University of California Press, 1979), pp. 57, 215–216.

33 Erving Goffman, *The Presentation of Self in Everyday Life* (Garden City, NY, Doubleday, 1959), p. 56.

34 Ibid., p. 66.

35 Ibid., p. 13.

36 Ibid., p. 75.

37 Ibid., pp. 46–47.

38 Ibid., pp. 107, 112.

39 Anthony Giddens, *Social Theory and Modern Sociology* (Stanford, Stanford University Press, 1987), p. 162.

40 Giddens, *The Constitution of Society*, pp. 72–73, 125.

41 Terence Hawkes, *Structuralism and Semiotics* (Berkeley, University of California Press, 1977), p. 22.

42 Giddens, *Central Problems in Social Theory*, p. 11.

43 Giddens, *Social Theory and Modern Sociology*, p. 63.

44 Ibid., p. 66.

45 Ibid., pp. 60, 62; *Central Problems in Social Theory*, p. 2.

46 Giddens, *Social Theory and Modern Sociology*, pp. 211, 216.

47 Giddens, *The Constitution of Society*, pp. 2–3; *Central Problems in Social Theory*, p. 43.

48 Giddens, *The Constitution of Society*, pp. 44ff.

49 Giddens, *Central Problems in Social Theory*, p. 55; italics in the original.

50 Ibid., p. 104.

51 William Sewell, Jr., "A Theory of Structure: Duality, Agency, and Transformation," *American Journal of Sociology* 98 (July 1992), p. 8.

52 Giddens, *Central Problems in Social Theory*, p. 82, italics in the original.

53 Ibid., p. 83.

54 Ibid., pp. 69, 88; *The Constitution of Society*, pp. 30–31, 258.

55 Giddens, *Central Problems in Social Theory*, p. 104; see also Sewell, "A Theory of Structure," p. 6.

56 Anthony Giddens, *The Consequences of Modernity* (Stanford, Stanford University Press, 1990), pp. 92–97.

57 Giddens, *The Constitution of Society*, pp. 50–51.

58 Giddens, *Central Problems in Social Theory*, p. 44, italics in the original.

59 Giddens, *The Constitution of Society*, p. 17; *Central Problems in Social Theory*, pp. 46, 65

60 Giddens, *Central Problems in Social Theory*, p. 117.

61 Ibid., p. 4, italics in the original.

62 Ibid., p. 56, italics in the original.

63 Ibid., p. 43.

64 Giddens, *The Constitution of Society*, p. 17.

65 Giddens, *Central Problems in Social Theory*, p. 64

66 Giddens, *Social Theory and Modern Sociology*, p. 61.

67 Ibid., pp. 221–222; *Central Problems in Social Theory*, p. 144.

68 Giddens, *Social Theory and Modern Sociology*, p. 69.

69 *The Giddens Reader*, ed. Philip Cassell (Stanford, Stanford University Press, 1993), pp. 137–140.

70 Giddens, *Central Problems in Social Theory*, p. 114.

71 Ibid., pp. 198–199, 203.

72 Giddens, *The Constitution of Society*, p. 110.

73 Anthony Giddens, *A Contemporary Critique of Historical Materialism, Vol. 1, Power, Property, and the State* (Berkeley, University of California Press, 1981), pp. 3–8, 19–20, 34, 37.

74 Giddens, *Central Problems in Social Theory*, p. 255.

75 Giddens, *Social Theory and Modern Sociology*, p. 146.

76 Giddens, *The Constitution of Society*, p. 116.

77 Ibid., pp. 135–136.

78 Giddens, *Central Problems in Social Theory*, p. 117.

79 Giddens, *The Constitution of Society*, p. 185.

80 Ibid., p. 17; see also Sewell, "A Theory of Structure," p. 6.

81 Giddens, *Central Problems in Social Theory*, p. 131.

82 Ibid., p. 142; italics in the original.

83 Giddens, *The Constitution of Society*, p. 197.

84 Karl Marx, *The Eighteenth Brumaire of Louis Bonaparte*, in *The Marx–Engels Reader*, ed. Robert Tucker (New York, Norton, 1978), p. 595; paraphrased in Giddens, *The Constitution of Society*, p. xxi.

85 See, for example, Sewell, "A Theory of Structure."

86 Jeffrey Alexander, "Cultural Sociology or Sociology of Culture? Towards a Strong Program," *Newsletter of the Sociology of Culture Section* 10 (Spring–Summer 1996), p. 4.

PART II

SOCIAL CHANGE AND MODERNITY

Giddens contends that the reworking of the basic concepts of sociology goes hand in hand with a rethinking of the nature of modernity. New forms of self-identity and social action shape and are shaped by the institutions and culture of the modern world. Modernity is a concept that has many strands, not all of which necessarily cohere. Perhaps the most apt description is encapsulated in Marx and Engels's prophetic words in *The Communist Manifesto*, where they outline the changes wrought by modern capitalism: "All fixed, fast-frozen relations, with their train of ancient and venerable prejudices and opinions, are swept away, all new-formed ones become antiquated before they can ossify. All that is solid melts into air, all that is holy is profaned."[1]

Giddens points to two sides of this new experience of modernity. First, new, post-feudal institutions associated with democracy and industrial capitalism arise, which must be flexible enough to adapt to social change. Second, a new culture of constant innovation and widespread reflexivity emerges. Such changes create new problems for the legitimacy of institutions and the exercise of authority, and problematize the formation of personal identity and the very knowledge that informs modern actions and beliefs. As the eternal truths related to religion and tradition disintegrate, modernity must create its own criteria for everything from ethics to law. The legitimation of modern authority cannot be borrowed from any other period, which is why modernity is so dynamic and ever-changing. This decline of tradition demanded a search for specifically modern principles of legitimation, resulting in the Enlightenment's enthronement of reason as the judge and basis of culture and institutions, and a theory of history as the progressive evolution of such a rationality.

While many theorists equate modernity with Enlightenment rationality, Giddens joins his fellow sociologists Touraine and Habermas in positing that such a view is too narrow. Modernity includes critical reactions to this rationality, expressed in a widespread romantic counter-Enlightenment, ranging from art to philosophy. The search for rational truth in the eighteenth and nineteenth centuries existed concurrently with claims that the immediacy of subjective experience made all truth relative. Habermas contends that the problem of modernity grounding its beliefs in its own consciousness first appeared in modern art, as eighteenth- and nineteenth-century artists contested the ancient notions of beauty as timeless and formal. This critique led in part to aesthetic romanticism, which stressed feeling and subjectivity over rationality and form. The romantic sensibility spread to other arenas of social life, as philosophers and social theorists reacted to the hegemony of rationality in the modern world. Rousseau posited that feeling and authenticity, rather than a cold, calculating rationality, should be the touchstone of modern identity. Daniel Bell contends that this romantic impulse was translated into a belief that individual fulfillment is the highest goal of the modern self. Bell sees this aesthetic self-realization as the major component of the culture of modernity.[2]

Indeed, subjective freedom, in its different guises, is a central ingredient of modernity. As theorists from Weber to Habermas recognize, this subjective freedom was based institutionally in modern capitalism and democracy, and represented conceptually in notions such as the citizen, entrepreneur, and ethical actor. But these different realms break apart as modernity emerges, and conflicts develop between them.

Further, subjective freedom is a poor basis for social order. The logic of subjective freedom has been carried to its limits in contemporary discussions of postmodernity. Authors inspired by Foucault and Derrida contend that modernity has been transcended by a postmodern era, which is tied to the rise of new institutions associated with electronic media, post-material values that no longer exalt economic growth, and new social movements, such as feminism and gay/lesbian liberation. Such a postmodern culture breaks apart all notions of consensus and community, and critiques the hegemony of rationality posited by the Enlightenment, criticizing its power to exclude and marginalize non-whites and women in particular. Postmodern culture tends to value social differences over common identities, and is especially concerned with the representations of groups, such as women and people of color, which have been excluded from "the philosophical discourse of modernity," in Habermas's phrase.

Giddens develops his theory of modernity in part through an analysis of the expansion of subjective, reflexive freedom in modern societies, and as a participant in the debates about whether modernity has been surpassed by a new postmodern world. He concurs with theorists such as Habermas, who argue that postmodernists do not appreciate the different dimensions and complexity of modernity. Modernity was never of one piece and has been internally conflicted from its origins. Giddens critiques the idea that a new postmodern epoch is at hand, and calls for a theory of late modernity in opposition to postmodern perspectives. He contends that much of the postmodern critique of modernity can be explained by the expansion of modernist subjective freedom, embodied in a reflexivity that is extended to more and more areas of social life, as traditions lose their authority and people must create their own world. Giddens's analysis of modernity rests upon a theory of social change extending from non-modern to late modern societies. He ties this theory to an exploration of the distinctive culture of modernity, the role of public life and democracy in late modern societies, and the changes for self and personal identity that new social movements such as feminism have created. Giddens contends that a critique of Marxism, which posited the revolutionary character of modern capitalism in comparison to other modes of production, is the best starting point for a theory of social change.

Notes

1 Karl Marx and Friedrich Engels, *Manifesto of the Communist Party*, in *The Marx–Engels Reader*, ed. Robert Tucker (New York, Norton, 1978), p. 476.

2 Jürgen Habermas, *The Philosophical Discourse of Modernity: Twelve Lectures* (Cambridge, MA, MIT Press, 1987); Daniel Bell, *The Cultural Contradictions of Capitalism* (New York, Basic Books, 1978).

4

THE STATE, CAPITALISM, AND SOCIAL CHANGE

The sociological tradition is grounded in the exploration of social change. Marx, Durkheim, and Weber believed that the study of history and society were inseparable; accordingly, their theories of history informed their understanding of social life. For each theorist, the distinctiveness of the modern world necessarily involved a comparison with the societies that modernity had supplanted. Durkheim conceptualized this change as the transition from a mechanical solidarity, based on cultures that were homogeneous, often legitimized by traditions and characterized by an undifferentiated polity, economy, and culture, to organic solidarity, founded on the division of labor and a culture of individualism and scientific rationality. For Weber, the traditional social world of custom and kinship has been replaced by the modern bureaucratic order, a rational system that encourages calculation and principled reasoning. Marx saw social change in terms of the succession of modes of production, from the Asiatic to the feudal to the capitalist, which in turn would be supplanted by socialism and communism.

Many contemporary theories of social change adopt some of these tenets of the classical theorists. For example, functionalists draw heavily on the insights of Durkheim and Weber. Parsons views social change in terms of the evolutionary capacities of societies to adapt to their environments, in large part through the growth of rationality, as the specialized, rationalized social roles of the modern world replace the undifferentiated premodern world of tradition. Giddens also looks to Marx in developing a theory of social change that can capture the distinctiveness of modernity. But Giddens believes that much of the classical sociological tradition, as well as functionalism, fails in this task.

Giddens rejects the evolutionary assumptions of functionalism and classical sociology; he particularly criticizes the functionalist inattention to issues of power and class relations. He considers the Marxist tradition to be a rich source for understanding social change, especially as compared to functionalism, and views Marxism as grasping the fundamental importance of class relations in capitalist societies. Yet Giddens finds the Marxist tradition wanting, as it too assumes an evolutionary develop-ment from "premodern" to modern societies. Marxism has an inade-quate understanding of the types of power associated with the rise of the nation-state and nationalism. Giddens turns to theorists such as Foucault to remove this lacuna. He moves beyond Foucault by locating power in terms of time-space relations and the global impact of modernity, which in turn influence social change.

This chapter will briefly discuss Parsons's view of social change, moving to a discussion of the Marxist tradition, including the contem-porary Marxist theorists Wallerstein and Harvey. After a summary of Foucault's analysis of the disciplinary society created by modernity, Giddens's theory of social change will be addressed. While Giddens distinguishes between tribal, class-divided, and class societies (see pp. 116–17), viewing them as roughly equivalent to different eras in human history, he rejects any evolutionary approach to social change. Giddens also advocates placing the dimensions of time and space at the center of social theory, in conjunction with the study of the city, capital-ism, and the nation-state.

Parsons and differentiation theory

Drawing on Durkheim and Weber, Parsons argues that differentiation is the major dynamic of social change, paving the path to modernity. Differentiation creates new and distinct arrangements for performing particular functions, which require the creation of new roles and moral norms as older ones lose their power and functions. For example, differentiation occurs in the economy when a service is not being sup-plied, or is not performing as satisfactorily as it might. In such a case, the social system is not functioning efficiently. Accordingly, a better service arises, which in turn helps the social system respond to the impairment of its equilibrium, and restores the system's balance. Successful differ-entiation allows the social system to integrate change and adapt to shifting needs. Differentiation remains subject to the social system's dominant values; norms may be changed, but not the underlying values which characterize the system.

In the specific case of modern agriculture, differentiation means the emancipation of people from ascriptive ties. In the preindustrial family farm, management is tied to the household, as the farmer decides what proportion of money he will allocate to the operation of the farm, family consumption, and education. With differentiation comes an expansion of choice. The farmer often becomes an employee, having a broader array of occupational options available to him, or offering a wider range of services for money. Education becomes the province of new, specialized institutions outside of the home, such as schools. The change in the composition of the family farm is justified by the higher level of efficiency and opportunity that differentiation brings with it. As the family farm changes its occupational significance, this new form of free labor must be institutionally regulated by the market system and contracts of employment.

In order for this system to be workable, strong legal and moral values must lie behind it (akin to Durkheim's famous discussion of the non-contractual bases of contract). These values need to become more universalistic, covering a wide range of different cases, to provide the firm cultural backing necessary for the modern social system. For example, a differentiating, modern social system requires new universalistic values privileging competence and achievement over ascriptive ties as a means for occupational success.

Historically in the West, the transition to modernity saw the differentiation of the premodern concentration of political, economic, and cultural functions in a centralized authority (usually the monarchy). These different realms developed their own specialized laws and institutions separately from one another as their shared religious and traditional context faded. Politics became tied to new legislative institutions for governing, the economy developed its own ways of functioning through the market, and religion became part of a cultural sphere separate from the government and the economy. A crucial factor in the successful differentiation of these subsystems was the development of universal laws, values, and norms which were able to coordinate the economy, polity, and cultural realms. The legitimizing force of religious tradition in turn differentiated into autonomous law, scientific method, and aesthetics, each supplying a version of cultural legitimacy for the social system.[1]

Parsons's theory of modernity emphasizes the rise of a universalistic rationality, more functional role complexity, and the autonomous functioning of the social system. His evolutionary approach posits that the West, especially the United States, embodied the ideals of modernity. It is the model of social, economic, and political development which other countries would, and should, follow. Parsons sees no great role for social movements in the rise of modernity. Often when analyzing social movements, Parsons views them as reactionary forces inhibiting the emergence of modernity, as demonstrated in his discussion of Fascism.

Giddens believes that the Parsonian approach, as a prototype of functionalist theory, illegitimately places the West at the top of the evolutionary tree, distorting the distinctive differences and integrity of other cultures and historical eras. For Giddens, there is no end-point toward which history is evolving. Parsons does not see that social change involves conflicts over power, class struggle, and a wholesale reordering of social life. Nor does he recognize the importance of social movements in shaping social change. Giddens contends that Marxism provides a better account of these fundamental processes. He turns to a critique of Marxism in developing a theory of social change which can account for the distinctiveness of modernity.

Marx

Marxism occupies a central place in debates about social change, often in opposition to functionalism. Marx develops a comprehensive theory of the dynamic of world history, the transition from feudalism to capitalism, and the inner logic of exploitation within the capitalist system. He places societies in their changing historical context, as their internal tensions and contradictions push social change forward.

Marx's complex *oeuvre* is difficult to summarize briefly, as the continuing debates about the meaning of Marxism demonstrate. Of fundamental importance in Marxist theory is the famous idea that all history can be understood in terms of class struggle. This is not a simple concept, and more elucidation of Marxist theory is necessary to fully grasp its meaning.

Marx believes that the problems facing any society are inseparable from the organization of the labor process. He formulates a materialist perspective on the social world, in that the material has primacy over the spiritual world, as matter conditions mind. Material factors are the driving force in people's lives. The production and reproduction of physical existence through labor is the most important feature of human society. As Marx states, "Life is not determined by consciousness, but consciousness by life."[2] To understand any society, it is necessary to grasp the labor process: the ways in which people transform nature through work.

• Marx contends that human history is the history of people producing their material lives. Human labor produces a "definite mode of life," and human nature is dependent on the material conditions of production. Marx believes that the labor process is socially organized in various ways in different societies. The manner in which production is organized forms the basis for the distribution, exchange, and consumption of goods, which vary from society to society. Every type of productive system presupposes a set of social relations as well as a particular method of controlling nature. The reproduction of a people through labor is not accomplished by isolated individuals, but by members of a society.[3]

As the organization of labor becomes more complex, a division of labor emerges. The division of labor separates the conditions of labor (the tools and materials) into different, unequal groups. It creates a more efficient economic system that allows a surplus to be created above that needed for subsistence. When a surplus develops, one group can live off the labor of another. Marx argues that classes arise when the surplus created by the division of labor can be controlled by a minority of people. For Marx, class is defined by ownership or non-ownership of the means of production in a particular society. He states that any community in which a minority controls the surplus is an unequal society. Further, the ways in which a ruling class extracts the surplus from another class provide insights into the type of inequality and exploitation generated in that society. Marx contends that in feudalism class domination occurs through coercion and traditional mechanisms, while under capitalism exploitation rests on seemingly impersonal phenomena such as the labor contract and the market. Marx and Engels write that capitalism "has pitilessly torn asunder the motley feudal ties that bound man to his 'natural superiors,' and has left remaining no other nexus between man and man than naked self-interest, than callous 'cash payment.'"[4]

The theory of social change

Classes develop different economic interests and so came into conflict with one another. Class conflict is the motor of social change. It takes place within different modes of production, which are the totality of material and economic circumstances that "condition[s] the social, political, and intellectual life process in general."[5] Marx differentiates between Asiatic, ancient, feudal, and bourgeois modes of production "as progressive epochs in the economic formation of society."[6] Each succeeding mode of production exhibits progressive technological growth, organizational sophistication, and rational understanding of the world. Marx distinguishes between the forces and the relations of production to explain these social changes. The forces of production are the technological and organizational capacities of a given society, while the relations of production concern the type of ownership of the productive apparatus of a society (whether ownership is private or public, for example). The relationship between the forces and relations of production cannot be abstracted from the social and historical context in which they occur. Most significantly, the forces and relations of production are in constant tension, and, in concert with class struggle, social change is impelled by their internal contradictions.

Marx is sometimes painted as a technological determinist, who believes that the development of technology within the forces of production determines the direction of social change. However, Marx argues that the relations of production are an equally significant factor in social change, for in one historical era they can contribute to the growth of productive forces, while in another epoch they may inhibit them. The relations of production often seem to be the natural and inevitable conditions of production during a particular historical period. For example, the lord–peasant relationship and its corresponding system of estates appeared to be the eternal order of life under European feudalism, while the possession and control of private property by individuals and firms seems to be the natural order in capitalism. Marx argues that such is not the case, and that these relations of production become fetters on the further development of the productive forces, and have to be "torn asunder," in his colorful language. Capitalism does not escape contradictions, but creates new ones, especially the split between the capitalist's private ownership of the means of production and the laborers' lack of ownership and their collective work to produce goods. Marx argues that capitalism is constantly racked by crises which destroy productive forces, throw people into unemployment, and create widespread hunger and misery. Socialism and later communism would institute a more rational organization of the means of production.

The theory of capitalism

Marx contends that capitalism is an inherently exploitative system, which he details in his labor theory of value. He states that a commodity's exchange value, or price, is directly related to the amount of labor embodied in it. As it takes a greater amount of work and more sophisticated labor to make cars rather than pins, cars cost more than pins. Yet making pins and making cars involve very different types of labor. To compare them, Marx believes that the concrete differences between types of work must be erased through the notion of abstract labor, whose value can then be calculated in terms of wages. Abstract labor allows the computation of socially necessary labor time, i.e. the average amount of time required to produce a commodity in a given industry. For Marx, commodities exchange at their values, or the amount of socially necessary labor time that it takes to make them.

Marx argues that the exploitation of labor can be understood through the category of socially necessary labor time. The worker is paid his/her full value as a commodity, for he/she receives what is necessary to reproduce him/herself as a laborer (the socially necessary labor time to reproduce his/her existence). Yet the worker produces more than is necessary to cover the cost of subsistence, for only a proportion of the working day is necessary to reproduce the worker's life. The rest of the time that the worker labors produces profits for the capitalist. For Marx, exploitation occurs entirely within the realm of production, as the worker creates revenue for the capitalist and does not receive his or her just share of production.

Such an exploitative system cannot last, according to Marx. He believes that capitalism creates a new type of class struggle that will lead to its transcendence. As the capitalist ruling class controls the state, revolutionary activity tends to take on a political as well as an economic form, as the proletariat struggles for control of the state as well as the economy. All previous revolutions concerned conflicts over the distribution of economic goods, rather than over ownership of the production process. The proletarian revolution would change the very nature of productive activity, abolishing classes by destroying the capitalist organization of production. Moreover, as capitalism spreads throughout the world in its search for markets, it creates a world-wide proletariat in its wake. Marx conceives of the proletarian revolution as a world-wide revolt in which capitalism is overthrown everywhere by a united working class.[7]

Marx shows that the rise of capitalism is not a peaceful process, but involves new sources of power and exploitation, compared to previous eras in history. The distinctiveness of capitalism lies in its world-wide search for markets, new types of class struggle, and the pervasiveness of commodity production in all forms of social life. Marx's work inspired a rich and diverse array of theories of social change, influenced after the 1917 Russian Revolution by the impact of actually existing Marxist governments. Wallerstein's world-system theory and Harvey's analysis of modern urbanism are two of the most important contemporary Marxist theories of social change, which expand on the international and urban dimensions that are not fully developed by Marx.

Wallerstein and the world-system

The legacy of Marxist theory is complex and diverse, as Marx's followers have interpreted the major features of his theory in a number of ways. One of the most interesting and influential recent developments is Wallerstein's world-system approach. Like many Marxists, Wallerstein dispenses with Marx's theory of inevitable proletarian revolution, instead focusing on the influence of the world economic system on political and cultural life. He criticizes social theories that view endogenous processes within countries or areas as the sources of social transformation, positing instead an intersocietal, economically based approach to social change.

Wallerstein states that divisions between the economic, political, and cultural realms of life are artificial, for they are determined by a "single set of constraints."[8] These constraints are tied to the international economic system, in which "the system and the people within it are regularly reproduced by means of some kind of ongoing division of labor."[9] Wallerstein distinguishes three historical instances of the world-system. The first he calls "mini-systems," because they did not control an extensive expanse of territory and did not exist for a long period of time. These relatively homogeneous cultural and social systems were governed by "reciprocity in exchanges." The mini-systems were gradually supplanted by world empires, which had strong political centers and encompassed many different cultures. Their economic system was based on extracting tribute from relatively autonomous local political units for payment to the imperial center, which in turn paid local officials for political allegiance and social control. The modern capitalist economic system is different from the other systems, for it involves multiple nation-states participating in a world-wide economy founded on the extraction of surplus through market mechanisms.[10]

Wallerstein argues that historically these systems have not been clearly demarcated. From about 8000 BC to AD 1500, all three types of systems coexisted, though the world empire was strongest at that time. From 1500 to 1900, the capitalist world-system became dominant. Wallerstein contends that by 1900 capitalism had created the first economically integrated world-system. Previous empires had a single political center and were economically differentiated. While the capitalist system has different political systems within it, its major distinction is that it creates a global economy that unites all of the world into one economic system. The capitalist world-system has two axes of domination – between wage labor and capital, in the classical Marxist sense, and also the international division of labor between nation-states. The international division of labor creates core countries (originally found in Europe, such as the Netherlands and later Britain) which harvest most of the world's economic benefits. Outside the core system of states exist the semi-peripheral countries, which are exploited by the core states. The semi-peripheral nations exploit the peripheral countries, which have little power in the world economic system. These latter areas were colonized by the European powers in their search for raw materials.

Wallerstein's world-system approach shifts theoretical attention away from individual nation-states toward the international division of labor within capitalism, while dispensing with evolutionary, endogenous theories of social change. Wallerstein argues that a broad, sweeping perspective is necessary to understand the emergence of capitalism and its differences from other types of social organization. Different world-systems do not replace one another in a systematic, easily documented fashion, but coexist in unusual hybrids in different historical contexts.

Harvey and Marxist urbanism

Though Marx briefly discussed the rural/urban nexus (for example, in *The German Ideology*), he did not formulate an urban theory. Harvey's work on the city attempts to develop a Marxist perspective on urban life. Harvey believes that classical social theory consistently short-changes the study of space in favor of temporal arguments. He wishes to correct this error by developing a materialist understanding of the generation of time and space in societies. For Harvey, neither time nor space can be understood apart from material processes. The objective conceptions of time and space which most social theory takes for granted are actually created through social practices which in turn reproduce society. Thus, every different mode of production has a distinctive version of time and space.[11]

Capitalism has distinctive methods of creating space. Before the capitalist epoch, urban areas were sparse. Class divisions had not yet developed a spatial dimension. For example, Philippe Ariès writes of medieval France as a time "when people lay on top of one another, masters and servants, children and adults, in houses open at all hours to the indiscretions of callers."[12] Social classes lived and interacted with one another on a daily basis. Capitalism changes these types of living arrangement. The constant accumulation of capital creates a whirlpool of ever-changing spatial configurations, as cities expand and contract with the movement of capital throughout the world. These processes threaten to disrupt "the spatial and temporal bases for reproduction of the social order."[13] The very nature of urban life changes dramatically in contradictory ways, as increased individuation accompanies a more spatialized class division. As cities develop, clear class distinctions break down and barriers between individuals are enhanced, and people engage in a kind of mad competitive scramble for success and prestige, as Tocqueville might state. Yet the capitalist city also fragments classes and races into distinctive neighborhoods by the construction of freeways and other modes of transport. The commodification of space destroys notions of space as a sacred and/or symbolic area, as land loses its particularity and becomes a form of "fictitious capital," a type of financial asset.[14] For Harvey, capitalism has created an "urbanized human nature," which has a specific sense of time and space, with money as the source of social power.[15]

Harvey analyzes the contradictory processes relating to time and space that capitalism produces. He argues that the separation of home and work arising with capitalist production created new public and private spaces, while the rise of the mass media has constructed a sense of universal simultaneity and a uniform time that spans the globe. Capitalism also produces a strange tension between the centralization of power and its spatial dispersion, since the social power accruing to money can be concentrated in any place and/or diffused throughout the world.[16]

In sum, Harvey accents the importance of space for Marxist social theory. The commodification of space and time changes people's very sense of place in the modern world, as capitalism creates a distinctive urban experience and consciousness. The whirlpool of change and fragmentation that seems to characterize urban experience, and which has been commented on by social critics from Georg Simmel to Walter Benjamin and postmodern theorists of city life, can be traced to the changes wrought by a capitalist process that destroys the fixity of space.

Giddens finds much that is attractive in the Marxist perspective. While a more thorough discussion of his relationship to Marxist theories of social change will be addressed later in this chapter, some general comments are in order here. Like Harvey, Giddens believes that the issue of space has not been sufficiently studied by classical social theory, in which time has priority over space. Giddens adopts the Marxist claim that class plays a major role in the stratification of modern societies, as labor exploitation still exists. Like Wallerstein, he believes that the study of social change is inseparable from the understanding of the world-wide system of capitalism, and that the spread of capitalism and urbanism throughout the globe has created a distinctive modern world. Yet Giddens contends that the Marxist tradition concentrates on the economic bases of social change to the neglect of other important factors, such as the rise of the nation-state and nationalism and the emergence of administrative sources of power, as found in surveillance systems. Though Marxists have struggled to conceptualize the nature of the state, developing a wealth of theories about its relative autonomy in relation to the economy, in many ways they still regard the state as "the executive committee of the bourgeoisie," in Marx's famous phrase.[17] To understand the state as a distinctive base of social power, Giddens draws on the work of Foucault.

Foucault and surveillance

Foucault formulates a strong critique of evolutionary and class-based theories of social change, as found in Marxism. He shifts the analysis of domination from the Marxist concern with class to a more generalized critique of power. For Foucault, knowledge and power are intimately linked, as there is no disinterested knowledge. He argues that the emergence of new types of power in the West is tied to processes of exclusion and control that are at the core of Enlightenment and social scientific rationality. When faced with an experience that seems strange or heterogeneous, such as madness, Western rationality tends to define it as abnormal, tries to separate it from the rest of experience, and domesticate and control it.

In Foucault's view, power is productive, as it produces its own objects and then disciplines and controls them. For example, state power defines certain actions as crimes, therefore creating the category of criminal, which gives rise to institutions to deal with criminality, and experts on crime, who then write books on it, and so on. The penal system does not reduce crime but actually defines groups of people as deviant. Social scientific knowledge determines normality and abnormality; as these categories change over time, they promote an ever-increasing number of new ways of controlling people.

Foucault locates the modern forms of power in the rise of a new type of state in post-Renaissance Europe. Before this time, definitions of normality, deviance, and the like were certainly common, but the social power of such definitions was limited, as the everyday life of people lay outside the scope of the pre-modern state and its legal regulations. Foucault argues that this began to change in sixteenth-century France, as the state became concerned with demographic issues, such as the nation's population, fertility rate, and the composition and morality of the family. Scientific categories for gathering information on people developed in this context, and the populace became subject to systematic, sustained attention and intervention. This supervision not only permitted information to be collected, but gradually allowed the populace to be manipulated and controlled as the power of the state grew. New juridical definitions of normality and abnormality arose, as the mad, homosexuals, and other "deviants" became increasingly subject to state control and punishment. This inner connection of rationality and social control was demonstrated in the great confinement of 1656 France, when every hundredth inhabitant in Paris was arrested and placed in an institution. All sorts of "deviants," from the insane to the unemployed, were indiscriminately secluded. A productivist ideology justified this process, as the state wished to rid society not only of deviants, but to make the people more productive and eradicate idleness.[18]

These institutions provided settings where the confined could be continually and systematically observed by those in power. For Foucault, surveillance is an inherent characteristic of modern institutions. The asylum and the prison are typical of such institutions, as they represent the emerging power of modern professions (such as psychology and criminology) which can engage in normalizing judgments by objectifying and defining deviance. Foucault posits an inherent connection between the human sciences and supervision, seen not only in the asylum and the prison, but also in the factory, the barracks, and the school, where a regulatory reason rules: those inside are the subject of surveillance by foremen, doctors, teachers, etc. Much of what passes for humanistic treatment in these institutions actually allows anyone considered deviant to be observed, manipulated, regulated, isolated, and controlled. These new forms of power attempt to penetrate the very psyche of people and mold them according to dominant conceptions of morality.

The rise of the social sciences and the emergence of new institutions such as the asylum and the prison contributed to the development of new disciplinary technologies, in Foucault's terms. Disciplinary technologies are procedures and operations by which the social world is classified and objectified. A good example is the school examination, which combines normalizing judgments and the surveillance of students by the teacher. The exam objectifies individuals, making them into analyzable objects. Individuals are then classified according to the results of the exam, and they often internalize these criteria for self-assessment.

For instance, these techniques for creating and maintaining differences are institutionalized in the tracking system of many elementary and high schools in the US, where students are grouped according to ostensible academic abilities. Such disciplines order human multiplicity, and create new fields to be disciplined ever anew.[19]

Foucault believes that any analysis of modern power must look beyond the Marxist fixation with class struggle and exploitation. He concentrates on the autonomous influence of the state in disciplining its subjects, and the important role of surveillance as a form of social control in the modern world, from the workplace to the prison. The domination of subject populations includes more than just economic exploitation, as it involves the power to invent knowledges which define what is normal or deviant, to sequester deviants in institutions apart from everyday life, and to try and fashion people's very identities in the shape of a particular vision of moral life.

Giddens agrees with many of the general themes developed by Foucault. Following Foucault, Giddens defines surveillance as the gathering of information relevant to controlling and directly supervising a given populace.[20] He believes that the rise of modernity is inseparable from new modes of power manifested in the extensive surveillance capacities of the state. Like Foucault, Giddens argues that a central form of modern power involves the capacity of the state to make and enforce moralizing judgments, and to "sequester" in asylums, prisons, etc., deviants who do not abide by the dominant moral code. Yet Giddens contends that Foucault, like the Marxists, discusses power and social change largely in terms of institutional changes. Giddens believes that such perspectives do not do justice to the independent importance of cultural changes, such as nationalism, that are major factors structuring the organization of the modern world. Giddens combines many Marxist arguments about the rise of capitalism with Foucault's concern with the relationship of power and surveillance into a comprehensive theory of social change, adding his distinctive concerns with time, space, and urbanism, and discarding any evolutionary remnants.

Giddens and social change

Giddens advocates a discontinuous theory of social change. Marx implicitly develops such a theory, but it remains untheorized because of his evolutionary emphasis. What especially interests Giddens is the distinctiveness of capitalism compared to other forms of social organization and historical eras. The arrival of industrial capitalism entailed an enormous increase in the scope and pace of social change. Giddens contends that the task of contemporary sociology continues the quest of its founders, i.e. to understand the specificity and dynamics of the industrial capitalist world. To succcessfully undertake such an endeavor requires a comparison of the present and the past, and a critique of the theories of social change that inadequately analyze the transition from "premodern" to "modern" societies. Giddens introduces a theory of social change that places time-space distanciation and issues of power at the center of analysis. He uses these concepts to investigate the rise of capitalism and the nation-state. Giddens, as is his wont, develops his perspective through evaluating the contributions of other theorists who explore the rise of capitalist societies. He focuses on the contemporary theorists Wallerstein and Foucault, but devotes much of his criticism to Marx. We have already touched on Giddens's criticisms of these theorists; now it is necessary to examine them in more detail.

Giddens and Marx

Giddens argues that Marx's approach demonstrates the radical nature of the social changes brought about by capitalism, as "all that is solid melts into air." For Giddens, the globalization of capitalism in the late modern age cannot be understood apart from Marx's analysis of capitalist production. Like Marx, Giddens contends that capitalism creates a distinctive sphere of the economy, consisting of private property controlled by private persons rather than the state. Capitalism commodifies land and labor, which creates a propertyless mass of wage laborers. The concentration of workers in factories and other workplaces allows managers and owners to better control labor, creating a sort of workshop despotism. The labor contract is the major means by which the employer exercises authority over the worker. The worker forfeits rights of the control of his/her labor upon entering the capitalist workplace, and becomes subject to the direct surveillance of the employer. Moreover, the worker cannot escape the power of the labor contract, as he/she has few other opportunities for making a living. Giddens also finds attractive Marx's notion of praxis, for he agrees with Marx that people must continually try to change a social world that is not of their own making. According to Giddens, this notion of praxis shows that Marx is cognizant of people as neither completely determined nor totally free agents.[21]

But Giddens rejects many of Marx's major assertions and theoretical assumptions. Like a number of other commentators, Giddens contends that Marx saw exploitation solely in class terms, thus underestimating the independent sources of domination associated with gender, race and ethnicity, and the control of nature. Giddens finds fault with Marx's historical materialism. He does not believe that history can be understood as the progressive, evolutionary development of modes of production, nor that the conflicts of all societies are caused by class struggle. For Giddens, Marx joined other nineteenth-century theorists in falsely positing a movement from simple to complex societies, while seeing the sources of social change to be endogenous.[22] Such evolutionary assumptions do not square with the historical record. In Giddens's view, history has no telos; there is no progressive march toward a better world that operates behind the backs of people's conscious actions.

Giddens argues, *contra* Marx, that only with capitalism does the material expansion of production become a primary necessity of social life. Class divisions, class struggle, the control of private property, and increases in production were not central processes in the everyday life of non-capitalist societies. Possession of what Giddens calls authoritative resources (control over the social world) rather than allocative resources (control over the material world) was the cornerstone of rule in these societies, and military confrontations rather than the evolution of the forces of production were often the major impetus for social change.[23]

Giddens argues that Marx did not adequately analyze the place of the nation-state in facilitating the rise of capitalism, nor its role as an independent source of power in the modern world. The modern nation-state provides the framework for the industrialization of war through the baneful merger of industry, technology, and war-making capacities, a process not theorized by Marx. This neglect of state-sanctioned violence is a curious lacuna in Marxist theory, for Marx does not examine why industrialists do not directly control the means of violence under capitalism, as had dominant classes in previous societies. According to Giddens, this oversight points to Marx's impoverished conception of the relationship of power to the nation-state.

Giddens contends that Marx does not give people sufficient credit for being able to understand and change their lives. Marx, like other evolutionary theorists, underestimates the knowledgeability of agents, and their role in changing the social world. Giddens believes, *contra* Marx, that people are not mainly tool-making creatures, and that control over the ideological dimension of social life (based on authoritative resources) cannot be reduced to issues of production and class. Nor can we assume, like Marx, that the next society will grow out of the existing social world. In a nuclear age, we need a new utopianism which rejects all evolutionary assumptions (a point that will be developed in the next chapter).[24]

According to Giddens, Marx's notion of the primacy of production in modern social life cannot capture the complexity of modernity. Capitalistic enterprise and industrial production are indeed two important institutional components of modernity. But they are on a par with the other two of modernity's major institutional settings: heightened surveillance and the centralized control of the means of violence. None of these four axes can be reduced to one another. Moreover, modernity creates a distinctive cultural condition not analyzed by Marx, which requires increased reflexivity on the part of organizations. As traditions break down, people realize that they do indeed make their own history. Organizations are then reflexively able to influence the shaping of social life. For example, the state reflexively monitors its constituents through the census, law enforcement, and the like, and creates policies to enforce social control.[25] Social theory needs much more sensitivity to the interplay of these dimensions of social life than is displayed by Marx.

The critique of Wallerstein

Giddens believes that in many ways Wallerstein improves upon some of Marx's more problematic features. He finds much of value in the world-system theory of Wallerstein. Like Wallerstein, Giddens believes that capitalism created an intersocietal system for the first time in history. Wallerstein also observes that a major feature of this system is the state-mandated separation of economics and politics.

But Giddens has many criticisms of Wallerstein's approach. Wallerstein does not sufficiently recognize that the world-system is a political and military order as well as an economic one; further, the world-system is not wholly capitalist, as it involves non-capitalist political formations as well. Giddens criticizes Wallerstein for neglecting the analysis of the role of military power and warfare among competing nation-states in forging the world-system. In general, Wallerstein does not examine in any detail the independent effects of politics and the nation-state on the world-system, nor does he adequately recognize the significance of the commodification of labor power. Wallerstein also fails to grasp the importance of the massive increase in capitalist and government surveillance techniques in shaping the modern world. In sum, Wallerstein tends to fall into a functionalist and economically reductionist argument, for he does not see that the state system which arose in the wake of absolutism is as important as the capitalist world-system to an understanding of social change.[26]

Giddens and Foucault

In many ways, Giddens believes that Foucault captures dimensions of social change neglected by Marxism. Giddens's arguments about surveillance seem especially close to those of Foucault. For Giddens, social change is tied to the rise of new types of surveillance, which contribute to the formation of new institutions. Like Foucault, Giddens believes that the centralization of surveillance activities in the state allows the creation of new categories of deviance which can then be disciplined and controlled. Foucault also recognizes that those deviants to be disciplined and punished are usually sequestered from everyday life in institutions such as prisons. The prison serves as a kind of template for other forms of discipline, including the factory and the military barracks.

While Giddens agrees with the general thrust of Foucault's arguments, he has several criticisms of his analysis. Giddens argues that Foucault tends to oversimplify the social changes that gave rise to the modern world. Giddens believes that Foucault replicates the postmodern total critique of modernity, neglecting the valuable freedoms that modern society has created, from freedom of association to freedom of contract. Foucault exaggerates comparisons between the prison and other institutions, such as the workplace. The workplace is not a prison-like, totally closed institution based on coercion, for the very existence of modern labor presupposes a separation of work and home. Prisons in general are a poor model for the modern disciplinary power of the state, as the prison is a total institution, in Goffman's sense, which attempts to control much of the prisoner's life, and leaves little leeway for independent action. There is much more freedom of activity in other less totalitarian institutions within capitalism, from the workplace to the state. This focus on the prison is also indicative of Foucault's pessimistic view of the capacities of people to understand and change their lives. Foucault's view of a "subjectless" society does not sufficiently take into account that knowledgeable agents engage in social practices which actively reproduce social relations.[27]

Giddens contends that Foucault does not go far enough in his analysis of the sequestration of deviance. Sequestration is not just tied to the control of deviance, but is a major part of modern societies. The sequestration of certain experiences is a far-reaching phenomenon tied to the regionalization of everyday life in the modern world, as issues around intimacy, sexuality, and death become privatized. The reality of death, illness, and the like is segregated in institutions, from the hospital to the asylum, and hidden from everyday life. This sequestration of experience makes ethical reflection on these issues much more difficult.

Like many in the Marxist tradition, Giddens believes that capitalism has profoundly influenced modern societies. Class relations occupy a central place in the distribution of social power, and the commodification of labor is a major process of social change as the market expands throughout the world to create a capitalist world-system. Giddens jettisons the Marxist belief in the evolutionary theory of history that culminates in communism, and he also rejects the proletariat as a revolutionary class. Like Foucault, Giddens contends that the modern world cannot be understood apart from the centrality of the nation-state, and its many forms of power, from the monopolization of the means of violence to its capacities for surveillance and the sequestration of experience. Giddens develops an approach to social change which extends many of these ideas. However, he believes that social change cannot be understood apart from changes in the nature of time and space, the rise of the city, and the transition from class-divided to class societies, processes neglected by Marx and Foucault. It is to these issues that we now turn.

Time-space relations

Giddens sees modernity as a juggernaut, a world of constant change. He argues that people must continually adjust to new circumstances and cultural change as new urban centers grow and others decline, and the mass media create the simultaneous experience of different societies. Accordingly, Giddens calls for a reconsideration of time and space in social theory, which he believes Marx, among others, neglected. Giddens replaces Parsons's problem of order with a consideration of how societies bind time and space together. Such "time-space distanciation," in Giddens's terms, means that all social systems must stretch across time and space, and how they do so fundamentally affects their type of social integration. The interconnections of social systems, which extend across time and space among people who are not in physical contact, to social integration, or face-to-face relationships, becomes a major issue in the study of social change.

Giddens argues that models of social change based on adaptation and evolution should be replaced with the analysis of "episodic character-izations and time-space edges." Episodes refer to changes in the structural transformation of societies which have a clear direction, say from class-divided to class societies. Time-space edges refer to the simultaneous existence of different types of societies involved in episodic transitions. Giddens also moves away from the endogenous models of social change so powerful in sociology, toward a theory which emphasizes "inter-societal systems" à la Wallerstein. Studies of social change must also be historically sensitive, as episodic transitions differ from one episode to the next.[28]

Issues of time and space are important for understanding differences between societies. In non-modern societies, traditional memory allows a kind of "storage capacity" which enables social experience to be collectively understood and power to be exercised. Storage capacity is the control of authoritative and allocative resources through the collection of information and knowledge. Giddens argues that storage capacity connects the present to the past and time to space, as it gives time and space particular meanings. Different conceptions of time and space do not simply evolve as societies "progress." Distinct societies live side by side, and change often occurs through the interaction of one society with another.[29]

Giddens replaces the sociologically commonplace idea that some societies are more complex than others with his notion of time-space distanciation, which can be used to categorize different sorts of societies without the prejudices involved in evolutionism. Thus, hunting and gathering societies have low time-space distanciation, for they involve face-to-face interaction, with tradition and kinship providing the major means of social integration. Food is usually consumed a relatively short time after it is gathered, and long-distance trade is limited. Agriculture extends time-space distanciation, as it permits the storage of food and increases in trade. Industrial capitalism stretches this time-space distanciation to unprecedented levels, as it ties the world together in an integrated global market-place.[30]

Time and space relations take place in particular locales, or physical spaces which maintain the typical interactions of a collectivity. Like Harvey, Giddens argues that capitalism fundamentally alters time-space relations by changing the settings in which social interaction occurs. Modern life in general has seen the convergence of time and space. Capitalism in particular turns time and space into commodities, which can then allow for the interchangeability of labor. The development of the clock is central to this process. Control of time is a major part of capitalist life. For example, the length of the working day is not determined by tradition, but by class struggles at the workplace. The commodification of time allows labor to be measured and controlled at the worksite; some versions of social science, such as Taylorism, are used to increase the surveillance capacities of employers. The commodification of labor and time extends time-space distanciation, as capitalism spreads throughout the globe.[31]

The rise of capitalism also transforms people's sense of place. Capitalism inaugurates the separation of work and home, while new spaces can be produced ever anew according to the needs of capital. The contemporary deindustrialization of urban areas in the US, such as Detroit, and the rise of new "high-tech" industries in other parts of the country, such as Austin, Texas, are examples of the ever-changing nature of urban space under capitalism. In sum, temporal and spatial processes wrought by capitalism shape how everyday life is experienced, while creating new categories of home and work. The rise of industrial capitalism depends on such transformations, for work must be clearly separated from leisure, and labor disciplined at the workplace.[32]

The emergence of modern society also involves a new consciousness of the independent role of history in structuring social life, and that people themselves make their own history. Giddens labels this reflexive invention of history "'historicity' – the controlled use of reflection upon history as a means of changing history."[33] Such a historical consciousness erodes the hegemony of taken-for-granted tradition over everyday life, as tradition becomes subject to competing interpretations. People can envisage new forms of community which they themselves have in part constructed and for which they are responsible. Historicity becomes an important component in the rise of modern nationalism, in that people creatively, and sometimes illegitimately, draw on shared interpretations of their experiences of the past to develop new forms of national consciousness. Nationalism will be more extensively discussed below (see pp. 120–1).

Giddens demonstrates that he takes space seriously by placing the study of the city at the center of his social theory. Urbanization is a "distinctive feature of all societies characterized by extensive time-space distanciation," for the city is the main locus of the state, a necessary center for the generation of power and a location for elites to consolidate their rule.[34] Giddens argues that the analysis of the city cannot be separated from the social whole in which it is embedded, and that the urbanization associated with capitalism is very different from that of precapitalist cities, which were more important as political and military centers than as a hub of economic activity. Capitalism changed the nature of the city, as migration to urban areas by immigrants in search of work destroyed the city as a distinctive social form. In a manner much like Harvey, Giddens argues that as city walls disappeared, space became commodified, and created space became the norm in capitalist cities. Cities are transformed by capitalist social relations: they are no longer distinctive urban enclaves, but are a kind of manufactured environment, as capital reworks the very constitution of urban life according to its needs.

Power and social change

Processes of social change invariably involve issues of power. Accordingly, Giddens argues that the "articulation of time-space relations" also must include the analysis of power. Giddens believes that power is not adequately examined by Marx, but he also wishes to avoid the excesses of the Nietzschean-postmodern conception of a ubiquitous social power associated with Foucault. To some degree Giddens favors Parsons's notion of power, in which rulers must win the confidence of the people in order to maintain legitimized rule. But Giddens states that political legitimacy can also be based on a pragmatic acceptance of rulers rather than a strong belief in them, and that violence can play a part in maintaining the rule of elites.[35]

Giddens sees the primary importance of power in somewhat Foucauldian terms, for power is productive as well as repressive. Power refers to the capacity of people to change the world. It is a part of all social life. Power does not necessarily involve exploitation or coercion, as it is also tied to freedom and interdependence. This constant interplay of freedom and constraint which is at work in any social situation Giddens labels the "dialectic of control." The resources available to different people will determine the extent to which they can exercise freedom or become subject to coercion.[36]

In formulating the dialectic of control, and tying it to the larger issues of structuration theory, Giddens distinguishes power from domination. While power relations refer to the "reproduced relations of autonomy and dependence in interaction," domination consists of the "structured asymmetries" of the distribution of allocative and authoritative resources available in such interactions. A social group's dominion over allocative and authoritative resources plays an important role in determining social stratification. However, these resources are not controlled by any single person, but are features of the entire society.[37] Power is best understood as a kind of storage capacity rather than simply a means of coercion. Writing represented a major advance in storage capacity, for it allowed the retention and centralization of information and knowledge, which in turn promoted the expansion of the surveillance capacities of institutions. The invention of money was another important step, as it permitted the storage of wealth that was necessary for the rise of capitalism. Giddens follows Weber in seeing informational innovations as central to the emergence of capitalism: for example, double-entry bookkeeping allows the maintenance of records of monetary inflows and outflows over time. Banks were able to combine double-entry bookkeeping with the extension of credit, thereby fostering capitalist growth. Marx erred in reducing all relations of domination to the control of allocative resources, and in not addressing the independent significance of the control of authoritative resources. Giddens sees the control of authoritative resources as the key ingredient in political rule in non-capitalist societies.[38]

Giddens believes that changes in communication technologies have greatly altered power relations and affected the development of societies. The invention and spread of printing and literacy allowed the expansion of information while creating a print-based culture. Printing increased the surveillance capacities of the state, as official statistics on subject populations could be gathered. The social sciences themselves became important in this context, as their methodologies contributed the rise of new surveillance and information-gathering technologies, which permitted an enormous expansion of reflexive monitoring in the state. The consolidation of the administrative unity of the state was tied not only to increased surveillance, but also to changes in communication, including the mechanization of transport and the growth of electronic media. For example, timetables developed on a wide-scale by 1900 with the rise of mass transportation systems (primarily railroads carrying freight as well as people), which changed time-space distanciation substantially.[39]

Giddens thus follows Foucault in recognizing the independent significance of administrative power, or the control over the timing and spacing of human activities, in the rise of the modern social world. In developing this notion of power, Giddens does not see it as referring primarily to the shaping of a people's moral sensibility, so important to Foucault, but rather to the capacity of institutions to indirectly control

the actions of people through manipulating the settings in which interaction takes place.[40]

Class-divided and class societies

Giddens believes that power functions differently in different historical
eras and societies. He criticizes the Marxist assumption that the dynamics
of all historically existing societies are determined by class struggle.
Giddens argues that this assertion obscures major differences between
capitalist and non-capitalist societies, and encourages the evolutionary
approach to social change which he finds so distasteful.

Giddens contends that classes did indeed exist in non-capitalist,
"class-divided" societies, but that class was not "a basic structural
principle of organization." Capitalist societies, conversely, are "class
societies," in which class struggle plays a central role. One way of
distinguishing between class and class-divided societies is through the
different ways that economic surplus is extracted, which Marx ties
exclusively to class and economic domination. Political and military
control was the most important means of exercising rule in class-divided
societies, for the threat of force was the predominant form of social
discipline, combined with the control of authoritative resources by elites.
In capitalist societies, the extraction of surplus occurs through the labor
contract, with social control dependent on the ownership of private
property.[41]

Empires such as Ancient Rome were characteristic of class-divided
societies, and they had greatly centralized political power. Yet this concentration of power was not extensive in comparison to the bureaucratic
centralization of modern industrialism. In empires, kinship relations and
military power were the primary means of social integration. Often, the
populace's major link to the ruler was through the payment of taxes
rather than via any strong ideological relationship. The dialectic of
control in empires consisted of elites loosely ruling autonomous communities. There was little direct and extensive power from the top
down, as the limited surveillance capacities of the state inhibited its
control of everyday life in communities. The ruler rarely directly com-
manded the leaders of local villages. This diversity of lifestyles comple-
mented a mosaic-like institutional setting, as the economy and the rest of
social life were not clearly demarcated, while the functioning of an
autonomous political realm was quite limited.[42]

Class societies contrast with class-divided societies in other fundamental ways. The expansion of material production through economic
growth rather than military conquest, the control of nature, and the
replacement of myth and tradition by historicity are primary components of class societies.

Capitalism, the exemplar of class societies, ushers in a distinct sphere of the economy. Giddens sees capitalism as a class society not only because of its new economic formation, but also, like Marx, because capital becomes the major form of private property and wage labor the primary type of work. The control of labor under capitalism is much more extensive than in class-divided societies, and capitalist labor sanctions become based on the fear of losing work rather than direct coercion. Following Marx, Giddens argues that capitalist exploitation exists in the labor contract. The separation of the economic and political spheres in capitalism frees the labor contract from political considerations. The worker is denied any rights in controlling the workplace, and the political realm becomes a distinct sphere of citizenship. While Giddens realizes that governmental policies affect the economic sphere, he believes that one of the major characteristics of capitalism is the "insulation" of the economic from the political realm, as employers attempt to keep relations between capital and labor non-political. This exclusion of the worker from control of the workplace and a clear demarcation between the political and the economic are not just incidental to capitalism, but its most vital characteristics.[43]

Like Marx, Giddens believes that capitalism entails the dominance of the commodity, as the logic of buying and selling spreads to personal and political life. This commodification process changes the very nature of personal experience. The commodification of labor and land results in their continual modification, and the creation of urban spaces according to the dictates of capital undermines any secure sense of place. This erosion of ontological security is advanced by the separation of work and home, and by the disappearance of tradition as a firm anchor for social routines. Capitalism transforms social routines, as they lose their connection to traditional ways of acting and thinking, and often become mere habits reinforced by economic constraint.[44]

The state

Giddens contends that Marx's greatest failure in theorizing social change lies in his neglect of the role of the state. Marxists see state power as associated with class domination, while liberals tend to see state power as involving the expansion of bureaucracies to regulate an ever-more complex economic division of labor. According to Giddens, neither of these perspectives grasps that the surveillance of populations and the control of deviance are major components of state action. Like Foucault, Giddens argues that, especially with the definition and sanctioning of deviance (such as crime), the state enters everyday life. State surveillance is an independent source of power in the modern world.

Thus, attention to the state is of utmost importance in understanding social change. Giddens argues that processes of state formation are a central component of the creation of new civilizations, contesting the Marxist belief that new forms of social organization arise primarily in conjunction with new ways of extracting surplus from the lower classes. Giddens defines state sovereignty as a political organization which can make laws and devise sanctions in a delimited territory, monopolize the means of violence, control governmental policies, and regulate to some degree the national economy. Giddens sees the state as a major "storage-container of time-space relations," which generates "power through the extension of time-space distanciation." The state's storage of authoritative resources is particularly important, as it allows surveillance of the subject population to expand. Surveillance is also an integral feature of capitalism through control of the workplace, though its origins are tied to the rise of the nation-state.[45] Once industrial capitalism is established, however, the state expands its surveillance capacities enormously.

Giddens also critiques the Marxist theory of the subordinate role of the state in social change, particularly in the rise of capitalism. Giddens shows how capitalism and the rise of the nation-state were intimately connected. In so doing, he distinguishes between the absolutist state, the nation-state, and nationalism.

Absolutism

Like Wallerstein, Giddens argues that the rise of the absolutist state was a key factor in the creation of a capitalist world-system, for it contributed substantially to the separation of economic and political realms. Giddens states that nationalism, the nation-state, and the absolutist state originated in Europe between the sixteenth and eighteenth centuries. Absolutism consisted of strong monarchies – a famous example of an absolutist King was Louis XIV in France, who allegedly equated the state with his person (*l'État, c'est moi*). Nevertheless, absolutism posited the ruler as a secularized political entity, which was vital to the emergence of any type of political sovereignty, including democratic citizenship. This form of rule contributed to a more generalized and expansive notion of state power. The absolutist state monopolized the means of violence, which meant that violence was excluded from the capitalist labor contract. The state maintained coercive punishment powers which were important in the creation of a wage labor force and the establishment of the rights of private property.

Absolutism allowed the expansion and centralization of administrative power. It developed new types of fiscal management and new mechanisms of law, as the ownership of private property became clearly separated from public control, and laws protecting private property came into being. The absolutist state centralized money-making power, which created a national system of credit. This system of credit contributed to the commodification of land, labor, and products by expanding the range of contractually guaranteed rights and obligations. Absolutism also rationalized and centralized the taxation system, thereby increasing the surveillance capacities of the state. The propensity of absolutist states to engage in war helped to bring about advanced technology, state centralization, and the spread of capitalism.[46]

The nation-state

Absolutism gave way to the modern nation-state in eighteenth- and nineteenth-century Europe, symbolized most dramatically in the overthrow of the monarchy in the French Revolution of 1789. The absolutist state coincided with the rise of early capitalism, but this form of the state was also tied to class-divided societies. Capitalism was not fully developed in the absolutist era. The nation-state arose with the expansion of capitalism, as the state replaced the city as the major power-container of society. The expansion of capitalism was dependent on the centralization of violence in state offices, as the police controlled populations internally while the government provided the military support for capitalist expansion abroad.

Capitalism could only gain world hegemonic power in the context of a new state system which created a framework of law and the fiscal guarantees of a pacified social environment. The nation-state carried this internal pacification process to a much higher degree than did absolutism. Internal control of the population involved the state ridding society of alternative sources of violence. While this was to some degree a violent process, it depended increasingly on new, more subtle forms of social control, such as the elimination of violence from the labor contract. Economic compulsion and workplace surveillance replaced coercion as the fundamental means of control of labor. This new type of internal pacification that did not depend directly on coercion was symbolized by the withdrawal of the military from internal affairs and the decline of violent forms of punishment.[47]

The nation-state had other ties to the creation of a capitalist world economy. In empires, independent political units were assimilated into the imperial system. As the nation-state became the accepted political unit in the sixteenth century, it enforced a legitimate monopoly on a delimited territory, rule sanctioned by law, and the control of violence. Diplomacy was the creation of a world-system dominated by competing nation-states, with seemingly "natural" frontiers and an internally coherent administrative government. The rise of the market required these stable institutions of rule and law, so that the entrepreneurship and the long-term investment central to capitalism could take place.[48] In sum, the political revolutions of the eighteenth and nineteenth centuries facilitated the expansion of industrial capitalism.

Nationalism

The rise of the nation-state was dependent on a new type of large-scale worldview, over and above one's local village or region. While Marx sees class consciousness as the major form of this abstract, modern collective awareness, he neglects the importance of nationalism as a competing *Weltanschauung*. Giddens states that Foucault, like Marx, also does not sufficiently grasp nationalism as a source of social and personal identity in the modern world. Nor have theorists of nationalism sufficiently analyzed its impact. Commentators on nationalism tend to fall into three camps. One group, including the sociologist Tilly, emphasizes its ties to modern, centralized states governing a delimited territory. The anthropologist Anderson, in the second camp, stresses the existence and/or creation of a shared language to facilitate a national identity and an imagined community. Finally, many authors discuss the psychological benefits of belonging to a shared national community.[49]

Giddens borrows from all three of these perspectives in developing his approach. He argues that nationalism involves a sense of linguistic homogeneity, or the shared beliefs and symbols held by a community. Giddens sees nationalism as a modern phenomenon, feeding on the rootlessness of modernity and what the anthropologist Geertz calls the "primordial sentiments" of social life. For Giddens, there are many dimensions of nationalism. As a political phenomenon, nationalism helps formulate the notion of a shared history for a people, in large part through elites' creation of a common language and shared narratives embodied in the invention of a distinctive national past.[50]

Nationalism is also linked to the administrative sovereignty of the state over a particular territory. This is why nationalist movements are invariably oriented toward political change. Further, nationalism is in an important sense a psychological phenomenon. Giddens states: "Nationalism is anchored psychologically in distinctive features of modern societies and its content is linked to the historicity they engender."[51] Nationalism builds on the traditional loyalties generated by villages or tribes as they decline and large-scale governments arise. Nationalism helps maintain a sense of ontological security as tradition fades, in part through identification with nationalist leaders in troubled times. Such leaders can manipulate symbols and ideological appeals, thus contributing to an aggressive nationalism, in contrast to a more egalitarian nationalism associated with cultural diversity.[52]

Giddens states that nationalism draws on modern ideas of the importance of history. This notion of historicity informs the rise of the modern nation-state, as it ties nationalism to the distinctive "cultural unity of a collectivity" as it has developed over time.[53] The history of a nation creates a symbolic narrative which defines a people's self-understanding, as they see themselves as the embodiment of a historical legacy. Historicity helps erode traditional forms of consciousness, linking history with nationalist claims to sovereignty.

Giddens is far from celebrating modern nationalism and the contemporary state. He views the nation-state with a suspicious eye, as its centralization of surveillance activities always points to the possibility of totalitarianism. The state also contributes fundamentally to the industrialization of war. Giddens believes that violence and war are central factors in the history of societies. Their relative importance was not recognized by the classical sociologists of the late nineteenth century because they lived in decades of relative peace before World War I. The horrible destruction and unprecedented carnage associated with World War I showed the damaging consequences of the association of war, the state, science, technology, and mass production. The war also reshaped European society, as it helped institutionalize class conflict by making labor movements a partner with governments in ensuring economic growth, and integrated large-scale science and technology with industrial progress. For Giddens, this was a logical outcome of the interdependence of military expansion and the growth of the nation-state.[54]

Capitalism reaches its zenith only when it combines with industrialism. Giddens defines industrialism as the use of inanimate sources of material power for commodity production and distribution, the mechanization of manufacturing production, and the centralized workplace. Capitalism provides the inner dynamic of industrial expansion. Industrialism also transforms nature through urban expansion. The urban created environment is the territory in which capitalism, industrialism, and the nation-state take hold.[55]

Giddens formulates a theory of social change and modernity which differs in important ways from Marxism, functionalism, and other major sociological approaches. For Giddens, modernity comprises the rise of capitalist industrialism, the nation-state, urban experience, the printed word, and most recently the electronic mass media. Modernity and capitalism have indeed created a "world-historical," interdependent globe, as Marx foresaw. But as we have seen in this chapter, modernity as a distinctive historical epoch outstrips Marx's economic understanding of it. Unlike Marx, Giddens views social change as a discontinuous process, as societies do not progressively evolve from one form to another. Social change must be studied in its historical context, as the distinctive time-space distanciation of particular societies influences the scope and pace of change. Economic and political institutions also develop side by side, reinforcing one another. Giddens accents the importance of the state in processes of social change. The state promotes the expansion of surveillance activities and military power, which are key to understanding the make-up of modern societies.

Giddens's call for historical specificity in the study of social change is indeed salutary. He is not always clear, however, regarding how these various elements of social change fit together (the military, state, and economy). More importantly, it is not readily apparent, given Giddens's discontinuous theory of history, what modern societies can learn from the past. As Giddens rejects evolutionary conceptions of history, he does not point to any strong cultural traditions which have a continuous historical existence and that modern people can draw on to create some sort of collective solidarity. His approach to history does not address in detail how cultural innovation comes about, in part "because it leaves no place for an elaboration of collective memories that could provide cultural resources and ideals."[56]

These issues become acute as the new culture of modernity arises in the transition from class-divided to class societies, and modern reflexivity becomes pervasive as traditions break apart. In the late modern world, everyday life is permeated by distant events, which both unify and fragment culture. In such circumstances, the old Parsonian problem of social order, seemingly relegated to the dustbin of history by Giddens, rears its repressed head. Specifically, Giddens must answer the question of what holds society together in the late modern context (the problem of social order), and why and how innovative cultural change can occur. Giddens attempts to address such issues in his analysis of the new social movements and life politics of late modernity (see p. 147). The cultural experience of late modernity, designated by Giddens as reflexive modernization, thus involves the reformulation of social solidarity as "all that is solid melts into air." We turn to these questions in the next chapter.

Notes

1 See Talcott Parsons, "Some Considerations on the Theory of Social Change," in *Talcott Parsons on Institutions and Social Evolution*, ed. Leon Mayhew (Chicago, University of Chicago Press, 1982), pp. 255–276.

2 Karl Marx, *The German Ideology: Part I*, in *The Marx–Engels Reader*, ed. Robert Tucker (New York, Norton, 1978), p. 155.

3 Ibid., p. 156.

4 Marx and Engels, *Manifesto of the Communist Party*, in *The Marx–Engels Reader*, ed. Tucker, p. 475.

5 Karl Marx, "Marx on the History of His Opinions," *The Marx–Engels Reader*, ed. Tucker, p. 4.

6 Ibid., p. 5.

7 Marx and Engels, *The German Ideology*, pp. 191–193. See also *Capital, Volume One*, in *The Marx–Engels Reader*, ed. Tucker, pp. 294–438.

8 Immanuel Wallerstein, "World-Systems Analysis," in *Social Theory Today*, ed. Anthony Giddens and Jonathan H. Turner (Stanford, Stanford University Press, 1987), p. 313.

9 Ibid., p. 317.

10 Ibid.

11 David Harvey, *The Condition of Postmodernity* (Cambridge, MA, Blackwell, 1989), p. 204.

12 Philippe Ariès, *Centuries of Childhood: A Social History of Family Life* (New York, Random House, 1962), p. 405.

13 Harvey, *The Condition of Postmodernity*, p. 239.

14 David Harvey, *Consciousness and the Urban Experience: Studies in the History and Theory of Capitalist Urbanization* (Baltimore, Johns Hopkins University Press, 1985), p. 13

15 Ibid., p. 35.

16 Ibid., pp. 9, 12.

17 Marx and Engels, *Manifesto of the Communist Party, The Marx-Engels Reader*, ed. Tucker, p. 475.

18 Michel Foucault, *Madness and Civilization: A History of Insanity in the Age of Reason* (New York, Pantheon, 1965).

19 *The Foucault Reader*, ed. Paul Rabinow (New York, Pantheon, 1984), pp. 197–205; see also Foucault, *Discipline and Punish*.

20 Anthony Giddens, *A Contemporary Critique of Historical Materialism, Vol. 1, Power, Property, and the State* (Berkeley, University of California Press, 1981), p. 5.

21 Ibid., pp. 1, 10, 53–54; Giddens, *A Contemporary Critique of Historical Materialism, Vol. 2, The Nation-State and Violence* (Berkeley, University of California Press, 1985), 133–134.

22 Giddens, *A Contemporary Critique of Historical Materialism, Vol. 1*, pp. 2, 59, 90,

23 Ibid., pp. 22, 107–108, 238.

24 *A Contemporary Critique of Historical Materialism, Vol. 1*, pp. 155–156; *The Nation-State and Violence*, pp. 3, 71, 334.

25 *The Nation-State and Violence*, pp. 5, 12, 17.

26 Ibid., pp. 167–170; *A Contemporary Critique of Historical Materialism, Vol. 1*, pp. 168–169, 197.

27 *A Contemporary Critique of Historical Materialism, Vol. 1*, p. 171–174; *The Nation-State and Violence*, pp. 182–185.

28 *A Contemporary Critique of Historical Materialism, Vol. 1*, pp. 23–24.

29 Ibid., pp. 5, 90–91.

30 For a good summary of Giddens's view of this process, see E.O. Wright, "Models of Historical Trajectory: An Assessment of Giddens's Critique of Marxism," in *Social Theory and Modern Societies: Anthony Giddens and his Critics*, ed. David Held and John B. Thompson (New York, Cambridge University Press, 1989), p. 84.

31 Giddens, *A Contemporary Critique of Historical Materialism, Vol. 1*, pp. 9, 39–40, 120–132. On Taylorism, see Harry Braverman, *Labor and Monopoly Capital: The Degradation of Work in the Twentieth Century* (New York, Monthly Review Press, 1974).

32 Giddens, *A Contemporary Critique of Historical Materialism, Vol. 1*, pp. 137–139.

33 Giddens, *The Nation-State and Violence*, p. 212.

34 Giddens, *A Contemporary Critique of Historical Materialism, Vol. 1*, p. 6.

35 Ibid., pp. 3–4; *The Nation-State and Violence*, p. 202.

36 Giddens, *A Contemporary Critique of Historical Materialism, Vol. 1*, pp. 27–29, 51.

37 Ibid., pp. 4, 52.

38 Ibid., pp. 4, 35, 94–95, 117.

39 Giddens, *The Nation-State and Violence*, pp. 172–174, 178–181.

40 Ibid., pp. 46–47.

41 Giddens, *A Contemporary Critique of Historical Materialism, Vol. 1*, pp. 7, 112.

42 Ibid., pp. 102–103, 162–163; *The Nation-State and Violence*, pp. 58–59, 68.

43 *The Nation-State and Violence*, p. 207; *A Contemporary Critique of Historical Materialism*, Vol. 1, pp. 121–124, 128.

44 Ibid., pp. 152–154.

45 Ibid., pp. 168–169.

46 Ibid., pp. 94, 181, 186–187; *The Nation-State and Violence*, pp. 115–116, 148, 152, 157.

47 Ibid., pp. 190–192, 288–289.

48 Ibid., pp. 80, 85, 90.

49 On the various types of nationalism, see Craig Calhoun, *Critical Social Theory: Culture, History, and the Challenge of Difference* (Cambridge, MA, Blackwell, 1995), pp. 231–282.

50 Giddens, *A Contemporary Critique of Historical Materialism*, pp. 13, 191.

51 Giddens, *The Nation-State and Violence*, p. 219.

52 Ibid., pp. 217–220.

53 Ibid., p. 216.

54 Ibid., pp. 236–237, 254.

55 Ibid., pp. 138–140, 146–147.

56 Kenneth H. Tucker, Jr., "Aesthetics, Play, and Cultural Memory: Giddens and Habermas on the Postmodern Challenge," *Sociological Theory* 11 (July 1993), p. 197.

5

THE CULTURE OF MODERNITY: FROM THE CRITIQUE OF POSTMODERNISM TO THE RISE OF THE NEW SOCIAL MOVEMENTS

We are all aware of the seemingly unavoidable changes that are now occurring in our lives. Commentators tell us of the fast-paced world in which we live, where an information super-highway, from television to the Internet, creates a new global village and increases symbolic and material contact between different cultures. Many authors believe that this new information age represents a postindustrial, postmodern world, characterized by the loss of old certainties in the context of the decline of industrial labor and its replacement by service work, the crisis of the nuclear family, the ubiquity of mass communications, and the ecological distrust of science. This ever-present change and sense of crisis translates into questions concerning the very nature of our selves and our communities, as demonstrated in the many debates on issues such as sexual orientation, multiculturalism, and nationalism. The lack of traditional moorings for our self-identity has accompanied the profusion of new identities, from gays and lesbians to religious fundamentalists, that influence societies throughout the world.

The threat of nuclear catastrophe, the problems associated with industrial growth and bureaucratization, and the decline in the legitimacy of established political parties have created the conditions for the rise of these new social movements. As industrial societies have entered crises, established political parties appear to be caught in ideological straitjackets, unable to respond creatively to new circumstances and problems. Economic growth has remained the *sine qua non* of politics, yet leaders find it increasingly difficult to legitimize their practices on the basis of technological progress and bureaucratic rationality. Economic growth itself has been harder to sustain in the context of the decay of the traditional manufacturing sector, the mobility of capital beyond national borders, and fiscal problems and currency instability. These difficulties are exacerbated by the breakdown of tradition and religion as important overarching belief systems, as well as the spatial fragmentation of urban centers.[1]

Recent social changes have led to debates over the very nature of the contemporary social world, encapsulated in the complex arguments around modernity and postmodernity. We have encountered postmodernism and poststructuralism earlier in this volume; in this chapter we will examine them in some detail. Debates on postmodernism coalesce around two related themes. First, have we entered a new postmodern era that is fundamentally different from the modern era? This question hinges on the assertion that a host of social changes are fundamentally altering our world, and "that traditional class politics and faith in progress are being replaced by 'identity politics' and 'new' social movements such as feminism, gay liberation, ecologism, ethnic revivalism, religious neofundamentalism."[2] Second, these changes have brought with them a challenge to the "philosophical discourse of modernity," as the conceptual frameworks of social science and the historical legacy of Enlightenment rationality have been challenged by new postmodern knowledges, which contend that reason is a form of illegitimate power which marginalizes and excludes cultural vocabularies that do not conform to its categories.

The sociological tradition is certainly no stranger to such concerns. The distinctive characteristics of the modern world, as different from pre- or non-modern social life, have been a major concern of sociologists since the era of Marx, Weber, and Durkheim. Yet it seems as if the late modern or postmodern era raises particular issues which call for a new understanding of the social world.

Giddens accepts this challenge, and he develops a theory of the distinctiveness of modern culture. Giddens rejects the postmodern claim of a surpassed modernity, stating that modernity's culture of incessant reflexivity creates a post-traditional social world. As modernity spreads throughout the globe, it encourages the rise of expert, abstract systems of knowledge, represented by the social and natural sciences. These expert systems fuel modernity's constant change and reflexivity, which disembed time and space from their particular context, re-embedding them in new ones. Giddens also sees new social movements, centered on a new life politics, as integral to the texture of late modern life.

Giddens shares many of these themes with contemporary sociological theorists, such as Habermas, Touraine, and Melucci. They also address the issues raised by the culture of modernity and postmodernism, but in a way which attempts to preserve the best of the modernist tradition while exploring the changes wrought by contemporary societies. These authors attempt to grasp the distinctive culture of late modernity. They believe that this culture is fragile, ever-changing, and different from that which preceded it. Contemporary society is a global society, due to the world-wide spread of capitalism, the mass media, and industrialism. Accompanying globalization has been the decline of tradition and a rise in what Giddens labels a new reflexivity, as more and more people realize that their identities and moral systems can no longer rely on taken-for-granted traditions, but must be actively created by themselves.

As new problems arise in modern culture, the old solutions no longer seem to work. These theorists agree with postmodernists that pro-gressive social change cannot rely on traditional liberal-centered state programs, but must look instead to some variant of new social move-ments in order to realize the democratic potential of late modernity. These authors are suspicious of technological projects that aim to modernize social life without attention to democratic participation and/ or acknowledging the salience of cultural traditions.

Yet these theorists do not embrace the postmodern agenda. In the face of strong postmodernist critiques of modernity and a decline in the optimistic prognosis offered by Parsons, Giddens joins his fellow sociological theorists Habermas and Touraine in viewing modernity as an unfinished project. They criticize postmodernists for equating ration-ality, universalism, and illegitimate power, without sufficiently differen-tiating types of rational discourse. Giddens, Touraine, and Habermas construct a narrative of modernity which culminates in a reformed vision of rationality, universality, and evolutionary development.

For Giddens, as for these other theorists, in the late modern era of highly differentiated and specialized Western societies, conflicts arise in the areas of information and communication. The line between public and private issues becomes blurred, as the questions of personal life are increasingly politicized. Reflexivity ties the self to society in ever-changing ways, which makes the creation of identity problematic yet potentially exhilarating at the same time. According to Giddens, new social movements draw on this reflexivity to bring issues of cultural identity, sexuality, and the transformation of personal life to the center of public life.

The culture of modernity and the sociological tradition

Though these concerns appear to be new ones, as indeed many of them are, the theorists of late or postmodernity also develop themes that have long constituted core questions of the sociological imagination. For the sociological tradition, modernity has been intimately connected to the emergence and exercise of rationality, which in turn is tied to new possibilities of freedom. Accordingly, Weber's argument that modernity and rationalization are linked to one another has been a key reference point for sociological theorists from Parsons to Habermas. In the wake of these classical interpretations of modernity, Parsons became the most influential sociological theorist of the distinctiveness of the modern world and its inner dynamics. He develops a theory of modernization which, drawing heavily on Weber, provides a powerful theory of social change. Before turning to Parsons's modernization theory, it is necessary to explore Weber's theory of rationalization in more detail.

Weber on rationalization

Weber argues that rationalization, the master process of modernity, results in a less magical, increasingly disenchanted world, in which science gains pre-eminence as tradition loses prestige. He contends that the rise of rationalism in the West was tied to the emergence of capitalism, the Protestant ethic, bureaucracy, and science. Rationalization came to define the subjective experience of Western peoples, as they began to understand and evaluate the world in terms of strategies for the best means to reach a given end. Such an approach encouraged viewing the social and natural worlds in terms of coherence, calculability, systematic planning, and efficiency, and acting accordingly. Weber was ambivalent about this rationalization process, as he believed that it promoted a more realistic and scientific view of the world, yet also created a more cynical, bureaucratic society which destroyed people's capacities to believe in the exalted moral values associated with religion.

For Weber, rationalization has two meanings that are connected yet analytically separable and sometimes in conflict. On the one hand, rationalization refers to the increasingly precise, formal understanding of the world through abstract concepts. Mathematical models of social and individual behavior are a good example of this type of rationalization. Weber also states that rationalization involves the rise of principled reasoning, in that many different areas of social life can be brought together under one unifying idea. Systems of law and morality are based on such principled reasoning and ethics. While these different rationalization processes can complement each other, they can also conflict, as when principled ethics and the calculation of the best means to reach a given end come into contradiction. Principled politicians often experience this contradiction, as they are forced to compromise their ideals in order to bring about some measure of social progress through bargaining with politicians of different viewpoints, or using means that they might abhor, such as war, to achieve their ends.[3]

Weber argues that rationalization produces other tensions. Rationalization opens up social spheres which become differentiated from their original religious context. In the modern West, the state becomes separated from the economy, and both are distinguished from religion and the family. This specification of differentiation processes is one of Weber's most lasting contributions to sociological theory. His famous argument in *The Protestant Ethic and the Spirit of Capitalism* not only shows the contribution of religion to the rise of capitalism, but also demonstrates that a rational, methodical conduct of life and an ethics based on conviction, while arising in the context of religion, have become autonomous from it. Thus, rationalization results in the differentiation not only of ethical reasoning, but also of art and science, from religion. Each sphere develops its own inner logic and standards of evaluation. For instance, in art, harmony and perspective in painting are examples of these internal criteria. An aesthetic outlook on life, seen in bohemians from turn of the century Parisian artists to the hippies of the 1960s, can compensate for rationalization in other spheres.

Weber contends that rationalization also results in the increasing independence of morality and law, along with their basic decision rules, from the context in which they are first formulated. Thus, in the modern West, the Protestant ethic has become transformed into formal law and a profane ethics of responsibility and conviction. Legal norms develop which do not appeal to magic, sacred traditions, or revelation for their justification. Instead they develop their own internal rational logic. Institutions also emerge in each realm which encourage and embody the rationalization process. Universities and academies arise for the advancement of science, galleries and museums for art, and the judicial system for law. The increasing specialization of these different spheres results in the rise of professions from law to business, which encourage a rational approach to planning. Moreover, as the Protestant ethic becomes a part of everyday life, it promotes a methodical approach to conduct and thinking. But these realms are far from functioning together smoothly, as they have different logics and decision rules which come into conflict. Weber also believes that rationalization processes in the modern world tend to destroy the possibility of an ethical life, represented most dramatically by his depiction of modern society as an "iron cage" which destroys people's sense of meaning.[4]

Though Weber is ambivalent about the extent to which rationalization promotes freedom, the differentiation brought about by modern society requires an individual who is flexible and rational. Because of the diverse institutions and knowledge-bases of modern societies, people must be able to engage in abstract, principled reasoning to impose some coherence on the complexity and tensions of modern life. This emphasis on individualism, along with the capacity to reason abstractly and easily shift from role to role, are hallmarks of the universalism that Parsons sees as the central component of the culture of modernity.

Parsons and modernization theory

Like Weber, Parsons is very interested in the ramifications of rationalization for the modern social order. Parsons is concerned with the sociological conditions for the emergence of universalism, especially the universalistic criteria for understanding and evaluating the social world and their relationship to a democratic, market-oriented, liberal social order. Universalistic criteria, embodied in standards such as principled reasoning and professional ethics which apply to everyone regardless of race, gender, or class, are for Parsons major achievements of modernity. Parsons does not adopt Weber's critical analysis of the problematic fate of meaning in a rationalized order, the view that modernity could create an "iron cage" of bureaucracy and rationality which extinguishes higher values and moral meanings.

For Parsons, universalism is related to the differentiation processes characteristic of modernity. As societies modernize, different societal "units" become autonomous, while simultaneously becoming more functionally interdependent. Thus, for example, the individual's personality becomes more autonomous from the cultural and social systems, as people decide their life courses for themselves. The person learns that different situations follow different sorts of moral rules, from the school to the family to work. But the individual becomes responsible for integrating these different contexts in his/her individual personality. Individuation requires greater distance between the person and his/her particular environment, whether material or moral. Each system (personal, social, cultural) follows its own rules of internal development as it becomes independent from the others, raising more and more problems of social integration.[5]

Thus, as complexity arises in the modern world, the normative integration of the various dimensions of society becomes more abstract and universal, akin to Durkheim's notion of the fate of the collective conscience in the transition from mechanical to organic solidarity. As Durkheim states, organic solidarity arises with the extension of the division of labor, requiring a more individualistic, flexible, rational person and "a widening of perspectives" on the social world.[6] Accordingly, the homogeneous collective conscience of mechanical solidarity gradually disappears.

Parsons concurs with Durkheim's analysis. From Parsons's perspective, socialization means learning these universal norms and standards through nurturing the development of rationality. An autonomous individual armed with universalistic principles can flexibly take on many different social roles, and quickly change perspectives as circumstances warrant. Socialization for modernity means learning to be rational and autonomous.

Postmodernism

A major challenge to sociological theories of modernity comes from the theoretical position of postmodernism. Postmodernism denies any meaningful continuities in history. As Habermas states, postmodernism is akin to "the anarchist wish to explode the continuum of history," demolishing theories of modernity in doing so.[7]

Gitlin points out that postmodernism refers to a certain fragmented constellation of styles and tones in cultural works, which are very different from modernist notions of continuity, speaking with a single narrative voice, and addressing one visual center. Postmodern characteristics, demonstrated in contemporary cultural work from MTV videos to rap music, include pastiche, a tone of blankness, a lack of emotional depth, and a sense of cultural exhaustion. The postmodern sensibility involves the ironic refusal to take anything seriously, and the pleasure resulting from the play of surfaces. In the postmodern world there is no search for unity, as postmodern approaches point to the constructedness of any cultural work. There is an emphasis on cultural recombination, for anything can be juxtaposed with anything else. The attitude of detachment best characterizes postmodernism.[8]

This cultural orientation intersects with the literary persuasion of many postmodern theorists, who tend to view social practices through the metaphor of the text. This position foregrounds the importance of language, for all of our social practices are constructed through our interpretations of them. Texts do not in any simple way reflect a pre-existing reality, but only have meaning in relation to other texts. Cultural discourses are increasingly about themselves rather than about any objective real world, as the self-enclosed world of advertisements referring to other advertisements so aptly demonstrates. The idea of a text can mean that there is no closed work of art, for texts are always being revised and extended. This emphasis on texts promotes a view of the world in which there is no final authority or controlling center, and no limit to the questions that may be asked. It frees thought from all constraints.

This push to free thought from boundaries is demonstrated in the postmodern critique of the social sciences. Rationality, in the service of society, has often been used as a means to exclude and distort the cultural and social value of relatively powerless social groups (such as minorities and the colonized). For postmodernists, any attempt at universal knowledge or a theory of historical evolution is illegitimate, as there is no overall meaning to social life that could render coherent historical progress. Rather, social science should investigate, and indeed celebrate, diversity, as different eras and social groups develop distinctive types of knowledges. Thus, history is made up of relatively random happenings, and social science can never penetrate to an essence behind the historical events and discourses that occur. Postmodernists reject the search for laws in history – but they go further and discard the very idea of an inner principle determining outward appearances, whether it be Freud's notion of the unconscious or Marx's idea of class struggle. Any such attempt to find an essence of society or the person is merely a form of social power which imposes a false coherence on the diversity of social life.

Yet this kind of philosophical and cultural postmodernism is only one part of the argument about the shape of modernity. Post-modernists also argue that "there are social transformations . . . that render the 'modernist' conceptual apparatus developed by the classical sociological tradition obsolete."[9] As Jameson argues, postmodernism posits that rationalization and the market have penetrated all arenas of social life, so that these processes cannot be opposed in the same old way. Resistance to capitalism, for example, cannot mean restoring something that is lost, or realizing some sort of future socialist utopia. There are no groups that are now seemingly outside of modernity, or that carry the key to thoroughly reconstructing society (as did Marx's proletariat). As postmodernists believe that all community and history is constructed, they give up ideals of transcendence, narratives about the meaning of history, and the possibility of a fully meaningful life.[10]

As we saw in Chapter 4, Foucault, as an exemplar of the postmodern perspective, argues that social science creates the models of deviance that it then attempts to control. In order to contest these social processes, the very nature of rationality and progress must be critiqued. Post-modernists thus place much importance on the emergence of new social movements as the potential sites of resistance to the imposition of categories and labels on people. Postmodern theorists of the new social movements often blame rationality as the modernist culprit that margin-alizes the discourses of the Other(s). Tied to racism, imperialism, and sexism, a differentiating rationality must be overturned by new types of postmodern knowledge. Further, these approaches to new social move-ments reject the structural differentiation so important to Parsons, as groups such as ACT-UP recreate and recode private relationships in a public forum, thus blurring lines between private and public spheres. Finally, many new social movements often criticize state reforms as an ideological justification of power relations.[11]

In sum, postmodernism refers to many different things. Postmodern-ism to some theorists means that we have entered a new, postindustrial world, which problematizes old assumptions, including ideals of social progress, the importance of class as a source of social identity, and the very idea of a unified self. This leads to the second major postmodern position. A new social world requires new knowledges. Accordingly, postmodernism destabilizes contemporary social theory. It values differ-ence, as there are no absolute values that command our allegiance. Post-modernism critiques all limiting assumptions in social and political life, especially those based on a rationality that seeks to exclude multiple perspectives on the world. It is suspicious of any evolutionary theory and all centralizing and unifying tendencies, whether in politics or in sociological theory, as it sees all knowledge as grounded in power relations. It celebrates a diversity of approaches to social life and decen-tralized social movements.

Though differences between modernity and postmodernity are far from simple, schematically the postmodern critique of modernity can be understood as follows:

1   The modern search for a stable community has been replaced by the postmodern concern with social differences.
2   The Enlightenment belief that rationality leads to a discovery of a timeless, placeless truth, which is not affected by history or social circumstances, is criticized by postmodernists, who celebrate a diversity of truths.
3   Modernists believe that the social and natural worlds can be clearly represented by language. Postmodernists believe that there is no such correspondence between linguistic categories and reality. Language is always metaphorical, it structures our very sense of "reality," and language itself is always changing.
4   Modernists believe in a coherent, stable self, while postmodernists deconstruct this notion of self, which is constantly changing and takes on different shapes according to class, gender, and racial differences, which are continually in flux.

Reconstructing modernity

Giddens and other contemporary sociological theorists such as Habermas and Touraine adopt a much more critical and nuanced view of modernity than does Parsons, while rejecting the most extravagant claims of post-modernism. They are sensitive to the complexity of the classical socio-logical theory of Marx, Weber, and Durkheim, which grasps the costs as well as the benefits of modernity. These authors recognize that modern culture does not simply reflect a modernizing or differentiating economy. Accordingly, they reconstruct the history of modernity, viewing it as an internally complex if not contradictory process, replete with problems and possibilities, that is far from complete. Like Weber, they are especially aware of the problems created by a rationality which destroys meaning. Like the postmodernists, they recognize that a major problem of modern culture has been the destructive potential of a rationality that is not sensitive to social and natural contexts. This anxiety is clearest in their distrust of a "productivist" notion of rationality – a positivist and instru-mental reason that promotes economic growth as an unquestioned social good while eschewing questions of the ends of social life. These theorists contend that such a conception of rationality not only destroys more critical versions of reason that can promote mutual identification and ethical reflection, but also undermines the conditions for self-government, largely by translating social questions into issues of technical, undemo-cratic policy. Such a critical view of the problems of an unchecked instrumental rationality has been developed in the theoretical perspective of Habermas.

Habermas on modernity

Habermas is the strongest defender of the legacy of modernity against the postmodern criticisms of it. Like Weber, Habermas views modernity and rationality as intimately bound to one another. He reformulates Weber's theory of rationalization, giving it a Marxist twist. Instead of the economy encroaching upon everyday life and creating alienation, as Marx argues, Habermas believes that the "system's" instrumental rationality potentially inhibits democratic, rational discourse in everyday life. Like Parsons, Habermas states that a universalistic rationality is a major achievement of modernity, which must integrate an increasingly differentiated and complex modern society. Unlike Parsons, Habermas contends that social integration occurs through the fallible and critical discussion of shared norms, rather than through the straightforward internalization of moral beliefs. He also recognizes the problems of modernity in ways very different from Parsons. Habermas sees in modernity tendencies toward a rampant instrumental rationality that destroys alternative, more democratic visions of social life.

Yet instrumental rationality is only one component of the modern project. *Contra* Weber, Habermas believes that the modern world has opened up the possibility of greater moral and practical insight into personal and social life, rather than simply supplying people with more efficient ways of ordering the world. In this way, Habermas reconstructs Weber's theory of modernity. Though seeing bureaucratization as inevitable, Weber did recognize that modernity is characterized by different types of rationalization processes with their own autonomous principles, as demonstrated in differences between the use of rationality and basic decision rules in modern science and technology, in art, and in law. Habermas views the rise of these different types of reasoning as the key feature of the modern world. Modernity cannot rely on traditional justifications of rule and action: it must ground its criteria for evaluation within its own history, for it cannot look to other eras for the justification of norms, values, and the like. The lack of traditional moorings for social action means that modernity is often experienced as a crisis, for creating normative beliefs out of its own resources poses continual problems. In such a context, the future is often seen in terms of unresolved problems, and people have a sharpened consciousness of missed opportunities and options.[12]

The complexity of modernity is heightened by the processes of differentiation which it opens up. Again drawing on Weber, Habermas argues that by the late eighteenth century in Europe, in the wake of Kant's philosophical revolution, morality, science, and art were distinguished from one another, institutionalized in different spheres, and separated from everyday life. Western modernity became based on a variety of forms of principled reasoning, embodied in the autonomous logics of theoretical (scientific), aesthetic (art), and moral/practical (law) problems and solutions. In each realm experts arise and specialized institutions are created (from art galleries and art criticism to courts and the legal profession), which often contribute to their isolation from one another. As these realms develop, tensions emerge between them. For example, the natural scientific criteria for decision-making can illegitimately spread to areas outside of it (as exemplified in the methodological debates around the viability of the natural science method for the social sciences, discussed in Chapter 2). Yet Weber equated modernity with the progress of instrumental rationality. He saw bureaucracy and formal rationality diminishing possibilities for freedom. According to Habermas, Weber did not grasp Durkheim's insight that modern, universal values and principles open up possibilities for new types of intersubjective agreement. Nor did Weber attend to Mead's argument that modern individuation involves the capacity for imaginative reasoning and varied role-taking.[13]

Habermas contends that Weber's narrow vision of modernity also blinds him to the significance of civil society. The civil society of the modern age represents a novel reality and a type of freedom different from that of the past. It embodies subjective and principled freedom, the cornerstone of modernity. In civil society, subjective freedom means the rational pursuit of self-interest; in politics, the equal right to participate in political decision-making; in the private sphere, ethical autonomy and self-realization. These processes also became complexly differentiated from one another and more difficult to integrate, again increasing the crisis tendencies of modernity. This freedom from tradition is often experienced as alienation from the moral context of life.[14]

For Habermas, despite these problems, the various rationalization processes in these spheres converge on an enhanced ability to think critically about moral life, which he ties to the universality of principled reasoning. In the modern world, different areas of life can be brought under a unifying rational principle, resulting, for example, in the spread of the doctrine of human rights throughout the world. This expansion of principled reasoning is also manifested in the ideas of democracy and political and social equality, which posit people as self-determining agents, capable of freely creating their social world.

According to Habermas, modern social solidarity potentially involves the free attachment to universal principles of justice, freedom, and equality, rather than tradition as the means to bind people to one another. These values inform Habermas's notion of communicative rationality. Communicative rationality dissolves the hegemony of tradition, and allows people to free themselves from unnecessary social, psychological, and natural constraints. As freely participating equals, people engage in a communicative action which allows them to achieve consensus on contentious issues.

In Habermas's view, in the absence of tradition, communicative rationality takes on the ethical role of coordinating diverse social action. It reconstructs the ethical context of life, while countering tendencies to personalize or instrumentalize all life problems. For Habermas, this communicative context informs the acquisition of knowledge, the transmission of culture, the formation of personal identity, and more general processes of social integration. Each of these dimensions has its own autonomous logic, which results in independent learning processes: these are possible because of the built-in idealization of language and its pragmatic capacity for solving problems. Experiences and judgments are formed on the basis of criticizable arguments that transcend local contexts and can be formalized as scientific and cultural knowledge.[15]

Habermas believes that the emergence of communicative action requires a particular socio-cultural context. He emphasizes that constitutional democracies must guarantee rights such as freedom of speech, assembly, and the like, while also stressing the importance of institutions ensuring that people can freely engage in democratic debate. Of central importance for Habermas is the existence of a rich, vibrant public sphere, which allows different voices to be heard in the context of egalitarian communication.

A strong public sphere is particularly necessary because of the new types of legitimation crisis facing contemporary Western societies. For Habermas, because of capitalism's tendency to enter into economic crises, exemplified in the Great Depression of the 1930s, the state has regulated more and more of economic and social life in an attempt to achieve economic stability, from the organization of education to the funding of scientific and technical research. In the modern world, the state must raise revenues to assure economic growth and avoid crisis, but do so legitimately. If the state cannot ensure the necessary support from its citizens to carry out its projects, it suffers a legitimation crisis.

Habermas contends that contemporary Western societies indeed are experiencing legitimation crises, as the many tax revolts in the West demonstrate. Citizens think that the state is responsible for economic growth, but they often distrust its capacity to deliver such growth, while simultaneously believing that they have a right to entitlements guaranteed by the government (from social security to welfare). Thus, the state contributes to its own legitimation crises by attempting to solve social problems through increased intervention. The state often fails in this attempt, as its planning capacities are limited by the power of private corporations. Moreover, state regulation politicizes old ways of life, as contemporary debates around family, schools, culture, etc. demonstrate. As the state regulates more of these realms and they become politicized, people realize that political decisions determine the allocation of resources. As citizens become more skeptical about state programs, they question the validity of cultural traditions from the benefits of social equality to the ideology of achievement through schooling that have underpinned the welfare state. While neo-conservatism, favoring conservative cultural solutions to social problems and a return to the free market, has arisen in this context, so have new social movements, which challenge the old welfare state notions of economic growth and class compromise as social panaceas.[16]

Habermas and social movements

Habermas contends that new social movements provide avenues for the development of new values and identities, as well as novel interpretations of social life, freeing participants from the iron cage of instrumental assumptions. Arising in a post-traditional and postindustrial society, new social movements represent the main vehicle by which a non-instrumental, communicative rationality can be brought into public life. Habermas rejects the working class as such a democratizing agent, looking instead to broad-based, non-productivist movements for the implementation of these goals. He believes that the new social movements associated with late modernity, such as feminism and environmentalism, have fundamentally changed the nature of politics.

For Habermas, social movements can be conceived as "processes through which latently available structures of rationality are transposed into social practice . . . structured by cultural traditions."[17] Contemporary conflicts between social groups are no longer primarily over the distribution of wealth, nor can they be adequately represented by conventional political parties or alleviated by more economic growth. Rather, conflicts are now in the realms of cultural reproduction, social integration, and socialization. Issues such as abortion, women's rights, and gay and lesbian protests bring to the fore issues of lifestyle, sexuality, and family. These protests often occur outside of the government, and demand either recognition of new lifestyles or the protection of threatened ones.

New social movements represent a transition from an old politics, based on issues of economic and military security, to a new politics involving the quality of life, equality, individual self-realization, and enhanced political and social participation. The old politics was defended by entrepreneurs, workers, and the professional middle classes, while the new politics is supported by the new middle class, the young, and groups with higher levels of formal education.

New social movements react to the internal colonization of the lifeworld, the penetration of economic and administrative rationality into everyday life. Groups most removed from the productivist core of the welfare state, such as students, the young, and the elderly, tend to be the most vociferous opponents of this colonization process. The critique of unlimited economic and industrial growth unifies these various groups, differentiating them from socialist and bourgeois movements which called for more production and an expansion of technology.

Habermas distinguishes between groups that wish to defend or extend an already rationalized lifeworld which has a great amount of communicative action (he places left-wing movements such as feminism in this camp) from movements defending traditional lifeworlds that are not rationalized (conservative fundamentalist movements support this position). Given these epistemological concerns about rationality, and viewed from Habermas's perspective of the colonization of the life-world, movements are as much struggling to define their relationship to the emergence of new forms of instrumental and communicative knowledge as they are responding to economic and social changes.[18]

In sum, Habermas contends that modernity establishes inseparable links between rationality and freedom, demonstrated in the great modernist accomplishments such as democracy and universal human rights. New social movements are expressing and attempting to implement these achievements in new ways. Habermas's championing of the legacy of modernity distances him from the postmodernists. His linguistic turn in social theory preserves the theoretical centrality of a critical rationality which can lead to new insights into moral and social life.

Giddens believes that Habermas's approach, while effectively conveying some of the major issues concerning modernity, has limitations. He rejects Habermas's evolutionary view of cultural development. Habermas sees the culture of modernity, embodied in communicative rationality, as concerned with establishing autonomy and justice. Such emancipatory goals are only one side of the culture of modernity, in Giddens's view. Modernity, in the guise of new social movements, also raises issues of life politics, involving lifestyle, sexuality, and cultural distinctiveness. Such questions are not well thematized by Habermas. Giddens contends that, despite Habermas's protestations to the contrary, Habermas shares Parsons's arguments about the internalization of norms, for both posit a relatively smooth fit between the needs of the individual and the requirements of society. In this model, power relations and conflict have little explanatory force. Most significantly, Giddens contends that Habermas's analysis of the colonization of the lifeworld suffers from an insufficiently complex view of the individual and his/her relationship to social power. Habermas gives little credit to people's capacity as skillful agents who can reflexively incorporate expert knowledge into their own lives, rather than being dominated by instrumental rationality.[19]

Giddens, like Touraine and Melucci, theorizes a reformed view of modernity that is much more critical than that of Habermas, without rejecting the legacy of modernity completely, as many postmodernists would have it. Giddens, Touraine, and Melucci believe that much has changed in the contemporary world, and that social science must change accordingly. They argue that new social movements raise novel issues of cultural identity in a global context marked by rapid increases in communication technologies and a recognition of the importance of cultural differences. Any adequate social science must be sensitive to these questions. These themes are taken up in Touraine's reconstruction of the history of modernity. Melucci, much like Touraine, also sees struggles over cultural identity and the control of communications as the key features of modernity. Touraine and Melucci thus grant a central role to new social movements in determining the very shape of the modern world.

Touraine and Melucci

Touraine and Melucci share many Habermasian themes, but develop distinctive approaches to the study of modernity and new social movements. Like Habermas, they see modernity as somewhat bifurcated between an instrumental, systemic reason and more culturally sensitive forms of rationality and social solidarity. They fear that instrumental rationality has the potential to destroy capacities for the creation of meaning among social groups. Accordingly, struggles over cultural identity and communication are the *sine qua non* of new social movements, which can only be effective by influencing the values and debates of public life. Touraine and Melucci reject the Habermasian orientation toward consensus, as they see social life as characterized by continually changing constellations of struggles over cultural resources.

Touraine builds an action-centered theory of society and social movements focused on a culturally oriented agent acting within a social framework marked by conflict and domination. According to Touraine, the two fundamental components of society are "historicity" – "the capacity to produce the [cultural] models by which [society] functions" (or the cultural orientations by which society is organized) – and class relations, "through which these orientations become social practices, still marked by domination."[20] Society and social structure develop as a result of these struggles.

Contemporary societies have entered a postindustrial era, and social movements have become the major innovators in this new type of society. The productivist and evolutionary assumptions of industrial society have been replaced by concerns with systems of communication. Social movements have correspondingly changed. Instead of the predominantly economic orientation of the labor movement, contemporary struggles center around the spread of "technocratic power" into all of social life, and democratic attempts to resist this control and formulate alternative paths of development.[21] Late modern social movements are now sociocultural rather than sociopolitical, reflecting a greater degree of reflexivity than past movements regarding the normative bases of society.

Touraine contends that the rise of this postindustrial society entails a new understanding of the history of Western modernity. He argues that the Enlightenment captured much of the modern project in its attempts to link the person, society, and nature through reason. Ultimately, this process culminated in an instrumental rationality which championed an historical progress that threatened to destroy possibilities of cultural creativity. For Touraine, such creativity is tied to subjectivation, the belief in the unique qualities of individual and cultural identity, the other important dimension of modernity. Subjectivation, first adumbrated in Christian dualism, developed antagonistically yet in tandem with instrumental reason. Touraine views Nietzsche and especially Freud as the major theorists of subjectivation, as they destroyed the illusions of a rational fit between subject and society, while bringing themes of the body, desire, and sexuality to public awareness in their critiques of the limits of rationality.

A critical subject that realizes its distance from social roles and jealously guards its prerogatives has generated the most liberating visions of social life. For Touraine, this subjectivation process, when tied to social movements, is a safeguard against both the standardizing potential of the market and the totalitarian dreams of a fully administered society. He argues that those in the sociological tradition influenced by Durkheim and Parsons who see a fit between society and the individual underestimate the capacity of modern subjectivity for resistance and creativity in opposition to existing social institutions. This modern form of subjectivity is demonstrated in the emphasis on cultural identity that is so important to marginalized groups everywhere inside and outside of the West. Yet a cultural identity shorn of its ties to rationality becomes reactionary. This necessary yet inevitable tension and complementarity between rationalization and subjectivation is the most important dynamic of modernity.

Touraine's reconstruction of modernity complements his analysis of postindustrial society. Touraine ties these themes to his earlier work, in which he argues that industrial society has been surpassed by a post-industrial era characterized by the predominance of mass consumption, mass media, and the circulation of cultural meanings apart from material products (what he calls a "programmed society"). As there is no fit between social structure and individual identity, old sociological concerns with social integration must be jettisoned in favor of his perspective that sees society as a contested field shaped by constant struggles over cultural meanings.[22]

Like Touraine, Melucci argues that contemporary societies are now information-based, as modernity has entered a postindustrial phase and new conflicts around instrumental rationality and cultural identity have surfaced. For Melucci, social life is characterized by chronic conflict, as people form movements and groups based on the possession of social and cultural resources, which are increasingly tied to information. Indeed, with the decline of class identities, production has changed its meaning. It now refers to the creation of culture as well as material objects.[23]

Melucci develops several criteria for understanding the distinctiveness of contemporary information societies. These include the following:

1   People are now very reflexive, which means that much of social life is self-consciously constructed. People create selves with only a minimal relationship to social structures, with few references to taken-for-granted traditions.
2   All activities of social life are influenced by transformations in the realm of information.
3   The globalization of information and capital has fundamentally changed the dynamics of social life and restricted the power of the nation-state.
4   Western societies are post-material societies, in which conflicts over cultural identities replace class struggles over the distribution of material resources.
5   Ethnic-national movements are now arising in opposition to these processes.[24]

This new information society breaks apart local sovereignty and traditions, promoting an increasingly difficult search for personal and social identity, which often conflicts with the instrumental rationality and efficiency demanded by the political and economic systems. The exercise of power is ever-more fragile in information societies, for people interact on similar communicative levels. Governments cannot always shield information from the public. The level of uncertainty and distrust of authority are very high in such societies. Accordingly, the search for a new identity can sometimes result in a return to fundamentalist religions.[25]

New social movements are central to the dynamics of modern information societies. They challenge the language and cultural codes that organize information, in opposition to the dominant society's definition of meanings. Like Habermas, Melucci argues that systemic knowledge is based on instrumental measures of efficiency and effectiveness. New social movements question these measures, evaluating system criteria in terms of standards of moral and social responsibility. They advance issues of cultural identity marginalized by this systemic logic, while raising the possibility of new types of non-instrumental communication as alternative forms of information and identity.

In sum, Melucci and Touraine raise several important issues for a theory of modernity and new social movements. They believe that modern societies are more fluid than those of the past. Modern societies exist in a postindustrial context, and cultural strife between diverse groups has replaced class struggles over the distribution of resources as central social conflicts. Modern societies are in chronic combat over the possession and very definition of cultural codes and information. New social movements are the primary agents and carriers of innovative discourses and practices in the struggles of the late modern era.

Giddens: modernity and new social movements

Giddens shares many themes with Habermas, Touraine, and Melucci regarding modernity and postmodernity. These theorists all critically engage the postmodern persuasion, arguing that modernity has not been superseded but remains an unfinished project, as modernist beliefs and practices are still central to contemporary societies. They believe that rational reflexivity has replaced tradition as the main form of social solidarity in the modern world. Each critiques a productivist rationality, tied to the historical legacy of the welfare state, that inhibits possibilities of democratic discourse and more fulfilling lifestyles, while recognizing new social movements as crucial carriers of such new beliefs and possibilities. Like these authors, Giddens sees fluid identities arising in a post-traditional order.

Giddens differs from Touraine, Melucci, and Habermas, in that he takes tradition more seriously than these other theorists. He ties his rethinking of the role of tradition in modern life to an analysis of the rise of a new, distinctively modern risk society, in which laypeople draw on expertise, re-evaluate it in terms of their own particular cultural context, and then utilize this knowledge to evaluate their everyday actions. These themes coalesce into Giddens's vision of an alternative developmental path for modernity, which he believes requires a new global sense of responsible agency and a rejection of the productivist ethos so central to industrial society.

Giddens and postmodernism

Giddens, more than these other theorists, takes seriously the post-modern criticisms of modernity and incorporates many of their themes into his approach. He grounds his critique in a careful discussion of the culture of modernity, which differs from Habermas's abstract rational ethics and Touraine's vague view of the postmodern impulse as the latest variant of the free-floating principle of subjectivation. Like Foucault, Giddens argues that modernity excludes and marginalizes particular groups of people who do not easily fit into its categories. Giddens agrees with the postmodern claims that the foundations of knowledge are fragile, that there is no inherent progress in history, and that new social movements are raising qualitatively new issues about social life. He believes that personal identity has also become less firm and more fragmented in the modern world, and he thinks that postmodern criticisms of modernist rationality are largely accurate. The "providential," all-powerful Enlightenment rationality of the modern world mirrors the divine Providence of absolutism that the Enlightenment criticized.[26]

Despite these favorable comments, Giddens disagrees with many postmodern tenets. He distinguishes between postmodernism and postmodernity. He states that postmodernism refers to recent changes in architecture, literature, art, and poetry, while postmodernity refers to recent institutional changes in the social world. He finds the latter more important, but he does not believe that postmodernity theoretically captures the meaning of these social changes. For Giddens, postmodernity cannot explain the intricacies of everyday actions, for it tends toward sweeping generalizations about the "disappearance of the subject" that give short shrift to the reflexive capacities of people to actively comprehend, organize, and change their lives. In Giddens's view, the contemporary pervasiveness of reflexivity makes useless the distinctions between modern and postmodern eras. Giddens prefers the idea of late modernity to that of postmodernity. The deconstructive impulse so prevalent in postmodern approaches is the logical extension of the reflexivity of a radicalized modernity, wherein reflexivity is inseparable from the reproduction of social relations. People do not live fragmented, unconnected lives; they still construct narratives about their selves, but they do so in "post-traditional" conditions which make such narratives much more problematic than in the past.[27]

Giddens's theory of late modernity

As we saw in Chapter 4, Giddens argues that early modernity consisted of industrialism, the use of material power and machinery in the production process, which is tied to the rise of capitalism, a system of competitive commodity production and wage labor. Industrialism and capitalism arise in tandem with the nation-state. Each institution, but most significantly the state, promotes a system of surveillance, the supervisory control of populations through bureaucratic means. Nation-states advance the surveillance of their subject populations through the constant reflexive, rational monitoring of their territories, as nations become increasingly distant from traditional forms of legitimacy. Modernity also results in the industrialization of war, with its terrible consequences. Modern wars have been carried out in the name of the nation-state.

For Giddens, late modernity involves many major social changes that distinguishes it from earlier forms of modernity, as it rushes toward the new millennium. The most important dimension of late modernity is the penetration of reflexivity into the reproduction of personal and institutional life, which informs Giddens's theory of reflexive modernization. Reflexivity radicalizes modernity, as traditions are rethought and problematized. In Giddens's theory of late modernity, reflexivity is inseparable from the texture of social relations. Social practices are constantly reformed in light of new information about these practices. Modernity's dynamism, its rapid pace and scope of change, is bound up with this reflexivity, as well as with the separation and recombination of time and space in social life. Social scientists, influenced by the heritage of classical sociological theory, have not sufficiently grasped the novel nature of these processes.[28]

Modernity separates time and space through new means of communication and transportation, recombining them in historically original ways. This time-space distanciation allows new connections between the global and the local to develop, and abstracts social relations from their ties to specific contexts. Social relations are constantly in flux; institutions are disembedded from their particular social circumstances. Such disembedding refers to the "'lifting out' of social relations from local contexts and their rearticulation across indefinite tracts of time-space." Abstract systems, such as monetary exchange and expertise, play a central role in this disembedding process, as they circulate independently of their practitioners and clients.[29]

The disembedding of social practices is tied to the contemporary interdependence of almost all cultures. Giddens argues that globalization is a major aspect of modern transformation, as modernity extends throughout the world. Globalization results in local actions being influenced by distant institutions and events, and the concomitant transformation of the local and personal contexts of social experience. Globalization is linked to the emergence of a post-traditional social order, in which traditions become more open to interrogation and change. The welfare state has been unable to meet the challenges posed by these social changes, as it responds to issues concerning production and the distribution of income rather than the new concerns about globalization and cultural identity that fuel the life politics of the new social movements, which will be discussed in more detail below. Lifestyle issues become dominant in the late modern era, as they respond to these cultural questions and "give material form to a particular narrative of self-identity."[30]

Despite continual change, individuals still attempt to maintain stable identities, and the creation of trust and the control of time become recurrent problems. As the future is severed from the past, the future must be directed or, in Giddens's term, "colonized."[31] The reflexivity of modernity makes this task difficult, as the social world and the self can be chronically revised as new information becomes available, and criteria external to modern institutions, such as tradition, are increasingly irrelevant in the formation of identity. Modernity creates "an internally referential system of knowledge and power," self-enclosed ways of understanding and acting that rely on their own histories for legitimacy, rather than on tradition or an adjustment to nature.[32]

The rapid pace and scope of change also means that expert, abstract systems and forms of knowledge become more dominant in everyday life. Reliance on these expert systems contributes to a kind of moral crisis in the modern world. In a manner reminiscent of Foucault, Giddens argues that although people reflexively utilize abstract knowledge in their everyday life, expert systems tend to sequester experience. These systems, often through expanding surveillance capacities, routinize everyday life by institutionally confining madness, sickness, criminality, and death, and separating the moral issues surrounding them from daily activities. Sequestration contributes to the meaninglessness that many people feel in contemporary societies, as individuals are denied contact with and answers to fundamental existential and moral questions.[33] Yet moral questions can never be completely expunged from everyday life. Ethical issues impinge on life during fateful moments of individual decision and action, such as marriage and illness.

Reflexive modernization and the rise of the risk society

In *Reflexive Modernization* (1994), written with Ulrich Beck and Scott Lash, Giddens further develops his theory of late modernity. These theorists define reflexive modernization as the increasing capacity of self-conscious individuals and groups to critically apply knowledge to themselves and their societies. As specialized knowledges become widely available in public life, people free themselves from social structures to define their own lifestyles and identities. This spread of rationality also creates new conflicts, risks, and problems of legitimacy, exemplified in modern risk societies.

Industrialization and the growth of science characteristic of modernity have ironically created a new sort of risk society. Science and industry ostensibly were to result in the advance of human control of nature and society. Indeed, human knowledge has penetrated the social and natural worlds, but people are not masters of their destiny. The awareness and calculation of risk is now a part of contemporary social life. Knowledge and modern expertise have not led to a greater control of social life, but instead resemble a spiral of ever new problems. Giddens argues that the reflexivity of modernity creates "circumstances of uncertainty and multiple choices."[34]

In Giddens's vocabulary, late modern social processes involving the double hermeneutic have resulted in a continual "displacement and reappropriation of expertise," which creates uncertainty and doubt in a world of multiple authorities.[35] Giddens believes that we live in an age of "manufactured uncertainty," not in the sense that our lives have become less predictable, but that the "origins of unpredictability have changed." More and more of our problems, from global warming to the possibility of nuclear war, are the products of human knowledge and practice, rather than the result of natural processes.[36] Modern peoples now recognize that science and technology are double-edged, providing benefits but also unexpected costs. The growth of science and technology encourages increasingly specialized expertise, which develops its own particular, internally referential ways of grasping and explaining the social and natural worlds. The problems created by science and technology can then only be solved by more expertise, whose unintended consequences create new types of manufactured uncertainty and contribute to the sense that modernity is out of control. The continual ecological crises spawned by technological development and economic growth are good examples of these problems. Giddens states that "modernity is inherently prone to crisis, on many levels," from self-identity to the potential of global catastrophe.[37]

Moreover, we now live in a risk culture because modern peoples utilize the concept of risk when organizing and acting in their lives. Risk has become diffused from experts to everyday life. As Giddens states, what is distinctively modern is not the existence of expertise in itself, but "the accessibility of expert skills and information to lay actors."[38] Many different futures can be created reflexively. However, the assessment of risk is difficult given the conflicting beliefs of experts. All of our activities are open to change and contingency, and no aspect of our lives is predetermined. We use calculations of risk in attempts to stabilize possible outcomes of our actions.

Tradition and reflexivity

Appeals to a nature outside of society no longer make sense, as new technologies create an artificial world where the natural and the social become indistinguishable.[39] In such a "post-traditional" order, self-identity becomes more fluid, problematic, and subject to democratic and rational discourse. In this context, the status of tradition changes, as the bases of legitimacy change with the coming of modernity.

Giddens believes that traditions are still important and must be taken seriously. Historically, tradition legitimized social power relations. Giddens argues that traditions have a binding emotional and moral force, for they are tied to memory and ritual. Tradition's truths are enforced by expert guardians and gatekeepers, such as religious figures. Tradition is tied to a "formulaic notion of truth," which links it to the sacred.[40] This notion of truth "renders central aspects of tradition 'untouchable,' and confers integrity upon the present in relation to the past."[41] Tradition is linked to repetition, and is most effective when it is not fully understood. It intersects with the psychology of compulsion, of which Weber's discussion of the driven and absurdly rationalistic character of Puritanical ascetic capitalism remains a splendid example.[42] However, the decline of traditions in late modernity results in the rise of a new form of pathology, that of addiction, ranging from drug abuse to eating disorders. Addictions arise as ritual loses its meaning and becomes empty. As an information society grows, traditions are rethought, pluralized, and problematized. In a post-traditional order, traditions must be "discursively articulated and defended," as they are competing with other discourses in a pluralistic environment. A tradition that is not defended rationally hardens into fundamentalism.[43] Fundamentalism is profoundly anti-democratic, and its rationales crumble when confronted with rational reasons that challenge its justification. Only when rational discourse prevails can power become "translated into authority."[44]

In the late modern context, traditions lose their taken-for-granted status. That they must be rationally defended furthers the crisis of industrial society, which extends to its very bases of legitimacy. Social reflexivity expands, creating a gulf between knowledge and social control. This situation leads to a greater sense of social and personal risk, and to more emphasis on bottom-up decision-making and flexible production.

New social movements

Giddens, like Touraine, Melucci, and Habermas, believes that the new social movements, such as gay/lesbian movements, the women's movement, and ecological movements, offer the best means of institutionalizing "bottom-up decision-making" and democratizing the modern world. In response to the problems of modernity, the new social movements place moral questions at the center of social life. Giddens emphasizes the importance of life politics, a politics of cultural identity and self-actualization, in new social movements, which concretely demonstrates the rethinking of tradition and expertise in the political and social life of late modernity.

Giddens sees a link between a more reflexive approach to emotional life, the rise of self-help groups, and more democratic societies. He argues that mainstream leftist programs advocating the redistribution of wealth will not eliminate poverty, and that governments should be oriented toward a life politics enhancing the "reflexivity of the individuals or groups they address."[45] In this uncertain world, Giddens, like Melucci, believes that the site of the reproduction of the dominant logic of societies is constantly changing, which also makes it much easier for conflicts to take on system-wide dimensions. The globalization of economies has weakened the nation-state and particularly the Western-style welfare state. For Giddens, life politics to some degree encourages this weakening of the welfare state, as it develops within new mini-public spheres which politicize gender and ecological issues, challenge experts, and create new risks and problems for the generation of trust.

Giddens believes that truly innovative social movements must offer the "utopian" possibility of changing the fabric and texture of human relationships. Overcoming inequality is not liberation; such an emancipatory politics must be linked with life politics.[46] For Giddens, emancipatory politics means eliminating the unnecessary constraints which limit the life-chances of particular groups. Power is hierarchical in this conception of politics, as social movements such as the labor movement attempt to eliminate economic and social oppression, and exploitation in the name of equality, justice, and participation. Autonomy is the major principle underlying emancipatory politics, which has as its goal a society where individuals are capable of free and independent actions.[47]

Emancipatory politics is still important, but it has been supplanted in some fundamental ways by life politics. Life politics assumes a certain level of emancipation from traditional hierarchies and the fixities of tradition. It is "a politics of choice"; whereas emancipatory politics is a politics of life-chances, life politics concerns the creation and implementation of lifestyles. Emerging in late modernity, life politics is "a politics of self-actualisation in a reflexively ordered environment."[48] Its main thrust involves the creation of a narrative of personal identity in a more reflexive world.

Life politics allows the "return of the repressed," as the sequestered moral and existential issues relating to sexuality, health, deviance, and the like become part of public discourse. New social movements bring these issues to the fore and remoralize social life, as reflexivity extends to more and more areas of society. As reflexivity expands, so do political conflicts. The rights of personhood, from the rights of the individual over his/her body to animal rights, become predominant, as life politics brings to public consciousness "the existential dimensions of self-identity as such."[49]

Emancipatory politics will not end with the rise of life politics. Life politics involves emancipatory issues, such as equal rights for women. Emancipatory and life politics can be joined in the sense that "struggles to emancipate oppressed groups can help liberate others by promoting attitudes of mutual tolerance which in the end could benefit everyone."[50]

Giddens contends that certain social and psychological consequences flow from life politics, which can help rescue modernity from self-destruction. The emphasis on economic growth so characteristic of the modern era has dire psychological consequences. For Giddens, industrialization has falsely equated happiness with the creation of wealth. He designates the dominant ethos of the West "productivism," where the primacy of industry creates a social world in which work defines life. Grounded in Weber's theory of the emotionally repressive aspects of the Protestant ethic and "this-worldly asceticism," productivism marginalized other traditions and ways of life as the West developed. In Giddens's words, "Following Weber, productivism can be seen as the ethos in which 'work,' as paid employment, has been separated out in a clear-cut way from other domains of life."[51] Labor, performed by males, meant that child-care, emotion-work, and the like became the domain of women in the family, and was rendered invisible in public discourse. Productivism defines a social system in which "mechanisms of economic development substitute for personal growth."[52]

Giddens rejects this version of the productivist ethic, and advocates a society which places more worth on emotional fulfillment rather than on maximizing economic growth. He distinguishes productivity, or the return generated by the investment of time, from the obsessive attempt to increase production for its own sake. Giddens contends that a productive individual can be a more autonomous individual, who can effectively integrate emotional and material well-being. Social and economic policies should accordingly be oriented toward strengthening individual autonomy, but always in a way that is sensitive to social context and that builds new traditions and protects old ones, while fostering the everyday allegiances of people to one another.[53]

Giddens, *contra* postmodernism, believes that for the first time in history emotionally healthy people can share universal, cosmopolitan values, such as the sanctity of human life, the preservation of different species, and a care for future as well as present generations. People can develop a sense of responsible agency, recognizing that they live in a risky world with no guarantees that social and ecological problems can be solved. New social movements as agents of change are central in realizing these goals.

This new agency involves a new vision of modern social development that is not tied to productivism. Giddens's "alternative development," while encouraging reflexive engagement with the problems of late modernity, would strive to protect endangered groups from destruction. This vision of development would improve the social position of women, protect the family as a resource, stress autonomous, preventative health care, and emphasize self-reliance, integrity, responsibilities, and rights. It would distinguish between two different sources of ecological destruction: the wasteful consumption of developed countries and the destruction of self-sustaining production among poorer communities. The ethos of productivism would have to be rejected, and the costs of economic growth taken into account in any economic development plan.[54]

Giddens sees the possibility of alternative paths of development as tied to the rise of life politics, which extends the reflexive project of the self and the contradictory character of modernity's "internally referential systems."[55] These factors make choosing one's lifestyle a difficult and complex process, while also complicating the possibility of social harmony in the wake of proliferating differences and points of view. Giddens agrees with many of the themes raised by theorists of late modernity and new social movements, including Habermas, Touraine, and Melucci. He shares with them a sense of the importance of globalization and the decline of the nation-state, and the centrality of new social movements in developing novel paths of social change. Giddens sees these trends promoting the detraditionalization of modern societies. As in Habermas's theory of legitimation crisis, Giddens views the reflexivity of late modernity as breaking apart taken-for-granted traditions, and creating new and chronic problems of justification for authority, which must be established in dialogic fashion in a public sphere.

But Giddens also differs in many respects from these theorists of new social movements. He places much more emphasis than they do on the knowledgeability of people in reproducing social structures, and their reflexive ability to transform their lives, even in the face of dominant systems of expertise. Expert discourses can be reinterpreted in the context of people's everyday life. For example, Giddens argues that self-help beliefs transform notions of intimacy, creating the egalitarian conditions for the exercise of democracy. Here Giddens also departs from Habermas, Touraine, and Melucci, for he stresses the emotional prerequisites for a rich, dialogic democracy, in addition to its institutional and rational dimensions. These themes will be more fully developed in Chapter 6.

However, Giddens's theory of modernity leaves some important questions unanswered. Giddens does not tie his theory of modernity and reflexivity to any particular cultural traditions. Because of this inattention to cultural continuity, he does not answer the question of whether or not there are distinctive cultural beliefs and patterns which contribute to the making of modernity. Giddens clearly wishes to avoid the Western ethnocentrism that has characterized so many sociological theories of societal development, such as Parsonian modernization theory. Accordingly, he does not explicitly confront the issue of the extent to which there are different paths to modernity in different cultures. Yet Giddens realizes that there is a distinctive culture of modernity, though it is defined more by what it replaces (tradition or religion, for example), or by rather vague references to reflexivity, than by any strong, positive exploration of its characteristic cultural qualities. Giddens thus arrives at a position almost similar to the early Durkheimian discussion of organic solidarity, as he gives the impression that strong cultural patterns disintegrate in the whirlwind of an ever-expanding modernity. As Giddens does not address the extent to which the reflexivity of late modernity may be informed by particular cultural traditions and systems of beliefs, he sidesteps criticisms of potential links between reflexivity, Western culture, and the imperialistic rationality that postmodernists see at the heart of Western modernity.

Giddens does not fully address these issues in part because he has no thoroughly developed theory of culture. As I have argued in previous chapters, he posits a kind of "Promethean subject" who is not embedded in a strong cultural milieu but is separated from social life and encounters a strange, ever-changing world and an unpredictable future. To the extent that Giddens deals with issues of cultural change, he looks to new social movements and life politics as agents of such change. However, he does not sufficiently theoretically ground how and why a new politics might emerge, as he has no "strong, socially grounded normative theory of interacting subjects."[56] Nor does Giddens address the differentiation of cultural systems so important to Weber, Parsons, and Habermas. This lack of theoretical complexity on Giddens's part contributes to his impoverished notion of culture and cultural conflict.

While Giddens lacks a strong theory of culture, he does address issues of democracy, as the new social movements and life politics are very concerned with the fate of public life in the late modern world. New social movements emerge in spaces outside the realm of the state and established political parties, advocating a richer and more participatory form of democracy. Life politics rejects a narrow, state-centered view of politics in favor of a broader notion of settling conflicts and/or values outside the state realm, promising new types of democracy which relate the personal to the political in different ways. Such considerations of the nature and fate of public life in late modernity are considered in the next chapter.

Notes

1 On new social movements and modern social conditions, see Carl Boggs, *Social Movements and Political Power: Emerging Forms of Radicalism in the West* (Philadelphia, Temple University Press, 1986).

2 Axel van den Berg, "Liberalism Without Reason?," *Contemporary Sociology* 25 (January 1996), p. 19.

3 See Weber's famous distinction between science and politics as respective vocations, in "Science as a Vocation" and "Politics as a Vocation," in *From Max Weber: Essays in Sociology*, ed. H.H. Gerth and C.W. Mills (New York, Oxford University Press, 1958).

4 Max Weber, "Religious Rejections of the World and Their Directions," ibid., pp. 267–301.

5 Talcott Parsons, "Integration and Institutionalization in the Social System," in *Talcott Parsons on Institutions and Social Evolution*, ed. Leon Mayhew (Chicago, University of Chicago Press, 1982), pp. 117–128.

6 Emile Durkheim, *Professional Ethics and Civic Morals* (New York, Routledge, 1992), p. 38.

7 Jürgen Habermas, *The Philosophical Discourse of Modernity: Twelve Lectures* (Cambridge, MA, MIT Press, 1987), p. 182.

8 Todd Gitlin, "Postmodernism: Roots and Politics," *Dissent* (Winter, 1989).

9 van den Berg, "Liberalism Without Reason," p. 19.

10 Martin Jay, "Postmodern Fascism? Reflections on the Return of the Oppressed", *Tikkun* 8 (November/December 1993), p. 41; see also Fredric Jameson, *Postmodernism, or the Cultural Logic of Late Capitalism* (Durham, NC, Duke University Press, 1991).

11 For a good overview, see Steven Seidman, *Contested Knowledge: Social Theory in the Postmodern Era* (Cambridge, MA, Basil Blackwell, 1994). See also Charles Lemert, *Postmodernism is not What You Think* (Oxford, Blackwell, 1997), pp. 108–110.

12 Habermas, *The Philosophical Discourse of Modernity*, p. 58.

13 Ibid., pp. 1–3, 20; Habermas, *The Theory of Communicative Action, Vol. 2, Lifeworld and System: A Critique of Functionalist Reason* (Boston, Beacon Press, 1987), pp. 160–166.

14 Habermas, *The Philosophical Discourse of Modernity*, pp. 31, 83.

15 Ibid., pp. 205, 316.

16 Jürgen Habermas, *Legitimation Crisis* (Boston, Beacon Press, 1975); see also Thomas McCarthy, *The Critical Theory of Jürgen Habermas* (Cambridge, MA, MIT Press, 1978), pp. 363–370.

17 Jürgen Habermas, *Communication and the Evolution of Society* (Boston, Beacon Press, 1979), p. 125.

18 Habermas, *Theory of Communicative Action, Vol. 2*, pp. 391–396.

19 Anthony Giddens, "Labour and Interaction," in *Habermas: Critical Debates*, ed. John B. Thompson and David Held (Cambridge, MA, MIT Press, 1982), pp. 160–161.

20 Alain Touraine, *The Voice and the Eye: An Analysis of Social Movements* (New York, Cambridge University Press, 1981), p. 25.

21 Alain Touraine, Zsuzsa Hegedus, François Dubet, and Michel Wieviorka, *Anti-Nuclear Protests: The Opposition to Nuclear Energy in France* (New York, Cambridge University Press, 1983), p. 120.

22 See Alain Touraine, *Critique of Modernity* (Cambridge, MA, 1995); and Kenneth H. Tucker, Jr., Review of Ulrich Beck, Anthony Giddens, and Scott Lash, *Reflexive Modernization: Politics, Tradition and Aesthetics in the Modern Social Order* and Alain Touraine, *Critique of Modernity*, in *Contemporary Sociology* 25 (January 1996), p. 12.

23 Alberto Melucci, "A Strange Kind of Newness: What's 'New' in New Social Movements," in *New Social Movements: From Ideology to Identity*, ed. Enrique Larana, Hank Johnston, and Joseph R. Gusfield (Philadelphia, Temple University Press, 1994), pp. 102–104. See also Melucci's book, *Nomads of the Present* (Philadelphia, Temple University Press, 1989).

24 Melucci, "A Strange Kind of Newness," pp. 110–111.

25 Ibid., pp. 112–114.

26 Anthony Giddens, *The Consequences of Modernity* (Stanford, Stanford University Press, 1990), pp. 45–46; Giddens, *Modernity and Self-Identity: Self and Society in the Late Modern Age* (Stanford, Stanford University Press, 1991), p. 6.

27 Anthony Giddens, "Risk, Trust, Reflexivity," in Ulrich Beck, Anthony Giddens, and Scott Lash, *Reflexive Modernization: Politics, Tradition and Aesthetics in the Modern Social Order* (Stanford, Stanford University Press, 1994), p. 197.

28 Giddens, "Living in a Post-Traditional Society", ibid., p. 57; *The Consequences of Modernity*, pp. 38–39.

29 Giddens, *Modernity and Self-Identity*, p. 18; *The Consequences of Modernity*, p. 139.

30 Giddens, *Modernity and Self-Identity*, p. 81.

31 Ibid., p. 111.

32 Ibid., pp. 144–145.

33 Ibid., pp. 9, 156.

34 Ibid., p. 3; see also Beck et al., "Preface," in *Reflexive Modernization*, p. vii.

35 Giddens, "Living in a Post-Traditional Society," pp. 60, 86–87.

36 Giddens, "Risk, Trust, Reflexivity," pp. 184–185.

37 Giddens, *Modernity and Self-Identity*, p. 184.

38 Ibid., p. 30.

39 Anthony Giddens, *Beyond Left and Right: The Future of Radical Politics* (Stanford, Stanford University Press, 1994), pp. 210–211.

40 Giddens, "Living in a Post-Traditional Society," p. 63.

41 Ibid., p. 104.

42 Ibid., pp. 66–67, 71.

43 Ibid., p. 100.

44 Ibid., p. 106.

45 Giddens, "Risk, Trust, Reflexivity," p. 196.

46 Giddens, *The Consequences of Modernity*, p. 156; italics in the original.

47 Giddens, *Modernity and Self-Identity*, pp. 210–214.

48 Ibid., p. 214.

49 Ibid., p. 226.

50 Ibid., pp. 230–231.

51 Giddens, *Beyond Left and Right*, p. 175.

52 Ibid., p. 247.

53 Ibid., pp. 178–180, 185; see also Anthony Giddens, *The Transformation of Intimacy: Sexuality, Love and Eroticism in Modern Societies* (Stanford, Stanford University Press, 1992), p. 3.

54 Giddens, *Beyond Left and Right*, pp. 159–163.

55 Giddens, *Modernity and Self-Identity*, p. 231.

56 Kenneth H. Tucker, Jr., "Aesthetics, Play, and Cultural Memory: Giddens and Habermas on the Postmodern Challenge," *Sociological Theory* 11 (July 1993), p. 197.

6

THE PROBLEMS AND POSSIBILITIES OF A DEMOCRATIC PUBLIC LIFE IN LATE MODERN SOCIETIES

While the new social movements discussed in Chapter 5 provide important vehicles of personal and social identity formation, they also serve a significant democratic function. New social movements can potentially revitalize a stagnant democracy by bringing new issues into public life. Indeed, the question of democracy now occupies a major place on the theoretical table. In the wake of the fall of communism in Europe, issues pertaining to democracy, civil society, and public discourse have become prominent in public and academic debate, from the ideological ferment in Eastern Europe to the sociological accounts of Giddens and other major theorists, such as Habermas and Bellah.

Democracy is often analyzed concurrently with capitalism, though the homology of democracy and capitalism is far from clear or accepted.[1] For example, in the context of the post-communist regimes of Eastern Europe, critics of the coupling of democracy and capitalism point out that the formation of a market economy, a democratic government, and a viable civil society follow very different logics. Many prominent East European dissidents single out the Western democratic tradition for praise, while criticizing the capitalist economy.

Thus, Václav Havel, the former Czech dissident and president of the post-communist Czech republic, critiqued the cold, gray bureaucracy of East European communism, which stifled individual creativity and self-expression and imposed its ideology on the people. While Havel advocates "living with the truth," or living with dignity and authenticity in opposition to the conformity of communism, he believes that such an authentic existence requires a public sphere where a non-conformist culture could emerge, a kind of parallel polis to that of the official communist government. As a realm which is potentially open to all and encourages the forging of common connections between people, this can be a truly democratic realm of interaction. Havel contends that the overcoming of communism means a broadening of democracy, where people become "proud and responsible members of the polis, making a genuine contribution to the creation of its destiny."[2] Like ex-Soviet dissident Alexander Solzhenitsyn, Havel believes that the unbridled consumerism associated with capitalism, as well as communism, poses a threat to true democracy.

The requirements for the maintenance of a vibrant democracy have also become a popular topic of discussion in the West. In the US as throughout Western Europe, many commentators contend that a veritable crisis of democracy is at hand, demonstrated in a range of factors from falling voting rates in elections to the seeming incivility of public life. A diversity of approaches to this democratic distemper have appeared, from the communitarian movement in the US to neo-conservative, market-based approaches throughout the West.

This new social context has prompted many sociological theorists, from Giddens to Habermas, to formulate complex theories on the problems of contemporary democracy. While differing in many ways, they all concur that the study and practice of democracy must move beyond its formal, representative parliamentary institutions. Giddens's approach accents democracy's extra-parliamentary and reflexive dimensions. He sees a vibrant political democracy as requiring an emotionally aware, sensitive citizenry. Giddens disagrees with many commentators, such as Lasch, Sennett, and Bellah, who see democracy threatened by a narcissistic concern with self-identity, self-fulfillment, and other private pursuits. He also disagrees with the Marxist tradition, represented in different ways by Lasch and Habermas, which views the possibilities for a democratic public life as being undermined by capitalism and/or "systemic" forces. This chapter outlines these various approaches to the problems and prospects of democratic public life. It discusses the theories of Tocqueville, Horkheimer and Adorno, and Arendt, three classical approaches that converge on the problem of the "decline of public life" in the West, though from different perspectives. Before turning to these classical theorists, a brief prolegomenon to the historical emergence of democracy and individualism will be presented.

The emergence of public and private spheres in the West

As we saw in Chapter 4, Giddens ties the growth of democracy to institutional changes in the West, from the rise of the nation-state to the emergence of capitalism. These changes also involved new conceptions of individualism and self-identity. In the wake of the European Renaissance, a new sense of the self emerged. Fixed, inherited social roles broke down, urban life gradually developed, and social mobility slowly became possible for non-aristocratic people. These changes were tied to a new understanding of individual agency, i.e. that one's actions could influence one's fate. Such a self-conception was intimately linked to the new institutional features of capitalism and democracy.

This new sense of self-autonomy was dependent on important institutional changes in the West. As Marx argues, the rise of capitalism resulted in the formation of new prominent social classes, the bourgeoisie and the proletariat. These classes formed "emancipatory" social movements, in Giddens's sense, which strove for equality and democracy, and the fruits of these movements were expressed most dramatically in the democratic revolutions in Europe and America in the eighteenth and nineteenth centuries. As democracy arose as a political system, public life became increasingly defined as an arena where decisions of common public interest could be discussed and debated by equals; Habermas labels this the public sphere. Alongside this public realm a new private sphere developed, centered in the family. In the private sphere, one could be an authentic, emotional, and sincere self, in opposition to the artificial role-playing that necessarily characterized the public self. This new sense of self was tied to the rise of the market as well as to democracy, for more people worked outside of the home in new occupations no longer linked to agriculture. This occupational change helped promote the idea that one engages in very different behaviors and roles outside of the home than inside it.[3]

This new constellation of public and private life created novel problems of political rule and self development in democratic societies. The public and private spheres coexisted uneasily, as tensions between them threatened to collapse one into the other. Never before had so many people been given the opportunity to govern themselves while having the possibility of changing their economic status; and this new political system, based on equality, emerged simultaneously with the inequalities generated by a capitalist economy and the creation of unprecedented wealth in the nineteenth century. Many authors believe that social inequalities, compounded by the pursuit of wealth and an over-emphasis on private life, contradict the major tenets of democracy and inhibit capacities for self-government. It is this conflict between individual self-fulfillment, a capitalist culture of consumption, social mobility, and wealth, on the one hand, and the requirements of a democratic political system, on the other, that concerns many prominent twentieth-century social critics. They argue that as the pleasures of private life become more important to people in the West, nations' capacities for self-government erode and democracies become fragile, weak, and governed by moneyed interests who promulgate their messages and encourage consumerism through the mass media. In the critics' view, this consumerist culture has metamorphosed into a new culture of narcissism informed by the "triumph of the therapeutic," in Philip Rieff's terms, which prizes a search for self-fulfillment over the cultivation of the capacities of self-restraint and concern for the common good necessary for practicing democracy responsibly.[4] Such issues were first broached in the thought of Tocqueville.

Tocqueville

Many of the contemporary critiques of public life in the West draw either consciously or indirectly on the thought of Alexis de Tocqueville. In his two-volume work *Democracy in America*, written in the 1830s, Tocqueville develops an appreciation of the potentialities of democracy in the US and a critique of the dangerous social and cultural factors that are also bound up with its development. He is among the first to criticize the thirst for money and wealth and the mediocrity of the arts that a democracy produces, which weaken participation in public life while simultaneously encouraging a culture of individualism and privatism.

Tocqueville contends that nineteenth-century European and American societies were undergoing a great transformation, as an aristocratic social condition gave way to a democratic one. Tocqueville does not mean only that democratic political institutions were replacing kingdoms. Rather, he argues that the change in social conditions entails a new culture and new ways of understanding and evaluating the world. In Tocqueville's view, aristocracies based on monarchy, inherited hierarchies, and traditional legitimations of social life, were gradually being replaced by an anti-traditional, materialistic, fluid democratic culture, whose overriding value was equality. While generally favoring this trend, Tocqueville does not believe that the rise of a democratic social condition necessarily results in a gain in freedom.

Tocqueville argues that democracies can only thrive, and indeed survive, if people participate in government and identify with their representative institutions. While Tocqueville feels that a democratic government requires the separation of political powers into executive, legislative, and judicial branches and guarantees of the rights of those with minority opinions, he also develops a theory of democratic liberty. He writes in the tradition of civic virtue, a theory of republican government which decreed that a vibrant democracy obliges a strong measure of public-spiritedness on the part of its citizens. Tocqueville believes that democracy demands that people be able to act together to make good laws and realize that their self-interest is inseparable from the communal interest. Such a concern for the common good has to be cultivated and constantly renewed in each generation, for democracy requires sacrifices on the part of the people. He contends that democracy calls for more than just representative institutions; it also involves concomitant changes in "the laws, ideas, customs, and morals" of a people if it is to be effective.[5]

Tocqueville believes that a thriving democracy demands that political life be infused in all aspects of the country, in order to make citizens "constantly feel their mutual interdependence."[6] He thinks that decentralized town governments, as in nineteenth-century New England, offer the best context for the realization of participatory democracy. Participating in the public world of the township forces people to consider more than their own interest. In Tocqueville's words, "Local freedom . . . perpetually brings men together and forces them to help one another in spite of the propensities that sever them."[7] Participation in local government gives people the crucial, irreplaceable experience of democratic life. In order to govern effectively, people must learn to work together.

Tocqueville fears that a type of democratic despotism can arise if citizen participation withers and local sources of opposition to the centralization of power erode. This democratic despotism does not have to rely on direct coercion and terror, for it involves the silencing of minority viewpoints in the face of the overwhelming force of popular opinion: what Tocqueville famously labels the tyranny of the majority. Tocqueville is also concerned that governmental centralization of power will work to deprive local communities of their rights and political efficacy, weakening citizen participation in the process. But for our purposes, Tocqueville's discussion of the problematic culture associated with democracies is most appropriate, for it echoes through much contemporary criticism of mass culture and the "culture of narcissism."

Tocqueville states that democratic despotism creates a depoliticized political culture. By centralizing power in the federal government, despotism promotes a passive and atomized citizenry who have no ties to one another. In such a context, people feel no attachment to the public good, and indeed selfishness and "general indifference" become "public virtues."[8] Despotism is possible when people are obsessed with their private lives, especially the desire for personal wealth, and care little about collective life.

When people are relatively equal yet no longer tied to one another, and tradition loses its force as an overriding cultural belief system, the pursuit of money and riches becomes more prominent. Tocqueville argues that the incessant striving for wealth is characteristic of the US, for nothing else holds Americans together. Money is something that everyone in a democracy wants to have. It is a means of distinction, yet it is a very transient one. This concern with money and social mobility gives Americans a particularly melancholy and restless character. As Tocqueville states, the American "clutches everything, he holds nothing fast, but soon loosens his grasp to pursue fresh gratifications."[9] Such a man in pursuit of wealth "is always in a hurry, for he has but a limited time at his disposal to reach, to grasp, and to enjoy it."[10]

This restless pursuit of wealth promotes a culture of individualism, rather than one of public participation in the common interest. There is little concern for past or future generations. Tocqueville feels that democracies encourage egoism, "a passionate and exaggerated love of self, which leads a man to connect everything with himself and to prefer himself to everything in the world."[11] Yet more insidious than egoism for a democracy is individualism. While egoism "originates in blind instinct," individualism "is a mature and calm feeling." Each person comes to believe that friends and family are the most important parts of his/her life, and that the public realm is at most a hindrance to the achievement of happiness in his/her private world. For Tocqueville, individualism saps the virtues necessary for participation in public life, and threatens to devolve into egoism. Individualism is the concomitant of equality, for it requires circumstances where people feel little attachment to one another and to their ancestors, but feel very strongly their own interest.

The culture of democracy and the market has other effects, especially on the arts. Tocqueville believes that democracies tend to promote mediocre works of art and handicrafts. He contrasted the position of the artist and artisan in an aristocracy and a democracy. In an aristocracy, the arts are a privileged sphere, where the artisan has a reputation to preserve. Guild ties ensure that the artisan "is not exclusively swayed by his own interest or even by that of his customer, but by that of the body to which he belongs." In such a context, speed of production is subordinated to "the best possible workmanship."[12] In a democracy, this social tie is destroyed, and for the artisan "the will of the customer is then his only limit."[13] But the customer also changes as well, as artisans and artists produce for an anonymous and expanded market rather than for a particular patron.

In effect, Tocqueville is arguing that the market promotes mass production. For Tocqueville, as people desire more products and works of art, the artisan and artist attempt to supply them, which induces them "to produce with great rapidity many imperfect commodities, and the consumer to content himself with these commodities."[14] Such quickly produced works of art and handicraft are often unchallenging and mediocre. As quality declines, people are more attracted to art and crafts for their novelty and shock value. Democratic arts also encourage a society of images, in that artisans attempt to give their objects "attractive qualities which they do not in reality possess." This social mirage is but a particular instance of an unstable democratic society obsessed with social mobility. As Tocqueville states, "In the confusion of all ranks everyone hopes to appear what he is not, and makes great exertions to succeed in this object."[15] Tocqueville's discussion of the tendency of the democratic arts to favor shock, novelty, and sensationalism over substance and continuity foreshadows many contemporary critiques of the mass media.

Tocqueville's criticisms of American democracy also have many affinities with contemporary analyses of the decline of public life in modern Europe and particularly the US. Though coming from very different theoretical perspectives, theorists such as Habermas, Lasch, and Sennett bemoan the decline of public life in the West, and its replacement by a culture of individualism and unchallenging mass media. These authors tie depoliticization to the rise of late capitalism and/or industrialism. They also share Tocqueville's belief that the love of money contributes to a mediocre mass culture which inhibits critical thinking as well as public participation.

The Frankfurt School

While also decrying the decline of democracy *à la* Tocqueville, the Frankfurt School critical theorists, working in the Marxist tradition, analyze the problems of public life in the West in terms of the rise of a new type of state and corporate capitalism informed by pervasive mass media. The critical theorists, including most prominently Adorno, Horkheimer, and Marcuse, differ from Tocqueville, in that they concentrate on the economic and psychological problems of the modern West, which they tie to the emergence of capitalism, industrialism, and instrumental rationality, rather than to a democratic social condition.

The critical theorists criticize the tendency of Marxism to harden into a dogmatic science concerned only with economics. An adequate theory of capitalism necessarily involves an analysis of the mediating links between society and the individual such as culture, the family, and educational institutions, in addition to deciphering the laws of the economy. The critical theorists see that capitalism not only affects the individual's "mind, his ideas, his basic concepts and judgments, but also his inmost life, his preferences, and desires."[16] In order to understand the complexities of social control, the Frankfurt School incorporated Freudian psychoanalysis.

In the view of the critical theorists, Marx had discovered the laws of capitalism and Freud had unearthed the laws of the psyche. Both demonstrate in different yet parallel fashion the dominated and degraded condition of people under capitalism. Freud, in ignorance of the social and political consequences of his theory, reveals how the mind is torn by conflict between the ego, id, and superego, proving that the inviolability of the individual proclaimed by capitalism is a mere fiction.

According to the critical theorists, the use of Freudian and Marxist theory needs to be tied to an analysis of social change. The Frankfurt School rejects the working class as a revolutionary agent in modern society, for the proletariat had become integrated into the social system. A new form of bureaucratic, industrial society insidiously squashes opposition, as a welfare state capitalism and state socialism replaces a liberal, competitive capitalism. In these new circumstances, the state and large-scale corporations manage more and more of everyday life.

Through the expansion of mass media, advertising, and schools, society penetrates everywhere into private life. A new type of rational domination results, expressed most forcefully in the manipulative, therapeutic ethos of the factory, bureaucracies, and schools.

The logic of capitalist expansion leaves no room even for the family as a mediating institution between the individual and society. The development of capitalism into its monopoly form and its convergence with the welfare state, the rise of mass culture, consumerism, and the mass media undermine the basis of the paternalistic, male-dominated family. For the critical theorists, the decline of the paternalistic family does not result in the emancipation of the individual, but rather subjects him/her to the total domination of an administered society. Authority does not disappear; it becomes more diffuse and oblique. This emergent form of authority is not based on harsh discipline within the family or the workplace, but involves therapeutic forms of manipulation disguised as liberation from an oppressive past.

The mass media play a central role in this process. Radio, television, and film create a mass culture that spread to all sectors of society and seem democratic and inclusive at first glance. However, the critical theorists argue that mass media follow the same logic as mass production, as they produce a standardized, uniform culture that has more in common with the commodified products of the assembly line than with the traditions of great art.

Mass culture is produced by large media corporations, which subject all of culture to their influence just as mass production supplants craft-oriented types of work. Mass culture gives everyone the same type of easily understood product and excludes anything that is different or difficult to understand. Mass culture creates people's very categories of understanding the world, as it increases the rule of quantification over culture. Consumers are regarded as statistical categories, while mass media products (such as television shows and movies) are calculated to be easily predictable. Accordingly, media products become formulaic and conformist.

The form of mass media inhibits critical reflection. The ever-changing, quick-cutting style of movies and television leaves no room for imagination or reflection, as the spectator is drawn into the onrush of facts and images. People react automatically, as if on the assembly line. In such a context, it is difficult to imagine anything new or different. As Horkheimer and Adorno state: "only the universal triumph of the rhythm of mechanical production and reproduction promises that nothing changes, and nothing unsuitable will appear."[17]

In sum, Horkheimer, Adorno, and Marcuse believe that people's capacities for rational thought and true creativity are being undermined by a new, pervasive corporate capitalism. Accordingly, they contend that a democratic culture requires a critique of mass media and state capitalism, while also maintaining a strong emphasis on rationality in the face of an irrational culture. These theorists' emphasis on the invasion of public and psychic life by administrative capitalism is in many ways similar to Arendt's critical analysis of the rise of the social and its dire effects on the possibility of a vibrant public culture.

Arendt and the human condition

The political theorist Arendt also criticizes the mass culture of the modern world and its effects on public life. Arendt takes seriously the claim that people are social animals, but critically evaluates this assertion from the perspective of Aristotle's contention that people are also political creatures. In her 1958 work *The Human Condition*, she states that a central dimension of human freedom is the autonomy of a public realm which guarantees that distinctive human actions will be allowed to flourish, the memory of which will exist over generations. Arendt traces her conception of the public realm to the ancient Greeks, who posit a rigid division between the public and household spheres. For the Greeks, the public arena, embodied in the polis, is the realm of free and equal participants who engage in distinctive ways of speaking and acting, creating the conditions for ever-new beginnings and great public deeds. It is a realm where public glory is sought. The household, conversely, is the sphere of necessity, structured by inequality and governed by absolute rule rather than freedom.[18]

Arendt argues that human excellence is inseparable from public performance in a common world. The public arena is this common world, where words and actions can be shared in a space that transcends the life-span of participants. In such a public realm, all members are concerned with the same subject, but from different positions and perspectives. In Rousseauesque fashion, Arendt argues that the public world is artificial, for its equality is created and sustained in the face of the unequal abilities of its participants. What makes the public world unique is that the particular identities of individuals are in some sense transcended when they participate in public life.

Arendt contends that a public realm requires mutual respect among equal participants, which also allows their distinctive qualities and abilities to flourish in public debate. The Greek polis not only furnished an arena for such activity, but also allowed great deeds to be remembered over time. This realm is indispensable to human life, as human nature requires speech and action, appearing and acting in the presence of others. In a way akin to the ancient desire for glory, the distinctive self is disclosed in public words and speech, in our capacity always to begin a new project. Such speech can only be confirmed and respected in the context of others, specifically our peers.[19]

This speech, which Arendt labels "action," produces narratives and stories that become part of a culture's self-understanding. Action must enlist others if it is to be effective, but it is inherently unpredictable and therefore creative and unique. Greatness comes from the performance of a deed or memorable words, not its motivation, as the latter is not unique. Action creates ever-new ideas that cannot be predicted, but also cannot easily be undone.[20]

Arendt views the rise of the "social" to prominence in human affairs as the major problem facing modern societies. She equates the social with the emergence of household activities, especially those concerned with the economy, into a dominating position in public life. Dating the rise of the social to the democratic reforms in nineteenth-century Europe and the US, Arendt contends that the dominance of the social in public life has all but obliterated the ancient Greek concerns with public distinctiveness and excellence. The public world, the world of freedom, has become controlled by the social, the realm of the determined, of the unfree.

The rise of the social to public prominence is synonymous with the emergence of modern mass society and mass culture. Mass society shatters the autonomy of the public realm, destroying the private sphere in the process, as all actions become leveled to the same common denominator. The social realm transforms all people into those who find their primary identity as jobholders and laborers, rather than creators of distinctive deeds. The necessity of laboring to produce and acquire products, encouraged by a pervasive consumerism, becomes all-encompassing in the modern world, destroying all other alternative visions and practices of human action.[21]

Arendt recovers a different sense of what public life means than that usually associated with politics today. For Arendt, public life should not be a realm of power-seeking individuals and groups dominated by interests in furthering their own power and economic considerations, but should be a realm of free human life, an arena where people can transcend their particular identities and create a new social narrative in conjunction with others. It is a world which is not predictable or determined, but is free and open to manifold possibilities. In opposition to the conformity of mass society, Arendt's conception of the public allows people to feel the exhilaration of creating a new social compact and new cultural traditions. Arendt contends that revolutionary situations have offered such a conception of public freedom, from the American Revolution of 1776 to the Hungarian uprising of 1956, when people acting in public spaces felt that they could found a new society.[22] A more recent example of the founding of such a public arena might be the American civil rights movement, which allowed voices that had long been silenced by slavery and oppression to be heard in American public life.

For Tocqueville, the Frankfurt School, and Arendt, the rise of the modern world has created new problems for the practice of democracy and a vibrant public life. The emergence of new institutions associated with capitalism and the nation-state centralizes social power and inhibits the possibilities of participation and/or distinctiveness in the public realm. Whether understood as democratic despotism, monopoly capitalism, or the hegemony of the social realm, centralized power and mass culture potentially destroy the social and psychological conditions for a vital public sphere where democratic freedom can be exercised.

Contemporary approaches

Contemporary perspectives on the problems and prospects of public life in the West, including those of Bellah, Lasch, Sennett, Habermas, and Giddens, develop many of the themes of the classical approaches of Tocqueville, the Frankfurt School, and Arendt. These contemporary theorists concur with the classical tradition's contention that a thriving democracy is made up of more than representative institutions. A vibrant public life requires non-governmental public spaces where people can come together to discuss issues of mutual concern, akin to the Greek polis, in Arendt's view. A democracy also needs a culture that promotes participation and a concern with the public good.

Contemporary theorists agree with the classical approach's disquietude that overly centralized power undermines the conditions for a democratic community. While Tocqueville feared that centralized government would inhibit democratic culture, many contemporary theorists also share the Frankfurt School's critique of corporate capitalism and, to some degree, Arendt's critique of the rise of the social. These theorists contend that centralized economic and political power undermines the capacities for democratic self-government, encouraging a culture of political passivity. Many modern theorists also concur with the classical critique of mass media, as a society based on images of wealth, beauty, and power makes rational, democratic discourse more difficult to achieve.

Bellah, Lasch, and Sennett share Tocqueville's view that modern democratic conditions tend to create a culture of individualism and selfishness. They add another dimension to this argument, however: they condemn the modern obsession with therapeutic understandings of personal and public relationships that is so widespread, especially in American society, critiquing the emphasis on intimacy that such a culture creates. Rather than rewarding true distinctiveness in Arendt's sense, public life has become a realm where celebrity status, based on the favorable image that one can project, overshadows great public deeds. Finally, Lasch and Habermas believe that the rise of modern expertise and abstract systems of knowledge tend to undermine the conditions for public debate, intellectually deskilling people so that they have trouble criticizing the technological imperatives of society.

While Giddens agrees with some of these arguments, he takes a more optimistic view of the future of public life, as he retains a belief in the capacities of people to actively change their lives. Utilizing his notion of the double hermeneutic, Giddens contends that expert and/or therapeutic discourses do not systematically deskill people, but rather are reinterpreted in the context of their everyday lives. Thus, the myriad self-help therapies available to the public encourage a more sensitive and democratic understanding of one's emotions, not the narcissism criticized by Sennett and Lasch. Giddens contends that such emotional flexibility leads to a more open self who is better able to democratically interact with others. These points will be developed later in this chapter. First, it is necessary to summarize the arguments of those theorists who see modern democracy as threatened by narcissism and capitalism, who range from Bellah to Habermas.

Bellah and democratic habits of the heart

Following self-consciously in the Tocquevillean tradition, Bellah and his colleagues attempt to write a contemporary update of Tocqueville's *Democracy in America* in their two works, *Habits of the Heart* and *The Good Society*. Like Tocqueville, Bellah explores Americans' mores and customs, what Tocqueville called "habits of the heart," to grasp the American character. These mores include family life, religious practices, voluntary associations, and participation in local politics. They shape the very sense of what it means to be an American.

Also, like Tocqueville, Bellah believes that American democratic institutions are threatened by an unchecked individualism. But he distinguishes types of modern individualism in a more differentiated manner than does Tocqueville. Bellah argues that the rich variety of American life has been lost as the rise of self-interest and a therapeutic sensibility have become prevalent in the US, exemplified in the "quest for self" which dominates American thinking. Bellah finds that individual freedom is indeed important to Americans, but it exists alongside a strong commitment to free institutions, family life, and the like. Bellah contends that an untrammeled individualism is actually undermining the conditions of freedom, and he advocates limiting the destructive side of individualism by revivifying practices and cultural traditions which are still part of the American heritage.

Bellah believes that Americans' attraction to individualism leaves them with few capacities to think coherently about moral problems. Thus, Americans have difficulty truly understanding the complexity of some of their basic values, such as success, freedom, and justice. They have not thought through exactly how economic success can be coupled with a successful public and private life, especially as most people now work in a bureaucratic setting where the relationship between the work they do and a larger, common good is not easily grasped. Americans also think of freedom negatively, as the right to be left alone to do as they please. As Bellah states, this view of freedom "leaves Americans with a stubborn fear of acknowledging structures of power and interdependence in a technologically complex society dominated by giant corporations and an increasingly powerful state." It does not allow Americans collectively to confront their future, but often makes them "nostalgic for their past."[23] Finally, Bellah believes that Americans have not devised a clear vision of justice in a society marked by social inequality and too many qualified people for too few jobs.

Bellah thinks that Americans have trouble dealing with these issues because they assume that people are isolated individuals detached from their social and cultural context. He argues that this is a fiction, as our sense of self develops in relationships, groups, associations, and communities ordered by institutional structures and cultural meanings. We discover who we are in such contexts, not in isolation. Moreover, most Americans are deeply involved in social relationships that involve interdependence and caring, yet they lack a language to clearly articulate the richness of their commitments to one another.

Bellah feels that Americans have arrived at this predicament by overemphasizing some aspects of their cultural life and traditions at the expense of others. Bellah distinguishes four cultural traditions that influence the ways that Americans experience and talk about their social and personal life. The first is the utilitarian tradition, exemplified by Benjamin Franklin, in which success is defined as getting ahead on one's own initiative. In this tradition, the sum of self-interested actions will result in the common good. Another important strand is expressive individualism, symbolized by Walt Whitman. This tradition posits a successful life as one rich in experience, sensual as well as intellectual. Expressing and exploring the self are the major goals of this tradition. For Bellah, the utilitarian and expressive traditions merge in the modern therapeutic sensibility. Some combination of these two traditions pervades American life, from its managerial and entrepreneurial ethos to the understanding of personal relationships.

The utilitarian and expressive traditions provide few resources for Americans to discuss their collective life together, as they focus on individual self-fulfillment and self-interest without a corresponding recognition of the importance of social cooperation. Two other American cultural traditions, the biblical and the republican, provide better collective cultural reserves. The biblical strand, symbolized by John Winthrop, sees success not as the accumulation of material wealth but as the creation of a community in which a genuinely ethical and spiritual life can be lived. In this tradition, character is very important, as true freedom is not freedom to do what one wishes, but freedom to do the good, the just, and the honest. The republican tradition, exemplified by Thomas Jefferson, stresses that a good society requires the political equality of self-governing equals. This strand fears great inequalities of wealth, which can corrupt the morals of the people. If the citizenry becomes solely concerned with money-making rather than participating in government, the Republic will fall apart.

Bellah believes that Americans have forgotten the republican and biblical traditions in their rush toward individualism. American citizens, and many politicians, view government and politics cynically, as a realm of self-interested pursuits. To counter this trend toward a destructive individualism, Bellah calls for a reawakening of the republican and biblical strands that are still a part of American life, as seen in people's desire for meaningful work, their wish to make a difference in the world, and their putting of loved ones over work life. If these traditions were strengthened, Bellah believes that government could be viewed as a center of ethical obligations and relationships, where a moral consensus on issues of mutual concern could be generated. Bellah contends that Americans must resurrect these traditions, as they represent ideals of a community of participating, active individuals who have an ethical relationship to the whole of society. For this concern with the common ends of society to be effective, institutions must change accordingly. From work to school, institutions place too much emphasis on technical skills, competitive individualism, and top-down management, all of which prevent people from experiencing the intersection and interdependence of personal and public welfare. American institutions must change so that people can recognize their mutual interdependence and actively participate in every aspect of their lives, and not view institutions as hindrances to their self-development.

Lasch and the culture of narcissism

Lasch, like Bellah, believes that Americans suffer from a lack of community, but he develops his argument in the context of the Marxist tradition, particularly the Frankfurt School, while drawing heavily on psychoanalysis. Like Horkheimer/Adorno and Marcuse, Lasch believes that psychoanalysis provides a window into connections between individual and social problems. Lasch also adopts the psychoanalytic postulate that the neurotic expresses in extreme form the psychological problems that afflict even the "normal" individual. Thus, Lasch examines the clinical evidence of psychiatry, finding that contrary to the obsessive, compulsive, sexually repressed neurotic of Freud's time, the current data point to the predominance of pathological narcissistic character disorders in the West, particularly the US.[24]

Lasch states that narcissism in its Freudian sense does not mean a surfeit of "egoism" but precisely the opposite. It is characterized by the absence of a strong ego, resulting in a weakened ability to distinguish between the self and the outside world. The narcissist does not internalize authority and therefore does not develop a strong sense of his/her own identity.

This personality is grounded in early childhood experiences. The narcissistic child does not examine the ideals which his/her parents represent. Beset by conflicting images of parental authority, the process of individuation is stunted, as the weak ego of the individual is unable to resolve these conflicts in a coherent, realistic fashion. The narcissistic personality is contradictory because of these unresolved antagonisms that beset it. The narcissist is blindly optimistic, yet projects the bad self and object images onto objects and people outside of him/herself, seeing the world as a dangerous place and people as untrustworthy.

As the obsessive-compulsive personality structure, with its Protestant-ethic-type emphasis upon order, asceticism, and self-sacrifice served the needs of capital accumulation during early capitalism, the narcissistic personality structure meets the needs of an advanced capitalist consumer culture. The process through which these needs are met, however, entails the transformation of all institutions which have traditionally stood between the individual and the economy. Particularistic loyalties and traditions are undermined, but such emancipation masks a more insidious and benevolent form of social control.[25] As overt oppression declines, a new degradation and dependency develop. Lasch sees modern societies as a veritable "war of all against all" in which the very real danger to physical survival combines with psychic distress to create a menacing, perilous existence. Neither remembrances of one's past nor hopes for the future are of much aid to the narcissist, whose very personality structure becomes a requisite of the society which perpetuates his/her oppression.

The rise of large, centralized bureaucracies reinforces this loss of power. The social conditions of capitalism, especially the rise of mass media and a society of images, contributes to the culture of narcissism which reflects the pervasiveness of the narcissistic personality. Such an environment, in which the individual is surrounded by unattainable images of beauty and wealth, reinforces a constant anxiety about personal appearance and the presentation of oneself to others. It promotes a conception of success in terms of celebrity and image-making rather than disciplined work toward an ideal. The narcissistic culture thus discourages critical thinking in favor of an obsessive concentration on the self. A therapeutic mentality complements the narcissistic personality, as therapy encourages people to be assertive and avoid dependence on others. This mentality does not allow people to develop strong, stable ties to one another.

Lasch's perspective clearly has consequences for the prospects of a strong public sphere. Lasch believes that, especially in the US, politics has degenerated into spectacle, as elections have become more like sporting events and horse races than the result of reflexive, democratic decision-making. Images of power overshadow reality, as politicians address symbolic issues that seem far removed from the everyday concerns of people. The culture of narcissism encourages a world of images which inhibit democratic discourse and encourage a privatism even more pervasive than that feared by Tocqueville. By adding a psychoanalytic perspective to his critique of society, Lasch, like the critical theorists, shows how the culture of narcissism crushes the psychological capacities necessary for the exercise of a critical rationality and democracy, undermining almost completely the possibility of people developing an art of association. The requirements of consumer capitalism and the personality structure of the narcissist fit into a coherent whole which leaves few possibilities for alternative paths of social change.

Sennett and the fall of public man

Like Lasch, Sennett's *The Fall of Public Man* (1978) sees narcissism as a powerful, modern social-psychological condition that inhibits the possibilities of a rich public life. Drawing on themes from Tocqueville and Marx, Sennett argues that the unfortunate distinctiveness of the modern world lies in its attempts to make the realm of privacy authentic. In a way reminiscent of Arendt, Sennett argues that such concerns fracture the fragile balance of public and private realms, as the autonomy of public life is effectively overwhelmed by the onslaught of psychological and intimate categories that invade the public sphere. These categories of intimacy undermine the "codes of impersonal meaning" that are necessary for public life, because such codes sustain people's psychological distance from one another. The ideology of intimacy redefines public life as the "mutual revelation" of a collection of personalities sharing their innermost feelings, effectively preventing people from grasping their own interests and interacting with others who are different from them. Public actions are now evaluated in terms of the character of the people performing them, not in terms of the rationality and consequences of the actions themselves.[26]

Sennett states that such changes in public and private life show the modern influence of narcissism. Like Lasch, Sennett believes that narcissism governs society, making it difficult for people to distinguish self from reality, and encouraging a self-absorption that collapses public and private realms. Sennett calls narcissism "the Protestant ethic of modern times."[27] Narcissism, like the Protestant ethic but reformulated in a therapeutic key, emphasizes the feeling, authentic self as the standard by which to judge the world. Accordingly, we only care about institutions to the extent that personalities embody them. He distinguishes such a narcissistic consciousness from Marx's notion of dialectical thinking, which requires a distance from the self so that beliefs can change in the face of changing social circumstances.

Sennett traces the fall of public man to the rise of capitalism and secularism in nineteenth-century Europe and the US. As the cosmopolitan city arose in the precapitalist era, it created a rich public culture with open public spaces. People were able to interact without feeling the need to know the innermost secrets of others. Capitalism's emphasis on wealth creation and mass production eroded this impersonal urban culture, as people came to believe that public life was inferior to the private world of the family and consumerism. Secularism, based on the immediacy of sensation, encouraged the search for clues behind appearance to find the true personality of the public figure. Sennett sees psychological imagery becoming clearly imposed on public events in the era of the 1848 revolution in France, when public figures were evaluated in terms of their authentic, personal commitment to the revolution rather than by their beliefs or acts.[28]

This ideology of intimacy has had dire effects on public life in the modern world. For example, city planners' attempts to create community in seemingly impersonal cities only results in class and ethnic stratification by neighborhood, as spaces for cross-cultural public interaction decline and people solely come to know others like them. The populace evaluates a politician on the basis of their reactions to his/ her personality, rather than the politician's convictions and programs. In such a context, class as a category by which to understand collective identity declines in the face of ethnicity and personality. The contemporary electronic media, while not the origin of such trends, effectively advance them by encouraging social passivity and isolation on the part of the audience.[29]

In sum, as cities become less hospitable to public life, the self becomes more important. An emphasis on authenticity and personality pervades private and public life. Yet this emphasis on the self cannot handle the burdens placed on it. In Tocquevillean terms, the individual retreats into the small circle of family and friends. More subtly, such a self projects its psychological categories into public life, thus creating a culture of narcissism and isolation. Societies with low levels of social interaction among different groups develop "destructive collective personalities" which effectively inhibit collective solutions to social problems and undermine the capacity of groups to fight the structural and impersonal bases of injustice.[30]

While Bellah writes a contemporary version of *Democracy in America*, Sennett and Lasch update the Marxist tradition's analysis of mass society, adding the critique of narcissism and its associated therapeutic ethos to the theoretical mix. Sennett, Lasch, and Bellah fear that the psychological self-absorption so characteristic of Western peoples destroys the possibilities for a rich public life by inhibiting rational, critical thought, and undermining the capacities of people to work together on issues of mutual concern. Sennett and Lasch contend that a narcissistic society encourages the understanding of public life in psychological and intimate categories, which distorts any true comprehension of the real working of capitalist power in the modern world. This theme of the collapse of public and private life is also taken up in the work of Habermas, but he develops a more nuanced perspective on these issues which distinguishes him from others in the Marxist and Tocquevillean traditions.

Habermas and the public sphere

Habermas develops one of the most influential perspectives on the rise and characteristics of modern public life, or the public sphere. For Habermas, people come together in a public sphere to discuss issues and problems of mutual concern. He agrees with Arendt that in some sense particular identities are left behind as people interact in public spaces, though his perspective on this issue has become more complex in his recent work. *Contra* Arendt, he does not believe that the desire to appear distinctive defines action in the public sphere.

For Habermas, capitalist society always held out the possibility of the transformation of domination into the rule of reason, guaranteed by an informed public opinion. Public discourse in an egalitarian public sphere would be the necessary component of a functioning democracy. The public sphere was crucial for the democratization of Western society, inseparable from the rise of the modern nation-state and capitalist economy. Constituted by independent property owners, the bourgeois public sphere guaranteed rights of speech, press, assembly, and privacy while providing the context (in principle) for the democratic and rational discussion of issues of general interest.[31]

Habermas argues that the bourgeois family represented, in idealized form, a private sphere of interaction free from outside interference. This familial "haven in a heartless world" provided a model for the small groups such as salons, lodges, and cafés where the ideal of a reasoning public first emerged in eighteenth-century Europe. As capitalism developed, property owners attempted to secure the necessary information regarding commodity exchange in the market, thereby demanding more information from the press.[32] Through newspapers, a large-scale, critical public grew which contributed to the formation of public opinion and promoted discussion based on principled argument. This in turn encouraged a more professional criticism in the public sphere, where law was interpreted as the expression of reason.[33]

For Habermas, rational public opinion provides a new principle of sovereign power. This universalistic rationality is not just another rhetorical strategy camouflaging elite interests, for it postulates a form of public authority which could guide state decisions without abolishing government. By bringing the control of the state under the guidelines of the franchise and public opinion, any rule of law has to answer to the sovereignty of the people.

According to Habermas, the public sphere declined as it democratized, for the incorporation of new groups such as workers created an unwieldy public space. The lack of substantive equality in the bourgeois public sphere made rational discussion difficult, and promoted corporatist, undemocratic bargaining between interest groups.[34] The interpenetration of state and society and the growth of the culture industry "refeudalized" the public sphere, as critical debate on public issues of mutual concern became subordinated to interest group bartering and charismatic politics.[35]

Habermas alters some of his views about the public sphere in his 1996 book, *Between Facts and Norms*, in which he states that he uncritically accepted the Frankfurt School's interpretation of the decline of modern culture and its associated one-dimensional view of rationality. Fearful of linking democracy to a specific community, Habermas ties communicative action to a "proceduralist" version of reason which does not prescribe any particular moral vision, but is grounded in legal norms. Democratic legitimacy follows a "discourse principle": "Just those action norms are valid to which all possibly affected persons could agree as participants in rational discourses."[36]

Habermas argues that communicative action corresponds to our pluralist, post-traditional world. Like Parsons and Durkheim, he believes that highly differentiated modern societies cannot be integrated solely on the basis of people's self-interest. Communicative action is now the major integrating force of modern societies. But communicative action provides only a fragile basis for norms; there is no supra-social, sacred, traditional guarantee of their stability in our late modern age. Moreover, social integration occurs not only through communicative agreement on norms and values based in the lifeworld, but also as a result of the system forces of markets and administrative power.

For many people, liberty appears threatened by system forces or an unchecked individualism. While Habermas shares this view, he believes that a democracy requires individual rights *and* an orientation to the common good; he links the two by his discourse principle. Rights cannot simply be understood as possessions accruing to individuals, for they imply mutual recognition within a legal community. The pursuit of individual interests must be clarified in public discussion, for any account of individual rights must take into consideration the different material conditions and possibilities for democratic discourse of specific groups. Rights of assembly, speech, and the like can only be effective if democratic communication can be realized. Private and public autonomy are inseparable.

While rights should assure a more just distribution of social wealth and new social entitlements, a discourse theory of rights and democracy requires shifting from a focus on the qualities, opportunities, and competencies of people to "the forms of communication" in which opinion develops and interacts with institutionalized decision-making.[37] Laws should be oriented to strengthening the democratic capabilities and prospects of those they affect.

This strong emphasis on public discussion presumes that a vibrant democracy is inseparable from a strong public sphere and civil society. In *Between Facts and Norms*, Habermas argues that the public sphere is the social space generated by communicative action. Civil society is the organizational component of the public sphere, made up of associations, voluntary organizations, and social movements. A robust civil society can only develop in the context of the rationalization of the lifeworld, the guaranteed autonomy of private life, and a liberal political culture. Habermas opposes populist movements which attempt to freeze this rationalization process in the name of a utopian past, for he contends that such movements inhibit possibilities for the spread of communicative action.

Habermas now realizes that many different public spheres exist, whose boundaries remain porous to each other. In the wake of the labor movement and feminism, the very notion of the public sphere has had to expand in order to remain a central institution of democracy. Because public life is now pluralized and open to new challenges, it can never be a realm solely of corporatist bargaining among organized interests, as Habermas saw occurring in the 1950s. Because the public sphere is the realm of communicative action, democratic legitimacy through debate must be part of its very functioning.

The emergence of new social movements has also changed the types of issues that are discussed in the public realm. Habermas gives a linguistic twist to C. Wright Mills's famous distinction between public issues and private problems, as Habermas recognizes that in contemporary social life public sphere issues are originally experienced and voiced as private sphere problems. Issues concerning the seemingly private notions of identity formation are part of the public sphere, seen in debates around gay, lesbian, and women's rights, for example. The public/private distinction is not absolute, and the problems of private life become thematized in the public sphere. What separates the public and private realms are not clear institutional distinctions, but "different conditions of communication."[38] This approach fits in with Habermas's recent turn to a procedural concept of rationality. Habermas believes that the democratic sovereignty of the public sphere cannot be embodied in specific institutions. Rather, it is found in democratic procedures that promote discussion and participation.

Habermas argues that the transformative potential of the public sphere is limited. Civil society and the public sphere can only change themselves, having at best an indirect effect on political institutions. Public influence is transformed into communicative power through political institutions, such as the legislature. This is why social movements in the public sphere must be "self-limiting," for the attempt to institutionalize new forms of social organization that change all of social life has proved disastrous, as the experience of communist societies demonstrates. At best, existing parliamentary institutions can be supplemented by new institutions deriving from these various public spheres, which could influence legislation on behalf of affected clients.[39]

Moving away from any essentialist conception of identity, Habermas argues that the public sphere(s) and popular sovereignty cannot be understood as a kind of collective subject writ large, but must be understood as a constantly shifting, subjectless interplay of democratic procedures, parliamentary institutions, and informal public opinion. Habermas contends that the major problems confronting constitutional democracies do not concern sustaining economic growth or creating a more efficient government, but involve nurturing a social solidarity and active, participatory public life threatened by unregulated systemic forces.

Cultural studies

In revising his theory of the decline of the public sphere, Habermas draws on the cultural studies perspective of the Birmingham school in the UK. As Habermas states, many mass media images and discourses "miss their target because the intended meaning is turned into its opposite under conditions of being received against a certain subcultural background."[40] This statement succinctly summarizes many of the major themes of the cultural studies approach. This perspective takes Marxism in a different direction than the Frankfurt School, for cultural studies views people as actively contesting and reinterpreting the meanings that they receive from institutions such as the mass media.

Like Marx, cultural studies theorists such as Stuart Hall, David Morley, and John Fiske argue that capitalist societies are divided by unequal power relations, though they consider gender and racial imbalances as important as class in the dynamics of social stratification. Subordinate groups struggle for social and economic power against ruling groups. A key component of this power struggle is the contestation over cultural meanings, as ruling groups "attempt to 'naturalize' the meanings that serve their interests into the 'common sense' of the society as a whole," through the mass media, schools, and the like. Cultural meanings are linked to groups unequally positioned in the social structure. Subordinate groups resist attempts at cultural homogenization that favor ruling-class interests; the cultural realm is not an arena of disinterested aesthetic discussion, but a place where struggle over the control of social meanings takes place.[41]

The cultural studies perspective distinguishes between the production, circulation, and consumption of cultural meanings. The fact that a meaning or message is a commodity produced by a capitalist ruling group does not mean that it will be interpreted in a single, unified manner, as production and reception are not identical. Hall argues that the dominant discourses promulgated by ruling elites are subject to different interpretations. Media texts, for example, do not have one single meaning, but can be read in different ways by people from different social backgrounds. Understanding a media message is a process of negotiation between the viewer and the media text. All meanings must be created by the audience, for a mass-produced text can only be made popular by viewers. Such reinterpretation of meanings is always political, even if only implicitly, for cultural meanings invariably involve social power. The most patriarchal of texts can be reinterpreted in a critical manner. Fiske cites a 1986 study by Michaels which demonstrates that Aboriginal viewers rejected the nationalistic and imperialistic themes of the *Rambo* movies, instead placing Rambo's actions "into an elaborate kinship network with those he was rescuing, thus making 'tribal' meanings that were culturally pertinent to themselves."[42]

The cultural studies perspective recognizes that some "preferred" social meanings, created by dominant groups, are more easily accepted than alternative, oppositional ones. They also concede that the commodification of cultural life criticized by the Frankfurt School, Lasch, and Sennett is indeed a major problem. But this approach holds out the possibility that people are capable of responding creatively and critically to the messages that they receive, and that such critical interpretations can form the basis of radical politics.

Giddens on democracy and public life

Giddens shares many of the themes addressed by the authors in the cultural studies, Tocquevillean, and Marxist traditions. Like the theorists of the cultural studies perspective, he contends that people can creatively reinterpret processes of commodification. As Giddens states, "Even the most oppressed of individuals – perhaps in some ways particularly the most oppressed – react creatively and interpretatively to processes of commodification which impinge on their lives."[43] Giddens agrees with the Tocquevillean tradition's emphasis on open, public debate and the necessity of cultivating democratic capacities in order to achieve a vibrant public life. He concurs with the Tocquevillean and Habermasian argument that progressive social change cannot rely on conventional, liberal-centered state programs, but must look instead to some variant of civil society, whether understood as the public sphere or as voluntary organizations, in order to realize the democratic potential of late modernity. In so doing, he shares Lasch's, Bellah's, etc. suspicions of technological projects that aim to modernize social life without attention to democratic participation and/or the salience of cultural traditions.

However, Giddens rejects the assumption of a decline in public life which characterizes most of these approaches. He severely criticizes the arguments advanced by Lasch and Sennett. His criticisms are in many ways similar to those of theorists in the cultural studies approach, who critique the assumption of a passive audience, in that Giddens contends that people are skilled agents who have the capacity to interpret the various dominant social discourses and practices in myriad, critical ways.

Giddens and Habermas

In many ways, Giddens's approach to public life and democracy is similar to that of Habermas. Like Habermas, Giddens views the rise of a public sphere in eighteenth-century Europe as a central factor in the emergence of modern democracy. In fact, the very notion of the nation-state is inseparable from a public sphere, as the nation developed alongside discourses about the nature of the state. Notions of citizenship had to be promulgated in a public sphere in order for the nation to come into existence, for such discourses defined the substance of political life, the general interest of the nation, and the particular cultural histories of different nations in a contested environment.[44]

Like Habermas, Giddens believes that a democracy requires a vibrant civil society and a number of different public spheres. Capitalism helps create a civil society relatively autonomous from government control. Because of class divisions, an effective civil society needs a number of different associations and institutional centers of rights and freedoms, which form distinctive but overlapping public spheres.[45]

Giddens, like Habermas, also ties his theory of democracy to a conception of rationality. He shares Habermas's distrust of a "productivist" notion of rationality – a positivist and instrumental reason that promotes economic growth as an unquestioned social good while eschewing questions of the ends of social life. These theorists contend that such a conception of rationality not only destroys more critical versions of reason that can promote mutual identification and ethical reflection, but also undermines the conditions for self-government by translating social questions into technical issues which foreclose democratic debate.

Giddens does not embrace Habermas's communicative reason as an alternative to instrumental rationality. He nevertheless argues, in a way similar to Habermas, that democracy is inseparable from the expansion of reflexivity, whose relentlessly critical and democratic character changes the status of traditional belief systems in the modern world. As we saw in Chapter 5, Giddens states that modern democracies exist within a post-traditional order, in which traditions must be "discursively articulated and defended" rather than taken for granted.[46] Thus, tradition cannot exist as it did before conditions of widespread reflexivity, for now tradition must be justified. Once rationally legitimized, tradition changes its very essence, for traditions can only be defended "in the light of knowledge which is not itself authenticated by tradition."[47]

Giddens argues that most theorists of public life and civil society do not grasp how the state and civil society have been linked together since the inception of the modern era. The very nature of the private realm is dependent on legal, state-sanctioned definitions of private rights and responsibilities. Changes in the private realm are dependent on changes in the state, and vice versa. Thus, it makes little sense to oppose the public and private spheres as in some sort of inherent conflict. Giddens rejects the Marxist contention, to some degree continued by Habermas, that private life is colonized by capitalist commodification. He also rejects the notion that public life is being overwhelmed by the private criteria of intimacy, as Sennett and Bellah argue.

Giddens's critique of the "Narcissistic society" perspective

As we saw in his critique of Elias's *The Civilizing Process* in Chapter 3, Giddens is suspicious of any theory which ties changes in personality formation closely to social changes. For Giddens, people have always had the capacity to be reflexive; what change are the social and cultural conditions in which they exercise this reflexivity. Further, Giddens argues that social theories influenced by Freud, such as that of Lasch, illegitimately project psychoanalytic concepts onto society, downplaying the extent to which all unconscious processes are altered by social practices. Giddens also argues that Sennett, Lasch, and Bellah miss many of the positive aspects of modern life. He contends that the public realm has "advanced with the maturation of modern institutions," increasing the possibilities of participation.[48] Modern urban life offers more diversity than in the past. For example, Giddens draws on Judith Stacey's 1990 work, *Brave New Families*, to demonstrate that people are reflexively creating new sorts of familial arrangements, as novel step- and blended families become increasingly predominant. The people forming these family types are not retreating from public problems, but actively constructing new social forms. This lack of attention to, or criticisms of, new family forms demonstrates a major deficiency in the theoretical approaches of Lasch, Sennett, and Bellah. These authors view people as passively conforming to changing social circumstances, rather than actively intervening and reflexively altering them. The late modern concern with the body can also be understood as part of this reflexive process, for it is a major aspect of the construction of social identity, rather than a narcissistic obsession with appearances.[49]

Giddens sees the modern concern with therapy as in some respects quite salutary. While he concurs with Lasch et al. in recognizing that therapy can promote dependence and increase the sequestration of experience, he also contends that therapy is an excellent example of modern reflexivity. Therapy is a resource for life-planning, a way of constructing the self in a post-traditional world. It often orients people to actively engage everyday problems. In addition, therapists are now very sensitive to issues of authority.

Reflexivity and democracy

Giddens's emphasis on the skillful reflexivity that people use to guide their lives separates his theory of democracy from the views of authors who see public life declining in the late modern world. Giddens distinguishes institutional reflexivity from reflexivity as a quality of human action, seeing both as central components of modern demo-cracies. Giddens argues that all humans are reflexive, but this means different things in different contexts. In non-modern cultures, reflexivity involves the appreciation of tradition as a means of continuity over generations. In modernity, reflexivity changes its character, as it becomes pervasive and widespread in a post-traditional order. Reflex-ivity "is introduced into the very basis of system reproduction, such that thought and action are constantly refracted back upon one another."[50] The administrative control and widespread surveillance of modern nation-states requires this new type of institutional reflexivity, which is an investigative and calculative attitude to system reproduction. The coding of information and the rise of new social scientific knowledge contributes to this institutional reflexivity, as the reproduction of societies becomes more subject to conscious control.

Both institutional and personal reflexivity are associated with the conditions of late modern life. With greater literacy and time-space distanciation, thought and action intertwine, and they cannot be separated. In Giddens's words, "The reflexivity of modern social life consists in the fact that social practices are constantly examined and reformed in the light of incoming information about those very practices, thus constitutively altering their character."[51]

Giddens recognizes that, despite its spread throughout the world, liberal democracy is in crisis in the West, as many people distrust politicians and do not care about politics. Giddens attributes this crisis of liberal democracy to structural and social changes that have changed the tenor of democratic life and institutions. Democratization in the contemporary world is influenced by globalization, detraditionalization, and the impact of new social movements. All of these social phenomena introduce people to new ways of life and a diversity of cultural experiences. They heighten social reflexivity, as new and changing information and knowledge circulate in myriad social and cultural contexts. Globalization links the local, regional, and international, bypassing the nation-state. Moreover, the expansion of social reflexivity forces changes in bureaucratic hierarchy, as people increasingly reject labor discipline in the name of greater democracy. These changes coalesce to encourage decentralization, the devolution of democratic power downward, as issues of cultural identity, personal life, and local politics become central to people's democratic experience.[52]

Given these changes, Giddens states that modern democracy must be rethought. His notion of reflexivity informs his vision of a new, vibrant public realm and its relationship to a democratic polity. Democracy is the attempt of people to control their lives through rational discussion, reflexively appropriating new knowledges in the process. For Giddens, democracy requires more than simply a set of representative institutions, for it also involves strong extra-institutional features tied to reflexivity. In a way reminiscent of Tocqueville and Arendt, Giddens states that democracy requires social circumstances which allow people to develop their capacities and express diverse talents. Individuals must be involved in determining their own conditions of association, rather than having such conditions dictated by the state. These features of democracy contribute to the notion of the person as self-reflexive and self-determining, or autonomous.

Institutionally, democracy requires the protection of citizens from arbitrary political and coercive power, while guaranteeing the expansion of economic opportunity. Democracy needs forums for open debate, which are a form of democratic education. Again, like Tocqueville, Giddens believes that exercising this type of participation can result in a type of legitimate democratic authority which enhances autonomy, for people themselves make the rules that they will follow. These forums allow reasoning from conviction rather than from emotion. In this context, decision-making can become accountable and rights and obligations specified, while being subject to continuous reflexive monitoring. Such a strong democracy allows non-violent distinctions between the criminal and the political to be drawn.[53]

Given the increasingly international context of democracy, it cannot be equated with a particular type of civic culture as the Tocquevillean tradition argues. Democracy is influenced profoundly by particular structural conditions. Moreover, democracy cannot be equated *tout court* with the nation-state and the liberal tradition. While liberal, representative democracy can be institutionalized in state structures, a more profound sense of democracy still has to be cultivated and created. This sort of democracy is not based on the opposition of the state and the market, but rather on the need for more radical types of democratization. Giddens calls this dialogic democracy: it takes place outside of the formal political sphere, and includes such phenomena as the democratizing of emotions.[54]

For Giddens, decentralization and the generalization of social reflexivity demand a new conception of generative politics, which is no longer based on the opposition of a welfare state vs. the market. Giddens's call for a more radical form of dialogic democratization can be understood in this context, for it allows people to take control of their lives. Giddens argues that the most important democratic social changes are occurring outside of the state realm. He is fascinated by the implications for democracy associated with the rise of new social movements centered on life politics rather than emancipatory politics. For Giddens, life politics creates a new type of personalistic democracy. True democracy requires a transformation of personal and emotional life. It demands the specification of rights and duties which are never fixed and need to be the focus of continuous, reflexive attention.[55]

The women's movement has played a fundamental role in the rise of this new type of "emotional democracy." Institutionalized in consciousness raising and self-help groups, feminism promotes the discussion of emotional life among equals. For feminism, a healthy emotional existence must dispense with repression and stifling gender roles. According to Giddens, such a democratization of emotional life is linked to possibilities of democracy at the global level. Giddens sees emotional democracy as especially important, for emotionally healthy people make good democratic citizens. In particular, self-help groups promote emotional democracy, and encourage decentralized authority and criticisms of bureaucracy.[56]

These notions of reflexivity and the possibilities for a rich, "emotional democracy" distinguish Giddens's notion of democracy from Habermas's theory of the public sphere. Giddens uses his concepts of reflexivity and the double hermeneutic to criticize Habermas's notion of the colonization of the lifeworld. According to Giddens, people can use expert knowledge in different and creative ways; personal life is not destroyed by impersonal systems, but often enhanced by them. For Giddens, the intersection of expertise and everyday life means that the personal is transformed, as self-identity "takes on rich new forms."[57]

The very nature of modern institutions is also bound up with trust in abstract systems of expertise. For example, we must rely on expertise associated with airplanes, automobiles, highway construction, and the like when using modern transport. The rise of modern expertise and abstract systems has not meant the invasion and colonization of personal life. Rather, everyday existence and abstract systems become deeply intertwined in the context of globalization. In such a context, new types of sociability develop. The relationship between expertise and everyday life is not simply one-way, as changes in day-to-day activities affect the ways that people interpret abstract systems, which can be continuously reappropriated and changed by them. As Giddens states, the relationship of the individual to expert systems is one in which "processes of reappropriation and empowerment intertwine with expropriation and loss."[58] Reskilling often characterizes this individual/expert system relationship, but it is always partial and in constant revision.

Giddens sees the late modern concern with intimacy as an important example of an emotional democracy which exemplifies the reskilling that comes with the everyday reinterpretation of expert systems. Giddens states that struggles around issues of intimacy help create the very social world in which people find themselves. The indeterminacy of modernity makes establishing a self-identity a particularly modern project for everyone, and this requires active intervention in the world. The late modern ethos of self-discovery is part of the transition to institutional reflexivity, the disembedding of social relations by abstract systems, and the interpenetration of the local and global that give a distinctive texture to late modern life. These reflexive activities create difficulties while simultaneously opening up new possibilities. Self-help books written by experts are part of this new reflexivity, as people interpret them in such a way that they "serve routinely to organise, and alter, the aspects of social life they report on or analyze." For modern people, biographies are reflexively organized around constantly shifting social and psychological information.[59]

Giddens shares many themes with the critical perspectives on democracy discussed in this chapter. He recognizes that a strong democracy requires more than representative institutions, as he emphasizes the need for free and open spaces for public participation, if democracy is to thrive. Giddens also shares the fear, expressed in various ways by different authors, that democracy is threatened by capitalist commodification. Yet, like the cultural studies theorists, he grants people the capacity to change and actively reinterpret their circumstances and lives as new information becomes available to them. He does not view capitalism, expertise, or mass media as monolithic monsters which prevent people from exercising their democratic capacities. He employs his notion of the double hermeneutic in this context, arguing that the findings of social science become part of laypeople's everyday life, incorporated reflexively into their milieu. This double hermeneutic implies that quotidian life is invariably changing, and can always result in something new. However, such a social atmosphere of constant change also points to the fragmentation of late modern social life, which makes personal and social narratives more difficult to create and sustain.

The problem of the maintenance of a strong sense of personal identity will be addressed more fully in the next chapter. Yet there are some other issues that trouble Giddens's theoretical approach to democracy. Like almost all of the authors in this chapter, Giddens tends to idealize a version of public life as the realm of free, open discussion. He does not see it as a realm of power struggles, in which not only do opposing groups vie for political control, but different people attempt to augment their cultural capital, in Bourdieu's terms. The notion that democracy invariably involves struggles over power in some form or other must be taken into consideration by any adequate theory of democratic public life. In addition, Giddens does not analyze connections between late modern democracy and its gendered, patriarchal history. Such considerations of the gendered split between a masculine, public sphere and a private, feminine realm, and the more general critique of social relations and social science raised by feminist analysis, will be addressed in the following chapter.

Notes

1 See for example the classic work of C.B. Macpherson, *The Political Theory of Possessive Individualism: Hobbes to Locke* (New York, Oxford University Press, 1962).

2 Václav Havel et al., *The Power of the Powerless: Citizens Against the State* (Armonk, NY, M.E. Sharpe, 1985), p. 91.

3 See Richard Sennett, *The Fall of Public Man: On the Social Psychology of Capitalism* (New York, Vintage Books, 1978).

4 Philip Rieff, *The Triumph of the Therapeutic: Uses of Faith After Freud* (New York, Anchor Books, 1961).

5 Alexis de Tocqueville, *Democracy in America, Vol. 1* (New York, Vintage, 1990), p. 8.

6 Ibid., p. 103.

7 Ibid., p. 111.

8 Ibid., p. 102

9 Alexis de Tocqueville, *Democracy in America, Vol. 2* (New York, Vingage, 1990), p. 136.

10 Ibid., p. 137.

11 Ibid., p. 104.

12 Ibid., p. 50.

13 Ibid., p. 51.

14 Ibid., p. 52.

15 Ibid., p. 51.

16 Max Horkheimer, *Critical Theory: Selected Essays* (New York, Seabury, 1972), p. 69. See also Herbert Marcuse, *One-Dimensional Man* (Boston, Beacon Press, 1964).

17 Max Horkheimer and Theodor Adorno, *Dialectic of Enlightenment* (London, Verso, 1979), p. 134.

18 Hannah Arendt, *The Human Condition* (Garden City, NY, Doubleday, 1958), pp. 25–31.

19 Ibid., pp. 49–58, 176–181, 197, 215.

20 Ibid., pp. 188–191, 206, 233

21 Ibid., pp. 38, 42–46, 59.

22 See Hannah Arendt, *On Revolution* (New York, Viking Press, 1965).

23 Robert N. Bellah, Richard Madsen, William M. Sullivan, Ann Swidler, and Steven M. Tipton, *Habits of the Heart: Individualism and Commitment in American Life* (Berkeley, University of California Press, 1985), p. 25.

24 Christopher Lasch, *The Culture of Narcissism* (New York, Norton, 1978), p. 42.

25 Christopher Lasch, *Haven in a Heartless World: The Family Besieged* (New York, Basic Books, 1979), p. 92.

26 Sennett, *The Fall of Public Man*, pp. 11, 262.

27 Ibid., p. 333.

28 Ibid., p. 25.

29 Ibid., p. 283.

30 Ibid., p. 238.

31 Jürgen Habermas, *The Structural Transformation of the Public Sphere: An Inquiry into a Category of Bourgeois Society* (Cambridge, MA, MIT Press, 1989), pp. 15–18.

32 Ibid., pp. 24–43.

33 Ibid., p. 54.

34 Ibid., p. 132.

35 Ibid., p. 195.

36 Jürgen Habermas, *Between Facts and Norms: Contributions to a Discourse Theory of Law and Democracy* (Cambridge, MA, MIT Press, 1996), p. 107.

37 Ibid., p. 408.

38 Ibid., p. 366.

39 Ibid., pp. 371–372, 484.

40 Jürgen Habermas, *The Theory of Communicative Action, Vol. 2, Lifeworld and System: A Critique of Functionalist Reason* (Boston, Beacon Press, 1987), p. 391.

41 John Fiske, "British Cultural Studies and Television," in *Channels of Discourse: Television and Contemporary Criticism*, ed. Robert Allen (Chapel Hill, NC, University of North Carolina Press, 1987), p. 255

42 John Fiske, *Television Culture* (London, Methuen, 1987), p. 316; see also Stuart Hall, "Cultural Studies: Two Paradigms," *Media, Culture, and Society* 2 (1980), pp. 57–72.

43 Giddens, *Modernity and Self-Identity: Self and Society in the Late Modern Age* (Stanford, Stanford University Press, 1991), p. 199.

44 Giddens, *A Contemporary Critique of Historical Materialism, Vol. 2, The Nation-State and Violence* (Berkeley, University of California Press, 1985), pp. 210–212.

45 Giddens, "A Reply to My Critics," in *Social Theory of Modern Societies: Anthony Giddens and His Critics*, ed. David Held and John B. Thompson (New York, Cambridge University Press, 1989) p. 275.

46 Giddens, "Living in a Post-Traditional Society," in Ulrich Beck, Anthony Giddens, and Scott Lash, *Reflexive Modernization: Politics, Tradition, and Aesthetics in the Modern Social Order* (Stanford, Stanford University Press, 1994), p. 100.

47 Giddens, *The Consequences of Modernity* (Stanford, Stanford University Press, 1990), p. 38.

48 Giddens, *Modernity and Self-Identity*, p. 174.

49 Ibid., pp. 174–178.

50 Giddens, *The Consequences of Modernity*, p. 38.

51 Ibid.

52 Giddens, *In Defence of Sociology: Essays, Interpretations, and Rejoinders* (Cambridge, MA, Polity Press, 1996), pp. 214–221.

53 Giddens, *The Transformation of Intimacy: Sexuality, Love and Eroticism in Modern Societies* (Stanford, Stanford University Press, 1992), pp. 185–187.

54 Giddens, *Beyond Left and Right: The Future of Radical Politics* (Stanford, Stanford University Press, 1994), p. 17.

55 Giddens, *The Transformation of Intimacy*, p. 186.

56 Giddens, "Risk, Trust, Reflexivity," in Beck, Giddens, Lash, *Reflexive Modernization*, pp. 191–193.

57 Anthony Giddens, "Structuration Theory: Past, Present, Future," in *Giddens' Theory of Structuration: A Critical Appreciation*, ed. Christopher G.A. Bryant and David Jary (New York, Routledge, 1991), p. 211.

58 Giddens, *Modernity and Self-Identity*, p. 7.

59 Ibid., p. 14.

7

FEMINISM, SEXUALITY, AND
SELF-IDENTITY

While many social theorists now view the public sphere as the center-piece of democracy, such discussions often downplay the extent to which a notion of the public presupposes a corresponding private sphere. Some feminist approaches not only focus on the public/private issue, but question whether this dichotomy is a gendered one. For example, in middle-class, mid-nineteenth-century Victorian Britain, the public/private split not only divided men and women into different social worlds, but also presupposed distinctive cultures and biologies divided by gender. A virile, active man participated in public life, while passive, emotional women controlled the household. Men focused on careers and public acclaim, and the destiny of women was marriage and motherhood. These differences were believed to be God-given, as men and women differed as radically in mind as they did in body. Cults of masculinity and domesticity presupposed one another, and reinforced the lack of rights and social power for women.[1]

Feminism arose in part to question this dichotomy between masculinity and femininity, and the social power that such division assumes. Contemporary feminism raises the issue of the extent to which modern institutions and social relations are gendered to their core, fortifying men's social power over women. Feminism, along with gay and lesbian movements, has brought themes of the construction of personal, gender, and sexual identity into the center of contemporary public discourse.

Giddens believes that feminism in particular has opened up the topic of modern self-identity to an unprecedented degree, as it has made people cognizant of the interconnections between personal life and political and social issues. With feminism, the body itself becomes sub-ject to reflexive awareness, as people become aware that the self is socially constructed as well as biologically given. Giddens states that the body becomes a subject of "continuous reflexive attention," from gender identity to sexuality, as people are now responsible "for the design of [their] own bodies."[2] In late modernity there are many options for bodily

appearance. This does not necessarily mean that some people are narcissis-
tically concerned with their appearance, but rather that "the self
becomes a *reflexive project*".[3] A person's identity is not given, nor simply
dependent on the reactions of others, but consists of "the capacity *to keep
a particular narrative going*": understanding where the person comes
from, and where s/he is headed is the major issue of self-development.[4]
For Giddens, contemporary concerns with the body and sexuality are
inextricably mixed with issues of self-identity.

Such themes are now an inescapable part of modern life. They are
demonstrated most clearly in the postmodern thrust of much
contemporary social theory that we have touched on throughout the
text. As Melucci argues, conflicts over meanings and the social construction of reality are pivotal issues of post- or late modern societies.
Issues around personal identity and sexuality intersect with the claim
that different cultural identities should be respected, which often
involves the assertion that different communities (whether of women,
gays, or minority groups) have different forms of knowledge. Such
arguments have become topics of controversy, as new knowledges are
asserted in the name of feminist, queer, and Afrocentric perspectives, for
example. A major right now is the right to be different. Identities can no
longer be taken for granted, as the widespread reflexivity characteristic
of information societies means that identities are fluid and changing,
and that their definitions are sites of contestation.

This chapter examines the issues of identity and sexuality as they have
been debated in the new context created by feminism. It explores
Freudian theory, which tied identity and sexuality together in a powerful synthesis that influenced later theorists who retained a psychoanalytic core while substantially revising some of Freud's major tenets,
such as the Frankfurt School's Marcuse and the feminist Nancy
Chodorow. This Freudian perspective has in turn been challenged by a
social constructionist orientation, which focuses more on institutional
and social power relations than on childhood experiences in explaining
gender dynamics. This constructionist orientation has been radicalized
in postmodern versions of identity and sexuality, ranging from
Foucault's critique of Freud to Butler's and Flax's postmodern feminism.
The chapter concludes with a summary of Giddens's critique of these
various theories, and explores his view of the fluid nature of contemporary personal and social identities.

Feminism

Issues of cultural identity, sexuality, and different ways of knowing tied
to gender erupted into public and academic consciousness in the wake
of decolonialization in the 1940s and 1950s, the civil rights struggles of
the 1960s, and the feminist movement of the 1970s. While all of these

movements have profoundly changed social life, it is feminism that has raised some of the most fundamental questions about contemporary societies, from the monogamous family to the "naturalness" of heterosexuality.

These changes have not been smooth or without sometimes contradictory results. For example, in the US women entered the workforce in great numbers in the 1970s and 1980s, and in doing so changed the nature of both the workplace and the family. In the wake of the feminist movement, they saw themselves as different from their mothers, and often rejected the domestic ideal of childrearing as their primary function. But women entered the workforce not only because of feminism, but also out of economic necessity. As real wages stagnated in the US beginning in the mid-1970s, both spouses had to work outside of the home to maintain their standard of living.[5]

In addition, changes in the nature of the workplace and the home have not kept pace with the new demands placed on women. Working women are still responsible for the vast majority of child-care and housework. Accordingly, many careers are still suited to men, for they have much more control over how much they will contribute to the workload at home. Job discrimination based on gender also still exists, as demonstrated in the reports on the "glass ceiling" inhibiting the mobility of women in the workplace.

Despite the social upheavals initiated by feminism, gender roles are still often taken for granted, and gender remains perhaps the most important fact of individuals' lives (for example, the first question usually asked of a newborn is whether it is a girl or a boy). Feminists have had to struggle with a myriad issues around gender, from how it is enacted in everyday life to its social meaning. With slogans such as "The personal is political," many feminists argue that questions of gender and sexuality pervade our everyday lives, and sexism in its various guises is among the most recalcitrant forms of social domination. Some feminists claim that our very forms of knowledge and rationality reflect gendered male assumptions that devalue women's experience and/or ways of knowing and inhibit possibilities for expanding, if not obliterating, the boundaries set by gender. Feminist analyses of gender are far from uniform, however, as demonstrated in the conflicts between a liberal feminism that sees women as essentially just like men, proponents of the "two cultures" approach who see fundamental differences between men and women and wish to validate women's distinctive capacities, and more recent postmodern feminists who often see the very category of gender as a remnant of oppressive social relations and masculine theories of knowledge which must be transcended. Analyses of gender have also been tied to new interpretations of the body and sexuality. Gay and lesbian movements and theories especially complicate simple notions of sexuality, further undermining any notion of the "naturalness" of gender. Many feminist discussions of gender begin with a critique of Freud's theory of sexuality and gender development, as he tied the two together in an explosive combination.

The Freudian tradition

Writing in late nineteenth- and early twentieth-century Austria and Britain, Freud is the most influential exponent of gender-based identities, as he argues that boys and girls grow up and mature in different ways. He sees unconscious desires connected to sexuality and its repression as the central causal factors in the formation of personal and gender identities. Freud also develops themes of the interplay of the unconscious, desire, and fantasy, which have been very important in feminist theory.

Freud contends that psychoanalysis introduces three new principles regarding the constitution of the psyche which distinguish it from other psychological theories. First, from the psychoanalytic viewpoint, mental processes are essentially unconscious. Our psychic activity is made up not only of conscious thinking, but consists primarily of wishing and feeling, which represent stored-up infantile desires that are repressed in adulthood. Second, impulses and instincts, which Freud terms libido, are the primary drives of the human organism. They are sexual in nature, and their repression plays a huge role in causing nervous and mental disorders. Third, such repression is recreated within every generation and every individual. This repression is fragile, however, and the ever-possible escape of unchecked sexual impulses might destroy individual and even social life. Only the sublimation of instincts can avoid social chaos and individual illness. Sublimation refers to the transfer of sexual gratification to social aims. Sublimation is the very basis of civilization, as its transformation of sexual instincts has contributed to the creation of the highest cultural, artistic, and social achievements of the human mind.[6]

Sublimation is a difficult process, in large part because people's entire psychic structure is based on procuring pleasure and avoiding pain, which Freud called the pleasure principle. The desire for pleasure rules the unconscious. The pleasure principle is tied to the release of the sexually charged libido, which constantly strives for consummation. The frustration of libido leads to neurosis and illness, as an inhibited sexuality grows more powerful as it is repressed. Freud formulates a tripartite theory of the mind in order to understand these processes, dividing the psyche into the id, ego, and superego. The id is pure libido, dominated by the primal search for pleasure. The superego is the conscience, represented by psychic images of society and parents. A sense of guilt develops in the superego, but it is often irrational, tied to unconscious fears of the loss of parental approval and physical harm. The ego attempts to negotiate between the demands of the pleasure principle of the id and the guilt of the superego. A most fragile mediator, the ego develops a reality principle as it seeks a diminished pleasure in adapting to the needs of reality. Maturity is based on the transition from the pleasure to the reality principle. The reality principle demands a rational accounting of pleasurable desires, adjusting gratification to social demands. Only fantasy escapes the clutches of the reality principle.[7]

These principles inform Freud's famous theory of the Oedipus complex. In order to mature properly and achieve an appropriate gender identity, a boy must renounce his desire for his mother and identify with his father. The boy makes this identification because of his fear of the power of the father, especially embodied in fantasies about castration. For Freud, such a renunciation of the desire for the mother on the part of the male child and the acceptance of the authority of the father is the basis of civilization, for it permits sexual energy (libido) to be sublimated and transformed into socially positive channels such as art and science. It also allows for the formation of the conscience, centered in the superego. Nevertheless, from Freud's perspective, socialization is not a happy process, for the superego tends to punish the self irrationally and viciously for imagined moral transgressions as well as real ones. The path to maturity, while exemplified in sublimation, also involves repression, ambivalence about sexuality, and unreachable desires which haunt the person even into adulthood. Morality for Freud expresses a kind of self-alienation, as the person internalizes parental authority while raging against this very authority. This psychic development allows males to develop relatively strong egos and renounce their emotions. According to Freud, adulthood means the attainment of sexuality centered in the genitalia, as the pleasures of sexuality move away from the infant's notion that the entire body is sexual and pleasurable.[8]

Freud did not devote as much thinking to the issue of female development. He tended to see females as more or less stunted males, who, because they do not undergo the Oedipal transition do not develop strong egos, have little capacity for holding strong values, and tend to be more emotional and sensual but more sexually passive than males. Girls find it necessary to renounce the mother in favor of the father, and eventually replace their desire to please their father with the desire to have children. Though Freud saw the relationship of the infant to the mother as a crucial one for psychological development, its importance and possible implications tend to be overlooked in the drama of the Oedipus complex.

In his later work, such as *Civilization and Its Discontents* (1930), Freud shifts from a concentration on the conflict between id, superego, and ego to a larger conflict built around the life instinct, or Eros, which consists of a wish for unity, and the death instinct, or Thanatos, which desires a return to a non-organic state. With his version of Thanatos, Freud develops the idea of a truly independent aggressive instinct, which he believes accounts for the prevalence of sadism and masochism in everyday life, and the destructive impulses which reign supreme in times of war.

At first glance, Freud seems to be a very poor candidate for feminist analysis. However, Freud's theories of the significance of the child's early relationship with the parents informs much later feminist theory, from Chodorow to Butler. His discussion of sexuality also accents the sexual repression and stunted emotional development of men demanded by patriarchy. Thus, issues of gender development, the repression of sexuality, and the importance of childhood identification with adults have played a central role in feminist and other critical analyses of gender, leading to formulations of Freud's perspective which result in new, radical theoretical terrain far from the master's own conservative convictions.

Marcuse and sexual liberation

Marcuse was intrigued by Freud's theories. He reformulates the conservative reading which Freud gives to his own approach, arguing instead that Freud's findings can lead to very different, radical conclusions. For Marcuse, Freud's theories of the psyche offer a new theory of liberation when combined with Marxism.

In his 1955 book *Eros and Civilization*, Marcuse undertook the typical Frankfurt School task of understanding how the state and society penetrate into the inner reaches of the psyche. Like his colleagues Horkheimer and Adorno, Marcuse argues that the rise of large-scale capitalism and mass culture results in new types of social manipulation, thoughtless leisure, and anti-intellectual ideologies, exemplified by corporate influence on everyday life, such as advertising. The emergence of mass society means the intrusion of social life into the private sphere, as the individual is evaluated and measured according to standardized skills, rather than through autonomous judgment and personal responsibility. In fact, Marcuse is attracted to Freud's psychological categories because they had become political categories in the industrial world. Images of the dominating superego shifted from parents to a depersonalized, bureaucratic authority as modern capitalist and industrialist domination congealed into a system of objective administration. For Marcuse, psychoanalysis demonstrates that the conflict between the ego, id, and superego is also a struggle between society and the individual, because psychological processes such as sublimation have a social content. Freud's work shows the inner connection between civilization and barbarism, progress and suffering, as the reality principle informing every human advance requires an increase of repression. Yet Freud does not make a distinction between historical contingency and biological necessity when discussing the reality principle. Nor does he distinguish between historical periods when analyzing the conflict of Eros and Thanatos.

Marcuse introduces two principles that take these distinctions into account, replacing Freud's pleasure/reality principle dichotomy in the process. The first principle presented by Marcuse is surplus repression, or the amount of sexual repression over and above what is necessary for the survival of a given society: this is akin to Marx's notion of surplus value. Marcuse argues that the amount of libido directed toward Eros and/or Thanatos differs according to the structure of society. Some societies require or demand more repression than is necessary. Marcuse believes that most repression is unnecessary, and thus is surplus repression. Second, Marcuse formulates a notion of the performance principle, or the prevailing historical form of the reality principle, which differs in distinct historical eras. Different societies have diverse types of reality principle, but these differences are the result of social factors, such as the control and distribution of social power, rather than biological necessities.[9]

A good example of surplus repression is found in Freud's discussion of genital sexuality. Freud believes that people learn to guide and restrain biological drives, and that the progress to genital sexuality is part of this process. Marcuse argues that the creation of genital sexuality results in the desexualization of the rest of the body, such as the pleasures associated with smell and taste. He states that this type of sublimation is in actuality a form of genital tyranny, as industrial capitalism requires a desexualized body to be able to perform instrumental labor. Marcuse associates the Protestant ethic with this genital tyranny, for the Protestant ethic increases guilt around the expression of sexuality, while also making procreation its most important function. This denial of sexuality is also a repression of life-affirming Eros; any decline in Eros necessarily results in an increase in the death-instinct, or Thanatos. Such an advance in Thanatos is largely responsible for the massive destructiveness of modern civilizations.

Marcuse contends that liberatory social change not only abolishes classes, but also eliminates the repressive constraints on sexuality. He states that modern societies are in need of a new rationality that will generate lasting erotic relations between individuals, breaking the hegemony of monogamy and the taboo on perversions in the modern world. The body needs to be resexualized, understood as an instrument of pleasure rather than of instrumental labor. In fact, the release of sexuality in a non-exploitative context would be a form of non-repressive sublimation, as work could be made more playful, Eros would be maximized, and the destructiveness associated with Thanatos would be minimized.[10]

In a later book, *One Dimensional Man* (1964), Marcuse is more pessimistic about the liberatory potential of a freed sexuality. He argues that through such mechanisms as advertising, capitalism has integrated sexuality into its very structure. Yet this is not an emancipatory development, as sexuality becomes commodified and functional for the status quo. Such immediate pleasures are no longer critical, as they confirm rather than subvert the existing order.[11]

For Giddens, Marcuse's belief that industrial society had become one dimensional shows the limitations of not only his approach, but of any approach based on Freud's theory that civilization is inherently repressive. Marcuse cannot theorize where contemporary sexual permissiveness originates, given the ostensible sexual repression of late modern societies. More importantly, theories like Marcuse's posit an image of society that is more monolithically resistant to change than it truly is, for the theory cannot account for the rise of new social movements such as feminism which raise fundamental questions about gender relations and sexuality.

Giddens argues that Marcuse in fact had little explicit to say about gender relations, as his vision of Eros was, like Freud's, a male one.[12] Yet, *contra* Giddens, Marcuse's theory still holds out the hope that a reawakened sexuality can inform a new sensuous rationality, which can be based on a return to a pre-ego stage of development, where oneness ruled.[13] Marcuse's belief in the positive importance of relationships before the Oedipus conflict damages the psyche has many affinities with feminist theories of psychic development that draw on Freud, especially the "Two Cultures" approach.

Feminism and the two cultures

Feminists have found much to criticize in Freud's analysis of gender development. Among the most prominent of the feminist criticisms was Chodorow's 1978 book, *The Reproduction of Mothering*. While Chodorow believes that Freud largely captures the socialization process for males, she argues that he misunderstands the ways that females develop a gender identity. Freud's approach reflected the sexist social climate of his time, as he took for granted the patriarchal, male-dominated middle-class family relations of the European nineteenth century as a model of all psychosexual development. The hierarchical family, like the stratified society in which it is embedded, reflects and reproduces the power of males. Freud's Oedipally produced ideology translates into male domination, as he discusses maturity in terms of masculine values such as the repression of the emotions, the performance of tasks over the expression of feeling, and an instrumental rather than a nurturing approach to social relationships.[14]

Chodorow accepts the contention that men and women inhabit very different cultures, but she attempts to validate a woman's culture that has been systematically repressed by a patriarchal society. Chodorow does not reject Freud, but reformulates his theory of female socialization. She sees the pre-Oedipal phase of socialization (the infant's relationship to the mother), as the crucial time and space of psychological development. Gender identity is rooted in the relationship to the mother in large part because of the structure of most families, in which mothers usually have responsibility for childrearing.

According to Chodorow, the connection to the mother is the first intense relationship for girls and boys, as it is all-embracing and the child's very survival depends on the mother. Yet children must to some degree break with the mother in order to develop into autonomous individuals. As Freud rightly understood, boys usually reject their mother and accept the paternal model as embodied by their father in order to develop the appropriate gender identity. Because boys repress this early relationship with the mother, they tend to define themselves as separate from others, they have rigid ego boundaries, they have trouble feeling, and they deny their connectedness and relations to other people because of their rejection of the importance of nurturing.

A girl during the Oedipal phase desires an identification with a male, often the father, to individuate herself from her intense relationship with her mother. But this wish for separation is less intense among girls, as they have a more continuous relationship with their mother than do boys, and thus find it easier to develop a gender identity. They do not have to completely renounce their relationship with their mother, and develop a different gender identity. Accordingly, girls do not need to create a strong, dominating ego, or deny their relationships to other people. Because of their less repressive socialization, nurturing remains an important part of the female personality, and women have a greater continuity of external relationships and more complex inner lives than do men.

While girls turn to males because they realize that is what their mother likes, they never completely transfer their affection to the father, and thus have a more ambivalent sexuality than do males. Women tend to have continuing close attachments to other women throughout their lives, for only other women can truly understand a female's complex inner life. The repression of the relationship to the mother, and consequently to other women, is never fully achieved. In fact, because men are incapable of meeting women's complex emotional needs, women unconsciously try to recreate their early relationship with the mother through having a child. In attempting to recreate the intensity of the mother/daughter bond, women demonstrate that they have a much stronger sense of a self in relation to others than do men.

Chodorow's analysis of mothering has had a powerful impact on much of the feminist literature, informing empirical studies from Lillian Rubin's *Worlds of Pain: Life in the Working-Class Family* (1976) and *Intimate Strangers* (1983) to Janice Radway's *Reading the Romance* (1984). Its echoes can also be heard in one of the most influential feminist discussions of moral development, Carol Gilligan's 1982 work, *In a Different Voice*.

Gilligan argues that women have traditionally been excluded from psychological theories of development. The influential developmental psychologists Jean Piaget and later Lawrence Kohlberg focus on the development of abstract reasoning skills and an understanding of formal rights as keys to cognitive and moral maturity. Erik Erikson sees the developmental task as one of individuation, developing an identity separate from that of others. Women often do not mature in these ideally-typical ways, and consequently are seen as deficient in terms of moral development. Borrowing from Chodorow, Gilligan argues that these psychological theories define all identities in terms of masculine characteristics, as identity is a task of individuation, separation from others, and the capacity to reason abstractly. Women's identity, on the other hand, is defined by attachment and threatened by separation, and ties reasoning closely to context.[15]

For Gilligan, women's moral development results in an "ethic of care," very different from the emphasis on abstract rules and rights characteristic of males. The ethic of care postulates that self and other are interrelated, and that care enhances this self/other relationship. Following Chodorow, Gilligan contends that women's different psychological development creates a self who acknowledges its needs while accepting responsibility for its choices. This simultaneous obligation to self and other dissolves the disparity between selfishness and responsibility, pointing the way toward a more intersubjective and affective notion of moral development than that found in the psychological approaches of Piaget and Kohlberg.[16] Women develop different "ways of knowing" than do men, based much more on empathy and a sensitivity to context than on abstract and rights-oriented reasoning.

These theories of gender intersect with the prevalence of gender differences in everyday life. Gender remains a crucial feature of the categorization of identity in everyday life. In the US, for example, Barrie Thorne argues in her book *Gender Play* (1993) that gender is the most important variable in predicting which groups children prefer to join. Girls hang with girls, boys with boys. Gender is a more significant factor in predicting group affiliation than either race or ethnicity.[17]

Further, boys' and girls' games are very different. Boys tend to play outdoors more than girls, they play more often in large, age-heterogeneous groups, and they play more competitive games. Boys enter into more disputes about the rules and outcomes of games than do girls. Girls' games tend to be less directly competitive, and their interactions in the play context are more concerned with sensitivity and sharing.

Boys are on the whole more rough and tumble than girls in their games, as much of their talk revolves around physical force and strength. Boys rank themselves into a hierarchy achieved through threats, insults, and challenges. Girls have a smaller, "best-friends" approach in groups, as they develop a strong network of friends. Among girls, best friends monitor emotions, share secrets, and become mutually vulnerable. Girls show tension less directly than boys, often turning to intermediaries or third parties to express their emotions, especially when conflict is involved.

While Thorne in *Gender Play* finds some support for the Chodorow/ Gilligan two cultures perspective, she criticizes their approaches as well. Thorne argues that studies of differences between boys and girls often rely on the most visible and dominant children in groups, thus skewing the portrait towards the most aggressive boys and the most other-oriented girls. In reality, there are many boys who are more passive than the more boisterous types. Multiple masculinities and femininities also often surface in groups. Moreover, interactions vary by context and activity, as girls often direct boys when playing house. When boys and girls work on a common project, gender differences are far less pronounced.

Theoretically, the approach developed by Chodorow and Gilligan has been challenged by the theory that all differences between men and women are socially constructed, not a product of the relationships of children to the mother and father. This social constructionist perspective has been radicalized in recent years by a new type of postmodern feminism, which also contests the Chodorow/Gilligan approach. Post-modern theories critique the notion that women and men have firm, different, and clear gender identities that can be easily demarcated. Gender is not a natural fact; it is socially constructed and culturally specific. In these critics' view, the "essentialist" theorizing characteristic of Chodorow and Gilligan often reflects the worldview of white, heterosexual, middle-class women. As feminism has become a broad-based movement, it has changed, and its notions of gender identity and sexuality have been shown to have class, sexual, racial, and ethnic biases. Recent changes in feminist theory and practice demonstrate that gender relations are not fixed, but can vary in different historical eras and with class and race distinctions, among others.[18]

The social construction of gender

An important strand in theorizing gender does not emphasize the significance of sexual differences rooted in deep, psychological child-hood relationships in the formation of gender identity, concentrating instead on the ways that gender is a learned behavior reinforced by the patriarchal structure of society. From this social constructionist per-spective, differences between men and women are not grounded in biology or in early childhood relations to the parents; rather, the social power held by men creates and maintains gender inequality. Patriarchal power relations divide the social world into the private life of the family and women, centered on emotions and nurturing, while the male world is the public sphere of work and politics. Such social arrangements help keep women subordinate to men. The social constructionist version of feminism criticizes gender role socialization which makes girls into stereotypical women and boys into stereotypical men, arguing that socialization patterns must change, and institutions and public life must become more open to women, if true gender equality is to be realized.

The social constructionist perspective has also been very influential in studies of masculinity. For example, in his 1995 book *Masculinities*, Connell argues that men's social privileges and power result from a "hegemonic masculinity" tied to institutional and cultural definitions of gender. In the modern world, Western colonialism has created a world-wide patriarchal order, as Euro-American definitions of masculinity displace local, indigenous understandings of gender. Yet Connell states that it is difficult to construct a single definition of masculinity, as it is constantly being challenged by feminist initiatives and alternative definitions. For Connell, gender is not a stable, biological essence. There are different masculinities which are redefined in every historical period. Masculinity is also tied to social relations, and cannot be separated from corresponding definitions of femininity. Thus, while men maintain power in different historical eras, exactly how they do so is a subject of empirical study.

Connell contends that gender relations are reproduced not only through childhood socialization, but recur over lifetimes and generations. Gender is a product of everyday interactions and institutional practices. Modern institutions are inherently masculine. As Connell states, the gendered nature of institutions is not only due to male control of wealth, income, state power, the means of violence, and cultural authority. The state is also a gendered, masculine institution because "there is a gendered configuring of recruitment and promotion, a gendered configuring of the internal division of labour and systems of control, a gendered configuring of policymaking, practical routines, and ways of mobilizing pleasure and consent."[19]

Further, Connell argues that gender inequality cannot be separated from the social construction of knowledge that serves to support a patriarchal social order. Many seemingly scientific studies of gender difference serve to make the concept seem natural, which effectively depoliticizes it and preserves the gender status quo. Hegemonic masculinity assumes a kind of compulsory heterosexuality; but this notion of sexuality is socially constructed, not grounded in biological universals. This focus on the role of knowledge in shaping social life has affinities with the postmodern critique of power and discipline. Postmodern theorists of gender develop this social constructionist perspective in some different directions, however. While they accept the gendered division of power in most societies, they are suspicious of the very categories of gender that many feminist analyses presuppose. They problematize the assumptions of the self, of sexual liberation, and of objective social science that much feminist analysis assumes. In doing so, postmodern feminists such as Butler and Flax have been heavily influenced by Foucault's discussion of sexuality.

Foucault and sexuality

Foucault's theory of sexuality intersects with his other concerns about the "normalizing" procedures that he believes accompanied the rise of scientific rationality in the West. Foucault contends that Western theories of sexuality, especially as represented in psychoanalysis and other medical and scientific perspectives, share the illusion that they are disinterested and objective discourses on human behavior. They do not recognize that knowledge is always grounded in power relations, and that all knowledge involves coercion, discipline, and normalization.

For Foucault, the rise of modern science intersected with the distinctive Western belief in the individual as the center of motivation and behavior, the focal point of scientific, legal, and philosophical traditions. Foucault believes that the individual is socially constructed, and our very concept of the person derives from scientific practices of normalization and confinement. This orientation informed Foucault's analysis of madness in *Madness and Civilization* (1965) and of the rise of social science in *Discipline and Punish* (1979): he argues that people were given distinctive identities and labeled through the normalizing practices of separation and confinement of the mad, and the categorizations and the descriptions supplied by schools, prisons, and other institutions devoted to the creation and reproduction of social scientific knowledge and practices. Foucault also contends that people turn themselves into individuals through active self-formation, which cannot be separated from the effects of power. It is in this context that Foucault discusses sexuality in *The History of Sexuality* (1980). He believes that sexuality became an obsession for Europeans in the nineteenth century because sex was seen as a key to self-understanding. Foucault analyzes the Western concern with sexuality as an historically particular experience, which involved new types of knowledge and new ways of conceiving and acting upon the self.

Foucault's discussion begins with a critique of the ostensible connection between sexual repression and the maintenance of social power relations, arguments advanced by theorists such as Marcuse and Wilhelm Reich. Foucault states that these theories posit an inherent link between capitalism and sexual repression, for the powerful sexual drives must be repressed in the interests of productive labor. Thus, a social revolution must involve a sexual revolution, as sexual and societal liberation combines "the fervor of knowledge, the determination to change the laws, and the longing for the garden of earthly delights. Because of sexual repression, merely speaking about sex appears to be a subversive act."[20]

Foucault contends that such approaches are wrong-headed. For him the real issue is not whether or not we suffer from sexual repression but why we so adamantly claim that we are sexually repressed, and why we see sexuality as a key to identity. Foucault finds it peculiar that sex is so important to people that they pay professionals to listen to them talk about it. He sees several problems with the sexual repression hypothesis. Foucault argues that power does not work through repression, but rather through its expansion and circulation. The discourses that arose around sexuality in the nineteenth century demonstrated the new types of power relations forming around sex and its ties to the creation of the individual, and should be the proper starting point for any inquiry. Foucault investigates those professions and disciplines which had an interest in promoting public and scientific discussions of sexuality so that they could better examine and discipline it, thereby enhancing their own professional prestige.

Foucault argues that the contemporary assumptions informing our discussions of sexuality posit that sexual desire and orientation is the secret key to our sense of self. He shows that this belief is historically constructed rather than an absolute truth. He turns to the ancient Greeks in order to portray a society that had a different understanding of sexuality and its place in social life. Foucault recognizes that Greek elite culture emphasized love between free adult men and boys. Yet this relationship was not understood by the Greeks in terms of a link between sexual desire and identity. The Greeks made no distinction between homo- and heterosexuality, for they did not carefully examine their sexual passions. Sexual preference was a lifestyle choice, a matter of pleasure along with eating, exercise, and marriage. Love between men and boys was an ethical issue in a distinctive way. For the Greeks, to lead a moral life meant to actively decide one's course of action. Sexuality was a part of this active mastery of life, and became a problem only if it was practiced immoderately, like over-eating. Sexual preference was not socially regulated, and was not considered the key to understanding the individual.[21]

Foucault argues that only with the historical transition to the Roman era did sexuality become a problem to be reflected upon and seen as the crux of the self, as marriage became a site of love rather than merely a political arrangement (as it had been under the Greeks). As Seidman states, "This narrowing of intimate culture was part of a broader change to a culture preoccupied with 'the care of the self' or with the shaping of subjectivity."[22] As discourses around sexuality gradually developed, they in turn generated an experience of sexual identity. In the nineteenth century, a discursive explosion around sexuality occurred. Foucault argues that at the root of this conflagration were agencies of social power, such as the medical profession, which encouraged the discussion of sexuality so that information on it could be accumulated. To gain mastery over sexuality, it was necessary to master the languages of sexuality.[23]

Foucault traces the genesis of the link between sexuality and discourse to the centrality of confession in Christianity. Christian confession tied discourse to self-examination, attempting to control desire itself through transforming sexuality into language. Christianity's evaluation of sexuality was eventually replaced by new technical and economic institutions in the West. As these institutions arose from the seventeenth- to nineteenth-centuries, sexuality was not simply something to be judged; it was to be actively administered. This new concern with sexuality was demonstrated in early modern administrative concerns with the birthrate, as sexuality became a site for potential government intervention.

The discussion of sexuality soon took on medical and criminal overtones in the eighteenth century, as schoolmasters and parents became concerned with the sexuality of children, and medicine, psychiatry, and criminal justice produced discourses around sexuality. Far from repressing sexuality, these new languages had the effect of encouraging children and others to discuss the issue with increasing frequency. For Foucault, the notion that sexuality is a key to identity resulted from the multiplication of new discourses around sex which made it an object of almost obsessive attention, rather than repression. Thus, religious confession metamorphosed into modern psychiatry, and helped create the notion that sex is the secret lurking beneath our actions, the key to unlocking our identities. The eighteenth-century discourses around sex created new categories of perversity, as children, criminals, women, and homosexuals came under unprecedented scrutiny. New professionals arose who created new scientific knowledges.[24]

In sum, Foucault believes that the power over sexuality is not based on prohibition, but on a proliferation of discourses around the subject. Educators and doctors attacked children's sexuality as if it were a disease. Their discourses created new categories of normality and deviance, which in turn defined people's very sense of identity. From the eighteenth century, every individual had a sexual biography which either conformed to or deviated from the norm. The study and discussion of sexuality demanded new medical experts, who increased their power through scientifically surveying children and others. Thus, the new type of power, based on growing numbers of studies, discussions, etc., required the surveillance of sexuality rather than keeping it hidden as a taboo topic.

For Foucault, the analysis of sexuality shows the intimate connection between knowledge and power. The production of power occurs through its expansion, not its repression. The gap between Foucault's perspective and Freud's, as well as most scientific perspectives, could not be wider. For Freud, to liberate individuals from the grip of unconscious forces requires the bringing of unconscious desires into the light of public discussion, because the secrets of people's actions lie beneath their conscious understanding. Knowledge of the reasons underlying repression causes the repressed to lose its motivating power over everyday life. For Foucault, the very opposite is the case. There are no deterministic causal factors underlying our consciousness. Power works by openly expanding and infiltrating different areas of public life, creating discourses which inform people's very sense of identity.

Postmodern feminism

Foucault's analysis has implications for feminism. He demonstrates that sexual identity is not an essential category of the self, but that it is constructed differently in different historical eras. Sexual identities are also tied to power; they are the effects of social practices and knowledges that determine "appropriate" types of gendered selves. Postmodern feminists in particular argue that gender identity results from discourses (often scientific) which posit dichotomous, essential male/ female differences. Like Foucault, they contend that such identities are socially created, and as socially produced they carry much force, and shape people's sense of self. Postmodern feminists also share Foucault's suspicions about the "normality" of exclusive male and female, or gay and straight, identities, for such strict, demarcated identities can regulate people's behavior and options. For these theorists, the idea of female and/or gay/lesbian liberation can be as illusory as the Marcuse model of sexual emancipation that Foucault critiqued.[25]

Flax and Butler are two of the more important feminist thinkers who work in the general terrain sketched by Foucault and poststructuralism, but who have developed new insights about sexuality and gender. Flax argues that essentialist ideas about a true male or female identity arise from the Enlightenment idea that rationality can mirror objective experience, when in reality this assumption of a transparent reason reflects the experience of white, Western males. Such a rationality that views some cultural constructions as "natural" can easily lead to the creation of categories of "normal" sexuality which can brand others, such as gays and lesbians, as somehow deviant and unnatural. Skeptical of all claims to truth and a fixed self, and in line with postmodern criticism of the notion of an essential reality outside of our perceptions of it, Flax's postmodern feminist theory demonstrates that gender is socially constructed. Moreover, feminist theory itself is tied to particular types of social experience (such as class and race), as its very diversity demonstrates. Men and women are both prisoners of socially constructed versions of gender, which must be transfigured for new identities to have room to flourish.[26]

Butler deconstructs the notion of gender even more radically. She argues that feminist theories that posit a distinctive women's culture close off possible experiences that might explode these very categories of gender. Gender identity is an illusion that ultimately relies on patriarchal and modernist assumptions about psychological development. There is no true self underlying actions; like Foucault, she believes that the self is an effect of power.

Butler turns to the French psychoanalyst Jacques Lacan for an alternative conceptualization of the development of the psyche. Following Lacan, Butler argues that unconscious psychological processes create radical discontinuities which characterize the psyche prior to the formation of the notion of a separate, unified self. This self is based on the repression of very different and often conflicting identifications with different people, such as parents. Because of these multiple identifications, the self is always unstable. But even Lacan views sexual differences as primary forms of psychic identification, even if they are less coherent than Freud believed them to be. For Butler, such a view of sexual difference is actually a norm of heterosexual coherence which limits possible sexual identities.[27]

Butler wishes to substitute the idea of fantasy identifications for the concrete identifications with the mother and the father on which so much psychological theory is based. For Butler, we identify with fantasies about the mother and father, rather than with their reality (which we can never know). We also have many different, and often conflicting, dream-like types of psychic identification. These fantasies constitute our very identities, for we derive our sense of self from identifications. But fantasies do not create a deep sense of self, only the chimera of one. To the extent that gender exists, it is because we repeatedly act in gendered ways which are socially reinforced, especially in our bodily actions (through clothes, ways of walking and talking, and the like). In Seidman's words, "Gender is a learned, situational performance whose dramatic effect is the illusion of an inner gendered self."[28]

We thus fabricate our identities mythically, through fantasy – and in doing so, we believe that we truly express a male or female gender. These fantasies about gender and self are reinforced by society, as in the images of men and women given to us by the mass media. Gender identities are tied to social power, for idealizations of men and women "are embodied in dominant cultural representations and social practices."[29] Butler offers drag as an antidote to the expressive notion of gender, for crossdressing mocks the very notion of a true gender identity. With drag, people can see the extent to which gender is fabricated and performed. Gender results from personal and social politics, and it is not a natural expression of an inner self. Gender coherence helps to maintain us in the straitjacket of imposed identity.[30]

From the postmodern social constructionist perspective, any notion of sexual or gender coherence is suspect, for it is tied to the repression of difference, whether in the formation of the self (as Lacan argues) or in the repression of alternative practices of sexuality (as Foucault contends). Giddens takes up issues of sexuality and personal identity, but places them in a theoretical framework very different from that of the postmodernists.

Giddens on the transformation of intimacy

Giddens is sympathetic to many feminist themes, as he sees women as "the emotional revolutionaries of modernity." He views changes in sexuality and gender as providing new bases of social identity in contemporary societies. He accepts the critique of Freud and feminist essentialism advanced by the postmodern feminists, though he is more critical of the psychoanalytic notion of the unconscious than are many postmodern feminists influenced by Lacan. Giddens believes that postmodernists err when they deconstruct the conscious self as a modernist, masculine illusion. Giddens contends that feminism and the conditions of late modernity converge to create a new, reflexive self that is the basis of possibilities for liberatory social change.

Giddens argues that the self is now a reflexive project in the West, as people draw on resources as diverse as therapy and self-help manuals to fashion their identity. Changes in conceptions of self and sexuality develop simultaneously. While Giddens shares Foucault's conviction that beliefs about sexuality influence social organization, he argues that Foucault, like postmodern feminism, falls victim to a one-way determinism in which people are not given credit as skilled agents who can create new identities. Giddens argues that institutional and individual reflexivity informs the intersection of sexuality and society, because sexuality enters social life in a way that cannot be controlled. Issues around sexuality are reflexively incorporated by people into their everyday life, often with unintended results. Foucault's discussion of sexuality ignores the struggles around it, as well as its potentially emancipatory character. Giddens believes that the creation of administrative power, whether through defining "normal" sexuality or labeling certain acts as criminal, is much more dialectical than Foucault imagines, as people are active agents who can oppose and change these very definitions, and more generally help shape the societies in which they live.[31]

Giddens also contends that the critique of any notion of the self as essentialist, shared by Foucault and many postmodern feminists, is misguided, for it misunderstands the social nature of language. As we saw in Chapter 3, for Giddens, language is pragmatic; it solves problems when used reflexively. Just because language is context-dependent does not mean that we cannot develop identities that cohere across time and space. Poststructuralism cannot grasp the fluid and intersubjective social practices of everyday life that inform the creation of identities. By emphasizing the centrality of texts, linguistic conventions, and fantasy identifications grounded in childhood, postmodernists do not account for the complexity of social interaction or comprehend the centrality of reflexivity in producing and reproducing these practices. Intimacy in particular is now infused with a reflexivity and democratic equality which requires the continual renegotiation of personal identities. By grasping the pragmatic formation of identities and placing them in their historical context, it is possible to see that male violence does not stem from patriarchy alone, but also from a context of democratic intimacy in which men have trouble negotiating an identity and lose many of their privileges.[32]

Giddens's pragmatic approach also rejects many of the tenets of Freudian analysis. According to Giddens, while the formation of onto-logical security in childhood is an important factor in achieving an autonomous self, unconscious desires have at best an indirect effect on social behavior, as they are invariably mediated by social practices. Thus, focusing on infant/parent relations cannot form the major explanatory basis of social behavior. While Giddens shares Chodorow's contention that men are defined by loss and separation from the mother much more than women, he states that femininity and masculinity are more intertwined than Chodorow recognizes. Giddens is thus much more amenable to the social constructionist perspective on identity and gender. As he states, "gender is constructed and reconstructed in the flow of interaction in day-to-day social life."[33]

Giddens finds Connell's ideas particularly close to his own views on the social construction of gender. Like Connell, Giddens states that masculinity and femininity are constituted and reproduced in the context of the power differentials of everyday, mundane life. Gender identity is best thought of as a property of institutions, as it is "embedded in the recurrent practices whereby institutions are structured."[34] For example, Giddens sees the separation of domestic and public spheres as instrumental in the reproduction of gender relations. Echoing Connell, he states that especially important in this respect is the sexual division of labor, as "segregated labour markets set up constraints upon job advancement through the influence of differential skills and other factors." The expectation that women will raise children and perform domestic chores limits women's opportunities, as gendered, unequal social relations are "incorporated within the various practices carried on in paid work and in the home."[35]

While Giddens is sympathetic to many of Connell's arguments, he develops a theory of sexuality and gender identity which draws on his approach to modernity and the self. For Giddens, sexuality is linked to the reflexivity of the individual, and is inextricably tied to the demo-cratization of personal life that feminism has helped bring about. This individualization of sexuality not only develops from the new scientific discourses that Foucault addresses, but is in large part due to the independent actions of women. Giddens develops a different version than Foucault of the history of sexuality in the West. In his view, as families became smaller, children were viewed as vulnerable. Accordingly, women grew in importance as caregivers of the family. Romantic love was a key aspect of this new familial situation. Giddens sees romantic love as "essentially feminised love," which raises the issue of intimacy in a profoundly new manner.[36] For Giddens, women promoted an expansion and democratization of the intimate sphere. This new intimate realm was far more complex than Foucauldian analysis recognizes, as it arose due to the actions of women rather than the workings of an anonymous power.

Giddens does see problems with this new private/public dichotomy, however. *Contra* Foucault, he argues that as sexual activity became tied to the nuclear family and freed from the constraints of reproduction, sexuality was "sequestered," in Giddens's word. It retreated behind public scenes and contributed to an increasingly intense private intimacy. According to Giddens, sexuality became privatized as the ideologies of motherhood and domesticity were invented. Sexuality's sequestration was due to the denial or confinement of female sexuality and the acceptance of male sexuality as unproblematic. Women were excluded from public life, and became managers of psychological and intimate transformations. Yet there were many tensions in attempting to keep sexuality sequestered. Perhaps the most famous example is that of Freud's famous studies of the sexual basis of hysteria in nineteenth-century Vienna.[37]

Giddens argues that the sequestration of experience is tied to modernity's break with tradition, as modernity's system of controls extends across pre-existing boundaries of social action. The sequestration of experience creates a greater need for ontological security grounded in routines. Sexuality becomes an important issue in the West not as an act of Foucauldian disciplinary power, but precisely because it connects the sequestration of experience and the transformation of intimacy. Identities, thought to be natural, are now recognized as socially created, and sexuality becomes a way of expressing these changing, fluid identities. Sexuality also puts people in touch with sequestered areas of existential experience. More open discussions of sexuality have contributed to more egalitarian relationships between adults and between parents and children.[38]

Giddens contends that everyday life in the West is being transformed by new types of social experiments. Sexuality ranks high among these new lifestyles, especially as it connects the body, social norms, and self-identity. In the wake of the expansion of reproductive technologies and the feminist and gay/lesbian movements, sexuality has become "plastic," a "decentered sexuality freed from the needs of reproduction."[39] A plastic sexuality can no longer assume the norm of heterosexuality, as gays and lesbians in particular have demonstrated that sexuality is "free-floating" and socially created.[40]

Giddens develops the notion of the "pure relationship" as an archetype for modern intimacy, as it is entered into for its own sake and is founded on the mutual emotional satisfaction of partners. The pure relationship is uncertain and based on the commitment of partners to one another, which is fragile in the conditions of late modernity. Its focus on the shared exploration of the self and the creation of shared histories involves both continual reflexive attention and the difficult task of the generation of mutual trust.[41]

This new type of relationship involves a new version of love, which Giddens calls "confluent love." Confluent love assumes an active opening up on the part of one partner towards the other. It replaces the patriarchy and gender imbalance characteristic of romantic love, for confluent love is based on equality. Giddens believes that sexual equality has been encouraged not only by feminism, but also by the proliferation of therapies and self-help books that permeate popular culture in the West. These books promote the self as a reflexive project which must be constantly reshaped and reformed. For example, psychoanalysis may not cure neuroses, but it "provides a setting, and a rich fund of theoretical and conceptual resources, for the creation of a reflexively ordered narrative of self."[42]

For Giddens, a reflexive self leads to a democratization of personal life, where relationships take on the characteristics of confluent love. The opening to the other is a basis for "democratically ordered interaction," in which equality characterizes the rights and obligations of intimacy.[43] The democratization of the private sphere provides the resources for a rich democratic life, for democracy must be socially and personally cultivated, and can only exist when individuals are sufficiently "self-reflective and self-determining."[44] Feminism has ushered in a type of emotional democracy, which translates into institutional democratic practices.

The distinctiveness of the modern self

Giddens believes that late modern social and cultural conditions create an unprecedented context for new types of self-development. He argues that in contemporary times people must answer basic existential questions without the support of traditional guidelines, including what the person should do, how s/he should act, and who s/he should be.

Giddens states that individuality, in the sense of the individual cultivation of personal capacities and tastes, has always existed in all cultures. What is distinctive about the modern self is encapsulated in the therapeutic ethos and practices of modernity. For Giddens, reflexivity is the most important characteristic of the modern self. We make ourselves, and build our own sense of identity. The self has a trajectory, as it develops through a "series of 'passages'" toward authenticity.[45] Self-development is "all-pervasive" and "continuous," as the narrative of the modern self is consciously constructed. We are all in a sense self-pioneers. This reflexivity extends to all aspects of identity, including the body. A key component of this reflexivity is that the self often approaches the world in a strategic way, as it calculates risks and opportunities. Such decisions must be made without any reference to traditional methods of self-formation, as the modern self is "internally referential," charting its development in terms of its own fallible, contingent history.[46]

This new identity is necessarily beset with many problems and possibilities. Giddens sees this self-creation neither as a loss of individual control in the face of social change nor as a limitless opportunity for novel types of self-identity. Giddens recognizes that many individuals feel powerless in the modern context, but he argues for a dialectical view of this process, as the rise of modernity has also generated new capacities for self-expression and empowerment.

Modernity undoubtedly creates dilemmas for the self. The interpenetration of the local and the distant creates an everyday self-consciousness which is "for the most part truly global."[47] The self must face the problem of unification versus fragmentation, of keeping a viable narrative operative in the face of globalization. The modern self confronts a dizzying array of contexts, which can contribute to fragmentation. But this can also result in a kind of "cosmopolitan person" who is capable of drawing on many different resources and experiences in the construction of an autobiographical narrative.[48]

Giddens argues that the formation of the modern self takes place in a social context where established authority is continually threatened by uncertainty and delegitimation. Giddens's theory of reflexive modernization states that as traditional forms of social control decline, laypeople develop a skeptical outlook toward all types of authority. The church, the state, and parents also compete with lifestyle models derived from the images of the mass media. The pervasiveness of such imagery leads to a conflict between its commodified, packaged version of experience and the personalized experience of people. The construction of the modern self takes place in the interstices of this dualism, in the overall context of the "standardising effects of commodity capitalism."[49] Commodification disembeds economic relations from everyday life while standardizing consumption patterns through processes such as advertising. Self-help therapies can also become pre-packaged, almost like commodities, when they encourage people to respond to personal and social problems in a stereotypical manner.

Giddens believes that market-driven commodification at least gives people some different choices among products and lifestyles. As he states, "mass produced clothing still allows individuals to decide selectively on styles of dress, however much the standardising influence of fashion and other forces affect those individual decisions."[50] Giddens contends that people can creatively and critically appropriate the images and products given to them by the mass media. He argues that "even young children evaluate television programmes in terms of their degree of realism, recognising that some are wholly fictional, and treat programmes as objects of scepticism, derision, or humour."[51] Yet the commodification of experience highlights the recurring problem of personal meaninglessness that modern people face. The stripping away of tradition leaves individuals with only their own resources to guide them; maintaining basic trust in the integrity of the self and others cannot be taken for granted.

Giddens's most recent theoretical observations owe a great deal to contemporary feminism. Giddens argues that feminism has not only fundamentally changed relationships between men and women, but has substantially influenced social relations more generally. Feminism has revolutionized personal relationships between the genders, making them more democratic and open to change. Democracy and openness practiced at the personal level give an important impetus to more overtly political demands for global human rights, contributing to the cosmopolitanism that Giddens believes is the most promising perspective for a more democratic future. Like the philosopher Richard Rorty, Giddens contends that globalization informed by feminism brings with it the prospect of "a cosmopolitan conversation of humankind," though the possibility of violence between peoples remains.[52] The personal/political intersection claimed by feminism has become a truism in modern life, as more and more people realize that there is nothing engraved in stone about sexuality and gender. Not only have sexual and gender relations become more "plastic," in Giddens's terminology, but self-development is now a project that is reflexively monitored and determined by individuals themselves. This project is fraught with new possibilities and challenges, as traditional roadmaps for the development of personal identity crumble in the face of the juggernaut of late modernity.

Giddens does not accept the postmodern feminist criticisms of sexuality and the self, however. For Giddens, the self is much more than a fiction, as people actively create and reproduce their lives, even if they do so in increasingly uncertain circumstances. Individuals still create narratives of personal development, and they need a sense of ontological security to do so. These invariant features of the human condition require social routines which can stabilize interactions over time; however, in his later writings Giddens is far less adamant about this social component of ontological security.

The issue of self-development points to a recurring problem in Giddens's analysis. Especially in his later work Giddens posits a strong self which heroically creates narratives of personal development in uncertain times. Such a perspective gives short shrift to the structural and cultural factors still at work in fashioning the self. Thus, Giddens relatively neglects the issue of the boundaries set by the cultural context in which people find themselves, on the one hand, and the powerful social structures that are at work in shaping personal development, on the other. Scott Lash contends that the reflexivity so important to personal development is circumscribed by the social structural conditions of class and race. Social-structurally privileged people have more possibilities of constructing their own narratives, for they have more social power.[53] Despite his critical discussion of the ideology of productivism and his appreciation of Connell's work, Giddens lacks a thorough discussion of the social bases and privileges of a hegemonic masculinity, in Connell's terms. An even more glaring lacuna in Giddens's analysis is any extended critical exploration of the role of race in legitimizing dominant conceptions of masculinity, and more generally in reproducing social stratification.

Nevertheless, Giddens's theoretical approach points to some promising directions for understanding the contemporary significance of feminism and modern sexuality. His approach demonstrates the myriad and complex ways in which self and society, politics and the individual, and social movements and personal identity intersect. As Giddens argues, feminism has connected the personal and the political in new ways. Rather than becoming a form of narcissism and self-absorption, the new personal politics can lead to a democratization of individual life, and to a recognition of the importance of human rights and democracy at the international level.

For Giddens, the impact of feminism has resulted in the gradual decline of the productivist ethic so central to the rise of industrial societies. As productivism fades, new values may come to the fore. The transformation of femininity and masculinity associated with feminism may lead to a new historical era where universal, cosmopolitan values reign, and a post-scarcity society may emerge, which recognizes that untrammeled economic growth can be harmful and counterproductive. A post-scarcity society validates informal economies which bolster local solidarities, and questions the dominance of paid work over other forms of activities, such as childrearing. Indeed, Giddens's model of equality rejects productivism in favor of the pursuit of happiness, which he defines as the realization of security, self-respect, and self-actualization. State and private programs should be based on such a concept of generative welfare which can contribute to the formation of a cosmopolitan and autonomous self.

Giddens believes that a post-scarcity society must be founded on an appreciation of cultural differences and a respect for local, indigenous heritages. He contends that the modern welfare state has not achieved these goals, and is complicit with the productivism that has so damaged the modern world. We now turn to a more detailed discussion of Giddens's critique of the welfare state.

Notes

1 Peter Gay, *The Cultivation of Hatred: The Bourgeois Experience, Victoria to Freud* (New York, Oxford University Press, 1993), pp. 289–297.

2 Anthony Giddens, *Modernity and Self-Identity: Self and Society in the Late Modern Age* (Stanford, Stanford University Press, 1991), p. 102.

3 Ibid., p. 32; italics in the original.

4 Ibid., p. 54.

5 See Arlie Hochschild, *The Second Shift* (New York, Avon Books, 1989).

6 Sigmund Freud, *A General Introduction to Psychoanalysis* (New York, Pocket Books, 1953), p. 27.

7 Ibid., pp. 319–322, 365, 421.

8 See Terry Eagleton, *The Ideology of the Aesthetic* (Cambridge, MA, Blackwell, 1990), p. 272; Freud, *A General Introduction to Psychoanalysis*, p. 219.

9 Herbert Marcuse, *Eros and Civilization: A Philosophical Inquiry into Freud* (New York, Vintage, 1955), Chapter 1.

10 Ibid., pp. 199–202, 208–217.

11 Herbert Marcuse, *One Dimensional Man* (Boston, Beacon Press, 1964).

12 Anthony Giddens, *The Transformation of Intimacy: Sexuality, Love, and Eroticism in Modern Societies* (Stanford, Stanford University Press, 1992), pp. 169–170.

13 Marcuse, *Eros and Civilization*, p. 230.

14 Nancy Chodorow, *The Reproduction of Mothering: Psychoanalysis and the Sociology of Gender* (Berkeley, University of California Press, 1978).

15 Carol Gilligan, *In a Different Voice* (Cambridge, MA, Harvard University Press, 1982), pp. 8–19.

16 Ibid., pp. 85, 94.

17 Barrie Thorne, *Gender Play: Boys and Girls in School* (New Brunswick, NJ, Rutgers University Press, 1993).

18 Jane Flax, "Postmodernism and Gender Relations in Feminist Theory," in *Feminism/Postmodernism*, ed. Linda Nicholson (New York, Routledge, 1990), p. 40.

19 Robert Connell, *Masculinities* (Berkeley, University of California Press, 1995), p. 73.

20 *The Foucault Reader*, ed. Paul Rabinow (New York, Pantheon Books, 1984), pp. 295–296.

21 Ibid., p. 340; see also Steven Seidman, *Contested Knowledge: Social Theory in the Postmodern Era* (Cambridge, MA, Basil Blackwell, 1994), pp. 218–219.

22 Seidman, *Contested Knowledge*, p. 219.

23 *The Foucault Reader*, ed. Rabinow, pp. 301–302.

24 Ibid., pp. 311–318.

25 Seidman, *Contested Knowledge*, pp. 217, 246.

26 Flax, "Postmodernism and Gender Relations in Feminist Theory," pp. 41–45; see also Flax, *Thinking Fragments: Psychoanalysis, Feminism, and Postmodernism in the Contemporary West* (Berkeley, University of California Press, 1990).

27 Judith Butler, "Gender Trouble, Feminist Theory, and Psychoanalytic

Discourse," *Feminism/Postmodernism*, ed. Nicholson, pp. 324–333; see also Butler, *Gender Trouble: Feminism and the Subversion of Identity* (New York, Routledge, 1990).

28 Seidman, *Contested Knowledge*, p. 252.

29 Ibid.

30 Butler, "Gender Trouble, Feminist Theory, and Psychoanalytic Discourse," pp. 335–339.

31 Giddens, *The Transformation of Intimacy*, pp. 28–30, 172–173.

32 Ibid., pp. 114, 122.

33 Giddens, "A Reply to My Critics," in *Social Theory of Modern Societies: Anthony Giddens and His Critics*, ed. David Held and John B. Thompson (New York, Cambridge University Press, 1989), p. 285.

34 Ibid.

35 Giddens, "Structuration Theory: Past, Present, Future," in *Giddens' Theory of Structuration: A Critical Appreciation*, ed. Christopher G.A. Bryant and David Jary (New York, Routledge, 1991), p. 215.

36 Giddens, *The Transformation of Intimacy*, pp. 44–45.

37 Ibid., pp. 177–178.

38 Ibid., pp. 180–182.

39 Ibid., p. 2.

40 Ibid., pp. 14, 34.

41 Giddens, *Modernity and Self-Identity*, pp. 89–97.

42 Giddens, *The Transformation of Intimacy*, p. 31.

43 Ibid., pp. 188–191.

44 Ibid., p. 185.

45 Giddens, *Modernity and Self-Identity*, p. 79.

46 Ibid., p. 80.

47 Ibid., p. 187.

48 Ibid., p. 191.

49 Ibid., p. 196.

50 Ibid., p. 200.

51 Ibid., p. 199.

52 Giddens, "Living in a Post-Traditional Society," in Ulrich Beck, Anthony Giddens, and Scott Lash, *Reflexive Modernization: Politics, Tradition and Aesthetics in the Modern Social Order* (Stanford, Stanford University Press, 1994), p. 100; Richard Rorty, *Contingency, Irony, Solidarity* (New York, Cambridge University Press, 1989).

53 Scott Lash, "Reflexivity and Its Doubles," in Beck, Giddens, Lash, *Reflexive Modernization*, p. 120.

CONCLUSION

Giddens sees expanded social reflexivity accompanied by the globalization and the emergence of a post-traditional world as primary characteristics of late modernity. New knowledges and new social movements become widespread and manufactured uncertainty increases. This contemporary social context calls for a new type of politics, in Giddens's view. The mobile and ever-changing nature of manufactured uncertainty means that it cannot be controlled by old political solutions, as problems can no longer be mastered in the Enlightenment sense of people's self-conscious dominion over the natural and social world. Accordingly, socialism is dead, and political positions from welfare-statism to neo-conservatism are dying. None of these political orientations supplies the theoretical resources necessary to confront contemporary social problems.[1]

For Giddens, life politics forms the basis for a new radical politics, which must be concerned with repairing damaged solidarities, and preserving and reinventing traditions which provide a meaningful context for people's lives. Trust must be actively won and created. Life politics is a generative politics, which dispenses with the traditional liberal/conservative division, and transcends "state provision versus privatization" as the primary solution to social problems. It means that people must reflexively create and sustain their own lives, often outside of the formal political realm.[2]

Giddens states that this new politics requires a rethinking of the modern welfare state. He argues that many conservative critiques of the welfare state are on the mark, for it has been unable to reduce poverty or generate income transfers, and has created large, bloated, government bureaucracies. The Western welfare state resulted from a class compromise between the working class and economic elites: realized in the 1950s, it embodied economic equality and rationality. The welfare state arose in tandem with a manufacturing economy. State officials recognized that new governmental measures had to be taken to protect people. Bolstered by strong industrial labor movements and the two world wars, which increased central government power, the welfare state attempted to manage social risk. It encouraged economic bargaining between large unions and big firms, mediated by a reformist government, in the name of national solidarity.[3]

Such a state is now outmoded, in Giddens's view. Most welfare state measures are based on dealing with failures of the government or the market, rather than confronting and solving problems at their origin. The welfare state promotes a gendered workforce, as the domestic work performed largely by women is not counted as real, paid labor. Moreover, the class issues informing welfare state policies are now less relevant for everyday existence. Welfare state programs are tied to the emancipatory politics of economic growth and redistribution of wealth, and are unable to deal with the new issues of cultural diversity and self-actualization arising from life politics that are becoming more central in people's lives.[4]

Because welfare state aid programs often create bureaucracies which are inflexible, inefficient, and serve the interests of bureaucrats rather than their clients, a post-scarcity type of politics and society is necessary. A post-scarcity society is concerned with more than economic prosperity, rejects the ideology of productivism central to the welfare state, and recognizes that out of control consumption is a world-wide problem. It sees markets as "signaling devices" which let firms know where more production is needed, but it is sensitive to the role of markets in creating the economic class divisions as was recognized by Marx. The dominance of paid work and economic concerns central to the welfare state must be replaced with new issues. Giddens calls for policies oriented to the building of new traditions, or the protection of old ones, as everyday allegiances have to be fostered.[5]

Giddens's model of equality moves away from a concern with productivism toward the pursuit of happiness, which includes a sense of security, self-respect, and self-actualization. Such a "generative welfare" is tied to a new individualism that is now widespread in the West. The new individual is not the egoistic, self-interested person caricatured in the 1980s "me-decade" of Reagan and Thatcher. Rather, new individualism refers to the quest for personal autonomy, in which the trust of others and of institutions must be actively won. The new individualism can potentially give rise to an autonomous self, based on self-confidence and a strong sense of ontological security which allows for the tolerance and appreciation of differences among peoples. It would involve a pact between rich and poor, based on a sense of mutual responsibility, the desirability of lifestyle changes for the rich and the poor, and an expansive notion of welfare oriented toward developing the autonomous self. Such "positive welfare" connects individual autonomy and collective responsibility. For example, a positive version of health care is proactive, focusing on preventing illness, rather than treating it. To achieve these ends, the state would have to work with a variety of self-help groups. Affected groups must be heavily involved in government programs, which must draw on "the reflexivity of the individuals or groups they address."[6]

In sum, the welfare system is tied to a notion of life as fate, which is influenced by external risks. However, this approach misrepresents the most fundamental issues confronting modern societies. Major contemporary social problems do not concern the funding of welfare institutions, but involve "how to reorder those institutions so as to make them mesh with the much more active, reflexive lives that most of us now lead."[7] For Giddens, social reflexivity must inform life politics and generative politics, if they are to be effective. This politics should adopt a utopian realism, aimed at combating poverty, addressing ecological problems, contesting arbitrary power, and reducing the role of force and violence in everyday life.[8]

Giddens on labour politics

Giddens believes that his vision of a new left politics can find a home in the British Labour Party, as it rethinks its traditions and policies in the wake of the decline of socialism. As he has moved to become Director of the London School of Economics, he has become an informal adviser to Tony Blair and an important spokesperson for the Labour Party. For Giddens, the possibilities for a refurbished Labour Party grow out of the problems faced by Conservatism.

Giddens argues that the Conservative political position outlined in the 1980s by Thatcher and Reagan is inherently contradictory, for it advocates an unrestricted free market in the economic realm, and traditional values in the personal sphere. Yet the play of the market undermines tradition, as Marx and Engels recognized in *The Communist Manifesto*. Giddens concurs with Marx and Engels's assessment that the market "sweeps away all fixed, fast-frozen relations, with their train of ancient and venerable prejudices and opinions."[9]

While Giddens finds Conservative solutions to modern social problems to be non-existent, he rejects the welfare-statist and socialist policies traditionally advocated by Labour. Giddens contends that Labour's major idea should concern "civic restructuring," and this still involves repairing the damage to communal solidarities inflicted by capitalism. But an effective, modern model of community must be based on the new individualism, in which people actively construct their lives more than they did in the past.[10]

Giddens states that these changes entail a rethinking of Labour's philosophy. Labour must break with Keynesian welfare-statism. Welfare provisions must be changed, so that one-parent families without fathers are not encouraged. The power of labor unions over the Party must be severed, and new types of partnership between unions and industry encouraged. Correspondingly, Labour should not be beholden to finance capital, and should seek to close tax loopholes which unfairly benefit financial elites.[11] Labour needs policies which sustain low inflation and long-term infrastructure investment. Socialist concepts cannot supply policies which result in these economic benefits. Giddens contends that socialism is theoretically impoverished, for, *contra* Marx, "political and administrative power does not derive directly from control of the means of production."[12] Accordingly, socialist goals no longer make sense, and any leftist party must rid itself of beliefs in the virtues of the planned direction of the economy, the socialization of the means of production, the coming to political and economic power of the working class, and the disappearance of private capital.

The decline of socialism is also tied to social changes. The decrease of the manual and industrial working class as a percentage of the working population, combined with the globalization of capitalism, have destroyed class as a major indicator of social identity. Moreover, class communities no longer cohere because of the prevalence of the new individualism. In Giddens's view, the new poor of the chronically unemployed and single mothers do not form a class-based community.[13]

What then is of value in the socialist tradition? Giddens states that notions of equality and democracy are still central to a left politics. However, they must be understood in new ways, as Labour should try to "foster new forms of social solidarity, cohesion, and civic culture."[14] State welfare programs will not solve social problems by themselves, and they must be put in the context "of a wider drive against inequality" of all sorts, from gender to race. He states that an integral component of this rethinking is the equation of socialism with an attitude of care for oneself, others, and "the fabric of the material world."[15] An attitude of care means recognizing and nurturing human interdependence, while also realizing the value of diversity.

For example, Giddens states that fostering strong families is indeed important for a healthy society, but that the nuclear family is not the model to emulate. For Giddens, strong families are based on a variety of kinship ties beyond that of the mother and father. Moreover, in some societies such as Italy, families become too concerned with their own affairs, which can lead to a lack of community involvement. For Giddens, this demonstrates that contemporary communities will necessarily be more diverse than in the past. Recognition of this diversity demands a strong sense of cosmopolitanism among people, as they must be able to value ways of life different from their own.[16]

According to Giddens, cosmopolitanism and the new individualism demand new Labour policies, which include modernizing the state, attempting to create wealth and not simply redistribute it, and dealing with unemployment while pursuing egalitarianism. In order to modernize the state, the central government must give up some of its power to a more active citizenry while respecting the constraints brought about by globalization. For example, new regulations about children's rights might have to be negotiated with local groups and international organizations. Problems of wealth creation and unemployment should not only be tackled by creating more jobs, but also by equalizing work time between men and women and the rich and poor. Greater gender equality in housework and childrearing and more flexibility in work schedules can help mitigate the culture of productivism that is anathema to Giddens, and reduce the dominance of paid work over other aspects of life. For Giddens, civic obligations can only be improved "in the context of a restructuring of jobs, work, and family obligations."[17]

While Giddens advocates more education to increase economic productivity, he is suspicious of purely vocational training. In Giddens's view, education should be wide-ranging and humanistic, encouraging a cosmopolitan attitude and enhancing "a wide range of life values."[18] Humanistic education will actually be more practical in responding to social problems than technical instruction, for it will teach people the value of engaging in preventative and caring activity toward oneself, others, and the environment. Such an education would encourage people to take responsibility for solving problems through their own actions, rather than relying on technical solutions formulated by a state bureaucracy.

This type of education would encourage a reflexive, productive citizenry, combat the predominance of outmoded social ideas and policies, and challenge the belief that economic growth can solve all problems. As Giddens states, "Contesting productivism while promoting productivity is the only route to follow if a low-inflation, low-growth society is also to refurbish itself and give substance to values of participation and equality."[19]

Giddens's odyssey has taken him from the reconstruction of social theory to the rethinking of the politics of the Labour Party. Such seemingly disparate interests have been linked by his continuing attempts to discern the main contours of modernity, which ties theory to practice. Yet Giddens's proposal for a new politics points to an interesting tension in his work. He recognizes that damaged solidarities must be repaired, but they can only be (re)constructed on the basis of the autonomous, Promethean self. Giddens's political stance replicates the inconsistency in his theoretical work between the power of society (as in the importance he attributes to social routines), and the autonomy of the individual. Despite Giddens's attempts to overcome the structure/agency duality, he has not so much resolved this discrepancy as wavered between the two poles of society/individual. In his earlier work, he stresses the centrality of social routines and large-scale social changes (such as the emergence of the nation-state) in shaping individual behavior. In his recent studies of modernity, he reverts to a view of the individual as almost separated from social structures, and as having transformative abilities that allow him/her to reshape social forces in his/her own interests. This conception of individual autonomy influences Giddens's conception of how people become competent members of society. For Giddens, "individuation is defined as either absolute creativity or absolute conformity. This view is very different than, say, a Habermasian perspective, which sees individuation as a moral and rational learning process structured by cultural traditions that serve as a resource and context for the emergence of shared meanings."[20]

This tension points to other difficulties in Giddens's thought that I have mentioned throughout the text. Giddens does not develop a strong theory of culture and its role in shaping behavior, nor does he formulate a convincing analysis of the relationship between cultural beliefs and social power. Thus, he does not extensively investigate how people create communal beliefs through shared history and memories. Such negligence impoverishes Giddens's analysis of the possibility of people creating different social arrangements than those existing in modern societies, for he does not sufficiently examine "the role of individual and collective memory, and the experience of collective and individual suffering . . . [as informing] any conception of cultural alternatives within modern society." His emphasis on people's capacities to reflexively monitor their life situations underplays the role of "a preexisting cultural milieu that determines the texture of social interaction."[21] Finally, joining these theoretical problems is the more concrete discounting of class issues in Giddens's analysis. He does not adequately explore the new class divisions that globalization has created, as economic disparities between countries in the North and South replace class conflict within nation-states in the West as major sites of contestation.[22]

Despite these criticisms, Giddens's social theory is a lasting legacy for modern sociology. His analysis and synthesis of a vast number of theoretical traditions have brought different schools of thought into contact with one another in ways that can only enrich each of them. He places new social movements and the social changes of late modernity into a coherent, powerful theoretical context, so that such changes do not appear to be haphazard. Giddens creates a sociology for the twenty-first century that is no longer insular, but reaches out to other disciplines in its attempts to capture the character of late modernity. It is a dynamic sociology which dispenses with old dualisms such as structure and agency. His social theory respects the knowledgeability of people, who always have the capability of making the world a better place.

Giddens has been criticized for not giving rise to a new school of social research, akin to that of Marx or Durkheim. But his research has been truly practical, as it informs his approach to politics and social policy. This might be Giddens's greatest legacy, as he ties social theory to practical activity in a way reminiscent of the classical sociological figures. For Giddens, social theory is not separate from political action, and its major themes and arguments must stand the test of practice.

Giddens's forays into Labour politics are suggestive of Marx's activities in the Workers' International union, Durkheim's involvement in the Dreyfus affair of early twentieth-century France, and Weber's attempts to influence German national policy at the end of World War I. Giddens's criticisms of these classical theorists does not prevent him from continuing perhaps their major message to modern sociology – that social theory does not preclude strong commitments to moral and political action, but indeed demands them.

Notes

1 Giddens, *Beyond Left and Right: The Future of Radical Politics* (Stanford, Stanford University Press, 1994), pp. 4–8.

2 Giddens, *In Defence of Sociology: Essays, Interpretations, and Rejoinders* (Cambridge, MA, Polity Press, 1996), p. 254; Giddens, "Risk, Trust, Reflexivity," in Ulrich Beck, Anthony Giddens, and Scott Lash, *Reflexive Moderization: Politics, Tradition and Aesthetics in the Modern Social Order* (Stanford, Stanford University Press, 1994), p. 186.

3 Giddens, *Beyond Left and Right*, pp. 74, 136–140.

4 Ibid., pp. 136, 143–144, 153.

5 Ibid., pp. 163–164, 185, 248.

6 Giddens, "Risk, Trust, Reflexivity," p. 196; *In Defence of Sociology*, pp. 229–230, 237.

7 Ibid., pp. 222–223.

8 Giddens, *Beyond Left and Right*, p. 246.

9 Karl Marx and Friedrich Engels, *Manifesto of the Communist Party*, in *The Marx-Engels Reader*, ed. Robert Tucker (New York, Norton, 1978), p. 476.

10 Giddens, *In Defence of Sociology*, pp. 243, 250.

11 Ibid., pp. 260–263.

12 Ibid., p. 228.

13 Ibid., pp. 246–247.

14 Ibid., p. 249.

15 Ibid., p. 248.

16 Ibid., pp. 245–246.

17 Ibid., p. 259.

18 Ibid., p. 266.

19 Ibid., p. 270.

20 Kenneth H. Tucker, Jr., Review of Ulrich Beck, Anthony Giddens, and Scott Lash, *Reflexive Modernization: Politics, Tradition and Aesthetics in the Modern Social Order*, in *Contemporary Sociology* 25 (January 1996), pp. 12–13.

21 Ronald Lembo and Kenneth H. Tucker, Jr., "Culture, Television, and Opposition: Rethinking Cultural Studies," *Critical Studies in Mass Communication* 7 (1990), p. 101.

22 See for example Robert J. Antonio and Alessandro Bonanno, "Post-Fordism in the United States: The Poverty of Market-Centered Democracy," in *Current Perspectives in Social Theory, vol. 16*, ed. Jennifer M. Lehmann (Greenwich, CT, JAI Press, 1996), pp. 3–32.

INDEX

Anthony Giddens and
Modern Social Theory